Coming Alive from Nine to Five in a 24/7 World

071

Coming Alive from Nine to Five in a 24/7 World

A CAREER SEARCH HANDBOOK
FOR THE 21ST CENTURY

Seventh Edition

Betty Neville Michelozzi

Linda J. Surrell

Robert I. Cobez

Boston   Burr Ridge, IL   Dubuque, IA   Madison, WI   New York
San Francisco   St. Louis   Bangkok   Bogotá   Caracas   Kuala Lumpur
Lisbon   London   Madrid   Mexico City   Milan   Montreal   New Delhi
Santiago   Seoul   Singapore   Sydney   Taipei   Toronto

The McGraw·Hill Companies

Mc Graw Hill   Higher Education

COMING ALIVE FROM NINE TO FIVE IN A 24/7 WORLD:
A CAREER SEARCH HANDBOOK FOR THE 21ST CENTURY

This book is printed on acid-free paper.

1 2 3 4 5 6 7 8 9 0 DOC/DOC 0 9 8 7 6 5 4 3

ISBN: 0-07-284262-8

Publisher: Thalia Dorwick
Senior sponsoring editor: Allison McNamara
Marketing manager: Leslie Oberhuber
Senior production supervisor: Richard DeVitto
Project manager: David Sutton
Designer: Cassandra Chu
Cover design: Joan Greenfield
Compositor: TBH Typecast, Inc.
Typeface: 10.5/12.5 Sabon
Printer: RR Donnelley-Crawfordsville
Cover image: "Variety of Careers" by David Sims/© Images.com/Corbis

Library of Congress Cataloging-in-Publication Data

Michelozzi, Betty Neville.
    Coming alive from nine to five in a 24/7 world: a career search handbook for the 21st
century / Betty Neville Michelozzi, Linda J. Surrell, Robert I. Cobez.—7th ed.
        p. cm.
    Rev. ed. of: Coming alive from nine to five. 6th ed. 2000
    Includes bibliographical references and index.
    ISBN 0-07-284262-8 (alk. paper)
    1. Vocational guidance. 2. Job hunting. I. Surrell, Linda J. II. Cobez, Robert I. III.
Michelozzi, Betty Neville. Coming alive from nine to five. IV. Title.
HF5381.M46 2003
650.14—dc22
                                                                            2003065179

Contents

Chapter 4

WORK: Challenges, Options, and Opportunities   93

Chapter 5

WORKPLACES/WORKSTYLES: Companies That Work   137

Chapter 6

TIMESTYLES/WORKSTYLES: Alternatives That Work   172

Chapter 7

THE JOB HUNT: Tools for Breaking and Entering   207

Chapter 8

DECISIONS, DECISIONS: What's Your Next Move?   279

Chapter 9
WORK AFFECTS THE SOUL: The Final Analysis   313

Preface

Coming Alive from Nine to Five in a 24/7 World is a unique handbook that develops, demystifies, and integrates the various facets of career/lifestyle search and choice. A handy reference book, it draws together into one comprehensive, practical, easily usable and reusable source the essentials of career/life decision making. Flexible enough to be adopted in whole or in part by individuals or groups, previous editions have been used in semester-long courses, workshops, individual counseling sessions, colleges, high schools, industry, and business. In short, *Coming Alive from Nine to Five in a 24/7 World* is intended for anyone searching for meaningful life activities: from students to retirees, from managers of households to managers of corporations, and from job trainees to career-changing professionals.

What's New   This updated version of *Coming Alive from Nine to Five in a 24/7 World* focuses on career preparation for the twenty-first century by providing valuable, practical tools, techniques, and strategies. It is especially relevant for those who wish to obtain their ideal employment in today's competitive job market. Using the same personal approach as earlier texts, the seventh edition expands awareness of the career search process as it relates to a person's whole life. A first for this edition is the inclusion of instructions and guidelines for using the U.S. government's new replacement for its venerable Dictionary of Occupational Titles (DOT) called the O*NET database, which is an online career research tool that enables people to sort through various factors to find compatible careers to pursue. Additionally there are unique, simplified comparison tables for the three major national sources of jobs and career information: the O*NET database, the Guide for Occupational Exploration (GOE), and the Occupational Outlook Handbook (OOH). The comparison tables help readers easily navigate these complex resources. New value and personality assessments are presented to further pinpoint relevant career alternatives. Also, this edition contains updated Web site information directing readers to useful, supplemental material to aid in researching careers, investigating companies, preparing job search strategies, and conducting successful job searches. All sample résumés presented, whether intended to be written on paper or sent electronically, show the latest style and format in order to present a job candidate's accomplishments favorably to elicit maximum interest.

Writing this new edition has provided us with an opportunity to develop new material, integrate overlapping exercises, eliminate what seemed less relevant, and update innumerable bits of data.

The book begins with an upbeat discussion of success and moves quickly into self-assessment activities. It then considers some of the major societal factors that influence work and workplaces. Changes in the workplace and the nature of work are happening very rapidly and the next hundred years will no doubt also be filled with change. This book provides a template for finding work that best fits one's needs and desires. It suggests job search strategies that may make the difference between getting or not getting the job. The book ends with strategies on how to make decisions that will support career success.

If this book is used as part of a workshop or course, the instructor's manual includes a discussion of study skills especially useful in a career course as well as other materials to facilitate the task of assisting students with this most important activity: reflection on life goals, including, specifically, career choice.

As the field of career management evolves, so too will this book. The two new authors will continue the fine tradition and legacy initiated by the principal author in this and subsequent editions, continually striving to make the book's contents relevant and practical. To this end, your comments and suggestions on ways to improve this book are encouraged, and we can be reached at the following e-mail address: comingalive@humaxsys.com.

B.N.M.
L.J.S.
R.I.C.

Acknowledgments

Acknowledgments are a very personal thing. They point out the impossibility of accomplishing anything of importance without the help of others. We, the three authors, want to thank those individuals who have contributed to previous editions. We are very grateful to the people who have helped us move forward on the seventh edition.

We would like to thank our supportive colleagues at both West Valley College and Mission College who gave helpful feedback, materials, and encouragement for the "birth" of *Coming Alive from Nine to Five in a 24/7 World*. Additionally, we thank the colleagues and friends from Santa Clara University, the Career Action Center, University of California Santa Cruz, the Santa Cruz County Office of Education, and Cabrillo Community College. Finally we thank all the students and clients over the last twenty-five years who have shown us what they needed for career satisfaction by sharing their life journeys. It is hard to believe that this is the seventh edition!

The people at McGraw-Hill have been great to work with, especially Leslie Oberhuber who patiently endured the incessant questions, comments, and concerns from new authors and always cheerfully offered wonderful suggestions and directions. In addition we would like to thank David Sutton, our project manager, and Cassandra Chu, our designer.

And a special thanks to the academic reviewers who use the text and made valuable suggestions and comments:

David Blessman, Clackamas Community College

Daniel Coons, Skagit Valley College

Anne E. Cox, Saddleback College

Tim Hatfield, Winona State University

William R. Holmes, Lamar University

Jennifer Jones, New Jersey City College

Beth Kaiama, Pasadena City College

Wai Ming Lai, Towson University

Rick Larson, James Madison University

Rose Wedner, Skagit Valley College

Francis Wood, Southeastern Louisiana University

Last, but certainly not least, we give special thanks to our family and friends who endured our struggle and supported us through the process. You all are wonderful and we thank you for your support.

About the Authors

Betty Neville Michelozzi acquired firsthand experience in career change and search when she left college chemistry teaching to become a college counselor. With two academic master's degrees to her credit she is now retired. She currently works with Habitat for Humanity Guatemala fundraising for land acquisition and taking groups there to build simple homes on the acquired land. She also writes poetry, occasional articles about social justice, and is presently dabbling in writing fiction.

Linda J. Surrell is a nationally certified career counselor with over twenty years in the career development field helping individuals find meaningful and satisfying work lives through career assessment, career counseling and coaching, and understanding changing workforce needs. With a master's degree in counseling psychology, she has worked as an instructor and counselor in public education, community college and university settings, and in a nonprofit organization serving the employment needs of professionals in the Silicon Valley. She developed a values assessment instrument that is used by individuals and corporations worldwide. She is on the adjunct faculty for the graduate counseling program at Santa Clara University. She enjoys sailing with her husband, Rob.

Robert I. Cobez is an international management consultant who develops and maximizes the leadership and managerial talents of individuals and teams to enhance their success. Having earned a doctorate in psychology and a master's in business administration specializing in business management, having worked in various management positions including cofounding a prosperous software company, and having counseled and taught thousands of clients, Dr. Corbez continually emphasizes that good career planning is a vital component for anyone desiring to achieve the best results in his or her career. When not consulting, coaching executives, conducting seminars, teaching, lecturing, delivery speeches, or writing, he enjoys sailing with his wife, Linda.

Introduction

A Letter to You

Career search can be a special time to orient and organize your life. It can be a time when you look seriously at yourself and what you have been doing. It can lead you to question how you intend to spend your life for a time, or your time for the rest of your life: to keep or not to keep certain goals, to change or not to change certain behaviors, to aspire or not to aspire to certain positions—all with a view toward life enrichment, with you directing your efforts and activities toward the career or job you want.

Career search involves more than simply figuring out what job might suit you best. (That is the short-range view.) Your perspective expands when you ask yourself what you want that job to do for you. Once you ask this question, you may very quickly find yourself face to face with some of your deepest values and motivators, which will help focus your subsequent activities and stimulate you to actively pursue your dreams. Do you want power, prestige, profit? Peace, harmony, love? Are some values incompatible with others? Can you have it all?

Can you work sixty hours a week moving up the corporate ladder, nurture loving relationships with family and friends, grow your own vegetables, recycle your cans on Saturday, jog daily, be a Scout leader, meditate, and play golf at the country club? How fully can all your interests and values be actualized in the real world? What is the purpose of work? What is the purpose of life? These questions lead to that all-important question, What do *you* want out of *your* life?

This text is written for those in transition, whether in college and looking to start a career, currently employed and looking for a better job or new career, in a layoff situation and looking to find the right job in a timely

PEANUTS reprinted by permission of United Feature Syndicate, Inc.

manner, or retired and contemplating returning to the workforce or volunteering for something personally satisfying. Readers will have an opportunity to learn a thoughtful and practical career and life decision process if they are willing to let go of behaviors that are no longer appropriate and risk new ones to achieve satisfaction doing what they want and love to do. A book about career choice is inevitably a book about life and all its stages, for people from age nineteen to ninety-nine.

Because a career decision is so important, some people approach it with fear and trembling lest they make a mistake. Others avoid the process altogether, certain it will nail them down to a lifelong commitment. Still others feel that any job will do just to get them started on something! And then there are those who feel that even if they did a thorough career search, it would turn up absolutely nothing. Some people may feel that the world is in such turmoil, with threats of repeated terrorist acts, more war, economic malfeasance, and failing economy, that a career search is beside the point. So does this mean that finding a career or job is impossible? Of course not! It does mean, however, that those looking to be successful in starting or changing their careers will need to take charge and actively manage this process. In reality, a careful career search can help everyone. It can help *you* to see many possibilities, develop flexibility, and gain a great deal of confidence. It can even help people who have already made a career decision better understand themselves and their connection to the work world. The result can be greater career and life satisfaction.

THE PROCESS

What process should you use in making a thoughtful career decision? Many people choose their first career using the "muddle-around method." They consider subjects they've liked in school: if it's math, then they'll be mathematicians; if it's history, they'll be historians. They consider the careers of people they know and ask the advice of friends—a good beginning, but not always a broad enough perspective. If Uncle Jim the firefighter is a family hero, a new crop of firefighters is launched. If the career seekers fry hamburgers for a time, they're tempted to judge the whole world of business through the sizzle of french fries. If models and airline pilots capture their attention, they long for the glamorous life those people seem to have. They may try one job, move from here to there, get married, have a family, and move again, trying different positions, grabbing different opportunities. Then one day, they aren't sure just how it all happened, but there they are: spouse, children, house, job—"the whole catastrophe," as Zorba the Greek said. And they may wonder, "Is this all there is?"

Some folks make very early decisions: "I knew when I was two that I wanted to be a chimney sweep." Although deciding early may work out well and satisfy the need some people have to firm up choices, in other cases it means the person has closed off options that might have been more satisfying. Career choice is sometimes treated as trivial. Adults ask six-year-olds what they want to be when they grow up. Are they going to sell shoes at Penney's or invade the corporate complex of Microsoft? Will plumbing be their outlet or travel tours their bag? Even while quizzing the children, many adults aren't always sure what their next career would be if they had to choose.

At least occasionally, however, the image of life's wholeness will flash before you. You see that work will affect your life in many ways. The ultimate question will eventually present itself: "What's it all about?" If you deal in depth with career choice, you are bound to slip into philosophic questioning of life's meaning. To do otherwise is to trivialize a profound experience.

STAGES AND STEPS

Because you are reading this book, you're indicating that "muddling around" is not the way you want to approach your career decision. There are stages and steps in the career search process. For many people, the journey begins with not an idea in sight. As you gather career information, you may reach a point where you seem to be engulfed by too many ideas; things may seem to get worse before they get better. Eventually you must lighten the burden by choosing. You simply can't follow every career in one lifetime. The calmer you stay, the more easily you will arrive at your decision point.

The steps you need to take to reach a career or life decision must be part of a clear, understandable, and reusable *system,* one that

1. Helps you articulate who you are and what you do well.
2. Describes the work world as simply and completely as possible.
3. Helps you see where your personal characteristics fit into the work world.

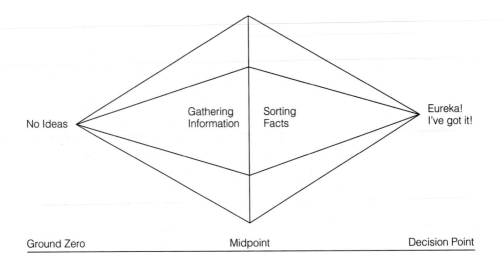

No Ideas ◄ — Gathering Information | Sorting Facts — ► Eureka! I've got it!

Ground Zero   Midpoint   Decision Point

Where are you on the Career Search Continuum?

_____ Ground zero: You have no idea what career to choose.

_____ You are gathering information about yourself, the work world, and the issues that affect work.

_____ You have gathered as much information as you can. Now you need to sort it out.

_____ You are sorting out the facts by talking to people and visiting workplaces in your areas of interest. You are reviewing the information and weighing the pluses and minuses.

_____ Eureka! You have decided exactly what you would like to do and where! You know it is possible.

The Career Search Continuum

4. Empowers you to secure the job you have chosen by improving your job-hunting skills.
5. Sharpens your decision-making skills, for you probably will make many decisions, and each choice leads to others.
6. Raises your consciousness about work as only one part of your personal journey, one aspect of your total lifestyle.
7. Addresses issues of global concern, showing how work is part of the world picture with its many challenges and how the solutions are provided by your work. Career planning breaks barriers and builds bridges.

In *Coming Alive from Nine to Five,* you will find such a system. It is based on identifying clear values that lead to good decisions. At first glance, this book may look like a conventional career manual. Read the book, fill in

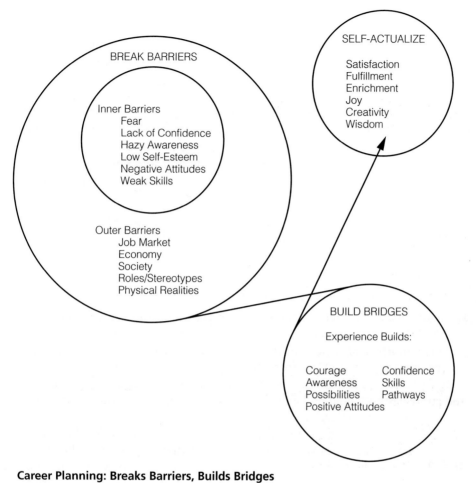

Career Planning: Breaks Barriers, Builds Bridges

the blanks, and (even if you're already over forty) you'll know what you want to be when you grow up.

You *will* find blanks to fill in as part of the process of getting to know yourself and the job world. You *will* find exercises to explore your needs, wants, and values, to discover your personality orientation. You will be guided to examine your past and select the activities you've enjoyed as well as the skills you've developed over the years. A job chart will help you to put *you* and *work* together in a meaningful way. A final inventory will collect all this "you" data and help you to see it as a unified whole. Armed with this valuable information, you will be given the practical tools and technical skills to actively target and get the job or career you want.

Each of these steps represents small decisions designed to fall into a general career pattern that is compatible with your personality. This in turn leads you to choose an appropriate educational pathway such as a college major; a career that will lead you into a field of your choice; and a lifestyle that both results from and supports your career choice.

No two people will do the process in exactly the same way. Some people find that doing every exercise will lead them to a career. Others may want to use this book for ideas but not follow it exactly. Some may wish to skip around, looking for what is most helpful as long as they are not doing so to avoid the issues involved in making a career/life decision. For example, those who find decision making difficult may want to read Chapter 8 for more structured decision-making exercises.

THE INTERNET: A CONVENIENT, POWERFUL, AND USEFUL TOOL

Using the Internet to help research your career opportunities while progressing through this book can be an efficient and practical way of uncovering valuable information quickly. The Internet can help you research companies and people and find useful information to make good career decisions. Relevant Web sites are mentioned throughout this book to augment the concepts and strategies presented and enhance your understanding about the career or careers you are investigating.

The Internet has given a new meaning to the word *research*. With access to the Internet, you'll have more information than you know what to do with. However, the Internet can become a "black hole" for your time. This can be especially true for those who have not carefully assessed their interests, motivated skills, values, and personal style. When researching on the Internet, follow these "rules" and you won't get overwhelmed with information.

1. Use reliable resources. Check the source and when it was last updated.
2. Set aside a short time period each day to do your research. Keep a record of what you have researched and learned each time.
3. Verify the information with more than one resource.
4. Don't pay for information on the Internet unless you are absolutely certain that it is information that you need and cannot get other places.
5. Finally, stay focused. It is easy to "go down a bunny trail" and end up researching something that is totally irrelevant to your career goal. When you find yourself "drifting" away, get yourself back on track *or* realize it may be time to stop for the day.

Being adept at using Internet search engines can provide you with relevant data in manageable quantities. Entering a simple query into a search engine could produce hundreds or thousands of links that would take hours to sift through for meaningful data. For example, using Google (**www.google .com**), probably the most popular general search engine around (as of January 2003), and entering the phrase, "resume writing tips"—in quotation marks as shown, to query for sites with an exact match—returned more than 9,200 sites. Adding the words "sample" and "example" to the query phrase and searching again reduced the number of matching sites to just over 1,000, which could be culled further with additional search parameters.

The Internet is a dynamic place, with Web sites coming, going, and changing. Be prepared to get the "HTTP 404" error, indicating that a link or site no longer exists, may have been moved, or may be renamed. If you type in a Web site address and get an error message, selectively deleting the rightmost sections of the URL and retrying may yield access to the site.

The Internet is an excellent tool and a means to help you become more efficient and successful on your personal journey to determine what your ideal work or career may be and assist you in achieving your work and life goals.

SUMMARY

This book also touches on some of the heavier issues of life. How can you fulfill your potential? Be happy? Be content? It deals with such issues lightly—sometimes whimsically—because life is meant to be joyful. After a good chuckle, you will get serious and *think* again because your life is also serious and sometimes even sad. Career search, then, is really a time to see who you are and where you're *growing*.

This handbook works best when the searcher approaches it in a relaxed, lighthearted manner. But a serious career search also calls for commitment and motivation. Those who get thoroughly involved will experience new confidence in themselves and greater clarity about their lives. Their goals will be easier to recognize and reach. Besides providing a living, a career can satisfy some of your deepest longings. The career search, then, will become a profound journey on the path toward self-actualization.

THE CAREER SEARCH GUIDE

Most people base career decisions on incomplete information. As you begin your career search, it may help to focus on some important questions.

1. Gather Information about Yourself

a. Needs, wants, and shoulds

What do you *need* to survive? What do you *want* to enrich your life? Do your *shoulds* help you or hold you back?

b. Interests and values

The choices you've made over your lifetime have developed into a strong pattern of interests. These reflect what you value most in life. Are your values clear?

c. Skills

Analyze your most enjoyable activities. Through repeated choices in your areas of interest, you have developed many skills. Of all the skills you have, which do you enjoy using the most?

2. Become Informed about Issues That Affect Your Career

a. What are the major challenges that face the world today?

b. What are the many positive and viable options already being taken to meet these challenges?

c. How do your values affect your work and your work affect your values?

3. Explore the Job Market: Where to Start

a. The job market

Interest and skill inventories lead you to an overview of the entire job market. What jobs fit your self-image?

b. Workplaces

What are the important characteristics of various workplaces? How do you find out which will work for you?

c. Job market opportunities

Check the job market outlook and relate it to needs and wants in society. Will there be a need for people to do the job you'd like? What workplaces will you choose? Do you have alternatives?

d. Information interviews

Have you talked to people in careers that interest you? Have you surveyed and evaluated possible workplaces? Does the survey show that you need to reevaluate your choices?

e. **Tools for the job hunt**

Do you know how to use the Internet? Can you portray yourself effectively through résumés, applications, interviews, and letters? Can you talk about yourself and your skills, abilities, and accomplishments? Can you develop an effective network of business contacts? Can you identify and meet the people who can hire you? Can you win the job you want?

4. Doing the Final Analysis: Wrap-Up

a. Decisions: Finalize your decision.

b. Goals: Set realistic goals with time lines.

c. Strategy: Develop a strategy for action.

d. Values/Philosophy: Review the whole picture to make sure it fits your value system, your philosophy of life and work.

SELF-ASSESSMENT

Before you begin your career exploration, discuss either in writing or with a group where you are on the Career Search Continuum (p. 4) and how you feel about doing a career search process at this time.

1. What are your strengths, weaknesses, concerns, and expectations going into the career search process?

2. What are your timeframe and the milestones you expect to reach along the way?

3. Who or what can you use as a support or source of advice?

1/

Needs, Wants, and Values

Spotlighting YOU

GOALS

- Define success in terms of your needs, wants, and goals.

- Examine important values in your personal and work life.

- Identify steps to help you decide on desired changes in your life.

- Understand your work ethic.

SUCCESS IS EVERYBODY'S DREAM

Everyone who begins a career search dreams of what he or she would like the process to achieve. Some simply want any job, the sooner the better. Others may be able to take the time not only to choose a career but also to get the education required. A career search will help you examine the kind of success that is right for you and help you achieve it.

The word *success* is so upbeat, so cheerful, so, well . . . successful! We certainly favor it over *failure*. Success, though an elusive concept, is compelling in its power. We chase it, we work for it, we long for it and for acknowledgment from others that we have it. But many career searchers forget to define this coveted quality in terms that are uniquely theirs.

What is success? Is it attained by high-speed movement? Go places, hit the floor running, travel in the fast lane. Is it beating the competition? Get ahead, be number one, swim with the sharks. Is it battle? Set your sights, maneuver, get to the top. Is it labels and logos? The right outfit, the right house in the right place with the right car? Is it power? Influence and direct the outcomes and fortunes in companies, control what others do, or enact laws through various political mechanisms. Media images of success bombard our consciousness; the successes that family and friends imagine for us confuse but compel us; our own half-formed dreams lure us up one pathway and down another.

These images can make the thoughtful person's head swim. Furthermore, society seems to demand one success after another without end. Yet achieving success is a basic human need. From getting a meal to making a deal, both the street person and the billionaire work each day to succeed.

Success Defined

Success has many layers and many definitions. We generally think of it in broad terms: a person *is* successful. We seldom ask what that means, what it consists of, how a person gets there, how that compares with our idea of success, and whether that is the kind of success we would enjoy. The fact is, success is "all in your head"; it is what matters most to *you*.

Some people see success as a secure niche they'll occupy when they have finished the hard work of achieving and changing. But we are all in transition and usually required to meet new challenges and draw on new abilities throughout our lives. No one stands still forever. Growth, marriage, family, divorce, deaths of significant people, degrees, promotion, transfers, new technology, layoffs, cutbacks, mergers, reorganization, management changes, company bankruptcy, illness, disability, retirement, societal and economic changes can affect life and careers and make us face new choices.

Success is different for everyone!

Goals that were appropriate for us at an earlier age fall by the wayside as we acquire and uncover new skills, as our values become more certain, as our experience opens up new horizons. What we view as a great and exciting success today may fall into a more modest perspective later in life as we move toward greater maturity and fulfillment. Our definition of success changes as we grow.

Sometimes people really are successful right now, but they aren't giving themselves credit. The powerful image of the dynamic, hardworking businessperson reaping tons of profits, prestige, and power can make other types of achievement seem trivial. Someone noted that today's maxim is "Nothing succeeds like excess." Artist Thomas Hart Benton lamented that the ideals and practices of the go-getter were ranked "above all other human interest."[1] We often honor the workaholic, who in fact may be quite self-destructive. We revere the ideal of individual success—being number one; but some may ask, at what price? We continually "up the ante" in the amount of material goods that make us look successful. We have to question these prevailing philosophies and ask, "Must success cost so much?" And further, "Must my success be the success defined by others?" Some people measure success in terms of their ability to simplify their lives, to live with less.

People often accept life roles based on stereotypes that may prove a stumbling block to success. You are born male or female, of a certain race and ethnic background. You may grow up in a certain religion. You are student, engineer, or cook. You become spouse, parent; you are divorced, widowed; you become a sage. Each person plays these roles differently. Some let stereotypes limit their actions and narrow their views. They may think that women should not . . . , only men can . . . , blacks are . . . , Muslims believe. . . . Stereotypes can be helpful in a general way—a doctor can fix your sagging back; a carpenter can fix your sagging door. But stereotypes often fail to show that people can exhibit a full spectrum of behaviors from timid to tough, from outgoing to introspective, from flamboyant to cautious, whether they are male or female, black or white.

Since the latter part of the twentieth century, stereotypes have been under scrutiny, bringing about a sea change in awareness. Women, minorities, disabled people, and older individuals have shown that they are capable of much more than people give them credit for. But we cannot assume that change based on this awareness is in any way universal. For example, the commonly touted adage that on the average women typically earn about 75 percent of what men do has now been dispelled after a close examination of the data. In the United States, women's salaries may be equal to or just a few percentage points below those earned by men in similar jobs when all factors are considered.[2] Most countries, unfortunately, fall far below those marks.

These realities can inhibit *you* when it comes to making career or life decisions. You may feel that because you are female or belong to a certain minority or are "too old" that you can't fulfill your dreams. Examining the attitudes that hold you back can give you the courage to move ahead toward success in achieving your goals.

At the very least, success is finding happiness, which may be defined as being reasonably content with the choices you have made in life. Unless you see more broadly, with a more penetrating look, you may simply continue searching for success—and hence, happiness—where they are not to be found. Through self-exploration you will begin to see how capable you are, how much more is possible for you, and how wonderful you are and can become on the road to success.

If you have grown accustomed to feeling "unsuccessful," find success by setting one small, short-term, realistic goal each day and achieving it: exercise for five or ten minutes; learn five dates in history; straighten out one drawer. And then congratulate yourself on your achievements. Expand your goals little by little each day.

Luck is preparation meeting opportunity![3]

Success also relates closely to failure. We achieve, and then we find ourselves looking at the next step. Some steps work, and some don't. What we learn becomes a part of our life experience. The steps that don't work are usually temporary, and they are also learning experiences. Thomas Edison tried hundreds of different filaments before he found one that worked in the electric lightbulb. When asked about all those failures, he said, "What failures? With every test, I discovered another material that didn't work."[4]

Failure often causes us to reassess our goals, strive harder, and hence attain greater success. Most successful people admit they have had some "good luck" that helped them along the way. Chances are they have had "bad luck," too. They have made some mistakes, but they were not defeated. Success comes most often to those who set realistic and reasonable goals and who work persistently and with enthusiasm.

Townes Duncan, chair and CEO of Comptronix, in Gunersville, Alabama, once said:

> Seymour Cray was a friend of my dad's. I asked him once what it was like to know the genius who had built the world's first supercomputer company. My dad said, "Well, actually, son, he wasn't so much smarter than me. He just made mistakes a hundred times faster."[5]

Sometimes people "fail" when actually they are resisting following the goals others have set for them. Failing becomes a way to exert independence. As surprising as it may seem, some people are afraid to succeed. Success brings more responsibility, higher visibility, and the expectation that the good performance will continue. Success requires continued effort to get there, to stay there, and to continue growing. The person who accepts failure, however, no longer has to keep trying.

Surprisingly, the setbacks we experience in life are often those that precipitate deeper, more valuable, and often painful insights into ourselves that cause us to make changes. Author Bill Cane asks, "Is it possible to accurately plot out a lifetime without budgeting in the possibility of change, darkness, and personal pain?"[6] When they look back, people are often grateful that a failure led them away from some serious pitfalls. People who never risk will never fail—or will they? Avoiding failure at all costs may be the greatest failure of all.

Be of good cheer. Do not think of today's failures,
but of the success that may come tomorrow.
You have set yourselves a difficult task, but you will succeed
if you persevere; and you will find a joy in overcoming obstacles.
Remember, no effort that we make to attain
something beautiful is ever lost.
—*Helen Keller, American essayist and lecturer*

CLARIFYING NEEDS, WANTS, AND VALUES LEADS TO SUCCESSFUL GOALS

All our activities are motivated by human needs and wants, and are based on our value systems. Work is one of the chief ways to fulfill those needs and wants, express our values, and find success. To start the career process at its roots, ask yourself what you *really* need. A genuine need is something you *must* have to survive, something you literally cannot live without. After these basic needs are identified, begin to look at your *wants*. Wants can enrich life beyond the level of needs. Then look at *shoulds*, those things others say you ought to do. Shoulds can create confusion about what we really want. What we want reflects our *values* and gives meaning to our lives. Looking at needs, wants, shoulds, and values can open a new phase of personal growth as well as clarify career goals.

Basic Needs Relate to Our Survival

We can divide all human motivation or needs into four areas: physical, emotional, intellectual, and altruistic or spiritual. These needs can be thought of as a hierarchy, with physical needs first on the agenda, then emotional, then intellectual, and then altruistic/spiritual, according to psychologist Abraham Maslow. All human beings have essentially the same needs. Minimal survival needs in each of these areas are the foundation for becoming a fulfilled and self-actualized person. If a person's most basic needs are unfulfilled, it is difficult for that individual to be motivated by higher needs.

> Even God cannot talk to a hungry man
> except in terms of bread.
> —*Gandhi*

Air, water, food, clothing, shelter, energy, health maintenance, exercise, and the transportation required for these necessities are the vital elements of our physical need system. We also must feel physically safe and secure, and we must have the time and usually the money to satisfy our physical needs in a dependable and orderly world.

Yet we've heard stories about orphaned infants whose physical and safety needs were met but who nevertheless died mysteriously. We've heard of old people "dying of loneliness" or of a person dying after learning of the death of a loved one.[7] Human beings need love, some kind of faith and assurance that they are lovable, and someone to give them courage in order to develop self-esteem and a sense of self and belonging.

POT-SHOTS NO. 179

I DON'T NEED
A GREAT DEAL OF LOVE
BUT I DO NEED
A STEADY SUPPLY.

Ashleigh
Brilliant
.COM

We fool ourselves when we say we have no need for others, that we can do it or have done it ourselves. Without the support of others, we would not have survived. Their caring helps validate our self-worth. The how-to-get-rich-quick, look-out-for-number-one, and win-through-intimidation books override the basic need that people have for caring and cooperative emotional support that "swimming with the sharks," "winning with weapons," and using "guerrilla marketing attacks" don't quite fulfill. A certain level of emotional nurturing is important for survival and growth.

We may tend to view intellectual needs as nonessential, but every culture has a system to teach its young how to satisfy their needs. Education begins when we are born and does not stop until we die. In this complex, fast-paced, high-tech world, it is ever more important for survival. Ideally, education leads to deeper knowledge and understanding of ourselves, others, and the world around us and to the wisdom needed to make good life choices. School is only one avenue to education, because people learn in different ways. Those who relate best to the physical world seem to learn through their hands. Some learn best through their ears, some through their eyes. Some learn best from the emotion-laden words of people they love. Media-lovers learn easily from books, pictures, diagrams, and other symbols. But however we learn, our intellect lights the way.

Altruistic needs—setting aside our own desires to meet the needs of others—sound as if they are only the frosting on the need cake and not a real need at all. But actually, a certain degree of altruism—looking out for others, winning by cooperation—is necessary for our individual survival. As we begin life and often as we age, we are dependent on the altruism of others. In a recent magazine article, authors Growald and Luks say that "scientists are now finding that doing good may be good for the immune system as well as the nervous system" and "may dramatically increase life expectancy."[8] There is no doubt that our individual decisions affect other people and the planet. Most societal problems are the visible product of many individual choices made without regard for the wealth and well-being of all. In an interview on *Bill Moyers' World of Ideas* on U.S. public television, the Rev. F. Forrester Church reminded us that our very survival depends ultimately on our seeing that our self-interest is the same as the self-interest of others and acting accordingly.[9] If you have survived modern life thus far, a good share of your basic needs have already been fulfilled. Many people have contributed to your well-being on all levels along the way.

When people reflect on their own needs and those of others, they often feel drawn to understand the problems that face them, to live a more meaningful life. They also sense that simply having knowledge does not imply that they will have the wisdom and will to act for their own good and that of others. A desire to develop morally and spiritually often results. As they search for answers to the whys of their existence, they may find motivation to live nobly and to accept with a graceful and adventurous spirit all that life brings them.

> I have the audacity to believe that people everywhere
> can have three meals a day for their bodies,
> education and culture for their minds, and
> dignity, equality, and freedom for their spirits.
> —*Dr. Martin Luther King, Jr.*

Needs Relate to Wants

Satisfaction of needs is absolutely necessary for life. A cup of water, a bowl of rice, and a few sprouts a day, one set of clothes, and simple shelter will do. Twenty percent of the world's people exist at this level on less than $1 a day.[10] Because most people choose not to live at a survival level if they can help it, they begin to search for the means to satisfy their wants. It's important to know what is clearly necessary for survival and what can wait—a great difference. Risks such as changing jobs are less frightening if you know that you can survive on very little. Once your basic needs are satisfied, you can work more calmly toward achieving your wants.

If all our needs and wants were completely satisfied, all the action in our lives would stop. Need/want satisfaction is not a straight line where at some point we have "finished." Some people find the struggle for survival needs so all consuming that they have only minimal time or energy left for the pursuit of emotional, intellectual, or spiritual needs. Others get so caught up with amassing great quantities of material goods that they neglect more enriching pursuits on other levels. The tiny, exquisite, and rewarding moments in life—a smile from a special person, a kind gesture, a word of concern, a work of insight and beauty—can be lost when we are constantly rushing for more. We have little time to savor and to taste the beauty that life brings us.

Survival needs get lost amid the surfeit of goods and services in which the postmodern person lives. The glitter of technology, the bounty of markets and malls, the ease of movement from place to place, the ever-present ability to be entertained all take enormous amounts of time and energy away from friends, family, work, personal enrichment, and growth. To gain perspective about abundance in the developed countries, consider that a person who earns $25,000 or more is in the top 1 percent of income in the world.[11]

In altruism, all the needs and wants come together: we share, we feel, we see, we do. We share what material things we can—our time, our security; we feel love, friendship, and compassion for and with others; we see with wisdom the common bonds, the connection of all people with each other and the Earth; we do what we can so that we all can be liberated into a more joyful life.

> A person is rich
> in proportion to the number of things
> he can do without.
> —*Henry David Thoreau*[12]

Needs and Wants Relate to Feelings and Shoulds

How does each person's unique set of wants evolve? Most wants come from the culture in which a person lives. Ideally people are taught by parents and teachers to find the balance called *common sense* that exists between going for everything that feels good, and reasoned judgment telling us that not everything that feels good is good for us. Life experience teaches us over and over that some things work and some do not.

Everyone has a range of emotional responses to life's events. Growing means learning to understand and manage these responses, not letting them manage you. Anger, for example, can be a natural response to adversity. Staying angry, "grinding" about bad luck, and plotting revenge keep a person from using "anger energy" in a productive and positive way to grow through the problem. It's obvious that impulsive people may act on feelings to such excess that they bring harm to themselves and others.

But it's less obvious that overly cautious people may become so dependent on rules that they are slaves to shoulds. When you say, "I should," you are implying that you neither need nor want to do this thing, but some force or some person outside you is saying you ought to. Shoulds are energy drains because they create a feeling of resistance and apathy. They cause people to shift responsibility for their choices somewhere else. When you make life changes, it's important to know whether your shoulds are value inspired. Shoulds will either evaporate as unimportant or, if value related, will be owned as a want.

Needs and Wants Relate to Values

Needs are survival minimums on the physical, emotional, intellectual, and altruistic levels. *Wants* go beyond survival to a place of enriched choices. When you make choices based on reasoned judgment, good feelings, and common sense, with no pressure from shoulds, you are clearly indicating that this choice is something that you value. Your decision is based on your core values, the principles that are the foundation of, and give meaning to, your life. *Values* are what you do and stand up for, not just what you say. Becoming aware of what you really value and cherish is a lifelong process. Some of your work values may change over time as your life needs and wants change, but your core values make you the unique person you are.

Defining a value and what it means to you is very personal. If your personal values have a dynamic relationship to your work and the values of your organization, you will be more satisfied. When they don't, your job performance may deteriorate, you may find yourself not wanting to go to work, you may manifest physiological symptoms including headaches, backaches, stomach pain, anxiety, fatigue, and ultimately complete burnout. It is important to evaluate your work values often. As changes occur in an organization, so might the values that were once important to you. Take, for example, an organization that was built on integrity and honesty, that put employees first, that ensured job security, and where everyone was one happy family. However, with a market downturn and a change in management, the new focus may be on profit and growth. No longer can the organization put the employees first, job security is out of the question, and unexpected layoffs happen. Being aware of the organization's values is important to your success and satisfaction at work. Being career self-reliant, meaning that you actively manage your career and all that it takes to make it successful, is more important today than ever before.

As your organization's values change, so may your personal work values. When you are young and single it may not be as important to you to have a balance between your work and family lives as it is when you are older and have a family depending on you. When thinking about what is important to you in your work, ask yourself these questions:

1. What kind of work environment is motivating to you and supports you to do your best work? One that is fast-paced, is aesthetically pleasing, requires a short commute time, or that provides the opportunity to make a lot of money?
2. What is the work content that is satisfying and engaging to you? Work that is challenging or creative, is on the leading edge, or requires physical involvement?
3. What kind of workplace relationships are important to you? A workplace where you are working as part of a team, working alone, developing friendships, or getting recognized for good work?

Awareness of your work values can help you evaluate job options with greater clarity and understanding.

Surprisingly, struggles, disappointments, worries, hopes, and dreams indicate a value area as well, for if something is not a value, it will not be of concern. Murky values can result in many conflicts. People who seem turned off, confused, indecisive, complaining, hostile, alienated, or "lazy," and who overconform or over-rebel probably have conflicts over values.[13]

Values are unique to each person. Sometimes your choices can lead you far from the kind of success you originally had in mind. Clarifying your values helps you avoid pitfalls on your journey. You don't want to find yourself halfway down the block before you realize you've turned the wrong corner.

Values Act As Motivators for Decisions

Your values lead you to make decisions about your whole life, not just your career. All the components of your lifestyle, including family, love and friendship, home and work environments, religious preference, education, work, and recreation reflect your personal values.

Your choices will in turn clarify and perhaps change some of your values and will thus influence your lifestyle in many ways. In your career, for example, you will learn new skills, change some behaviors to fit your new role, make new friends, and learn a new vocabulary. Recent college graduate Dan Anderson chose to teach English for a year as a volunteer in the African country Namibia. He found the people impoverished in a material sense but rich in joy and relationships. His discovery led him to rethink the values he had acquired as a typical American college student. Your work can lead to new involvements and even new ways of seeing yourself.[14] In fact, work roles are given such importance that some people find it hard to relate to a new acquaintance without knowing what that person does for a living.

Most important, the ideal work you choose will fulfill many of your needs and wants and will directly reflect your values. Without needs and wants to motivate them, people would not work. Most people work for money to fulfill their basic needs. Some people work because the work is intellectually satisfying. Others go to work to be with people, to be noticed, to be approved of, and for a whole host of individual enticements. Those with enough resources to fulfill their basic needs and wants then work for enrichment and for the good of others.

It may seem difficult or impossible at times to align your lifestyle with your values. Life is not always obliging. Writing the great american novel may be on your dream agenda, yet you find yourself typing engineering specs. Your choice says that you value feeding yourself and your family over feeding your love for writing.

Sometimes you can feel very alone when you struggle with a values-related decision. Clarifying your values and their order of importance can eliminate a great deal of conflict as well as help you set goals. When you have realistic goals, you have a far greater possibility of actualizing your dreams. With this book you will be clarifying many values as you learn about yourself and your own characteristics. You will be making decisions based on those values. And achieving your needs and wants in harmony with your values spells success. This process is bound to enhance your personal growth.

> The unexamined life
> is not worth living.
> —*Socrates*

PERSONAL GROWTH

Getting acquainted with yourself—your feelings, needs, wants, and most cherished values, changing shoulds to wants or dropping them—is a continuous process of growth. Growing as a person means adjusting but not losing our dreams and desires as we explore the realities of the world. It means expansion into new and exciting areas of life. Never before in the history of humankind have people of all ages had such opportunity for growth. People now live longer, are more affluent, have access to vast amounts of technology, and are more aware of possibilities. People are going back to school at ages seventy and eighty and even ninety, getting degrees, starting businesses, publishing their first books, painting, initiating nationwide political action groups, or teaching swimming. One very energetic eighty-year-old took a careers and lifestyle class to help plan the rest of her life.

The alternative to growth is stagnation, which results in a diminished life wrought with self-doubt, put-downs, and lack of confidence; many *shoulds* that close out others by viewing them in a narrow way; and many demands that create tension, guilt, and anxiety.

Growth is not always easy. Sometimes exploring these ideas and feelings with a trusted mentor, coach, or counselor can help you learn to channel your energy in positive ways and to accomplish your goals more effectively.

Reviewing past experiences can uncover important clues to your skills and interests as well as promote growth. Your "free spirit" years, those beginning at about age five or six when you became independent enough to make some choices, are especially important. You weren't worried about what people thought of you. What gave you satisfaction then and what proved disappointing? Some people find great motivation in striving for success in what was once a so-called area of failure. Timid speech students become noted speakers; inept Little Leaguers become strong athletes.

Times of transition can be fearful periods in which life seems so empty that we'd give anything not to face reality. But when we do face it, we are amazed at how much more there is of all good and joyful things. We begin to like ourselves better and are able to care more for others. We gradually begin to see life differently. In a sense, we create our own world. Ken Keyes, Jr., believes that "a loving person lives in a loving world."[15] Self-awareness leads to self-acceptance, which leads to self-confidence. Then we are on the way to self-actualization.

Self-Actualization

When minimal needs are fulfilled on every level, when our wants are becoming reality, when our shoulds have dissolved or turned to wants, when our feelings are helping rather than hindering the process, endless vistas of growth seem to open up for us. Psychologist Abraham Maslow said, "We may still often (if not always) expect that a new discontent and restlessness will soon develop, unless the individual is doing what he's fitted for. A musician must make music, an artist must paint, a poet must write, if he is to be ultimately at peace. What a person can be, he must be. This need we call self-actualization."[16]

A self-actualizing or growing person might be described as follows:

- Is authentic, open, doesn't hide behind roles or masks
- Is ruled neither by ego nor emotion
- Is simple, natural, with little need for status symbols
- Is autonomous, centered, not pulled along by every fad
- Can make decisions, take responsibility
- Takes life seriously, with a generous touch of whimsy
- Can see through the pretenses of others with a benign view and maybe even a chuckle
- Is emotionally balanced, enjoying peak experiences, delighting in people, art, nature, yet able to "get the job done"
- Feels secure, worthy, cared about, respected, connected with others
- Is not burdened with the anxiety, guilt, or shame that go with shoulds
- Is spontaneous, passionate, creative, an enjoyer of life—yet is moral, ethical, concerned
- Sees all useful work as dignified and treats all workers with respect
- Takes time for self-renewal and relaxation
- Can be alone or in a group with equal ease
- Values self as well as others
- Is able to find common ground in opposing views and to help reconcile people's differences
- Values privacy, yet feels one with humankind
- Tends to form deep personal relationships, based on love and caring, with other self-actualizing people
- Has a basic set of beliefs, a philosophy of life
- Acts not out of greed, fear, or anger, but out of love and caring for the whole world

The possibilities for an enriching life are endless. Maslow intimates that when people have good homes, clothing, and food, many will take time for intellectual, artistic, and altruistic/spiritual interests. But in affluent, consumer societies, people may miss the enrichment that comes from growth in these areas.

As they find balance and sufficiency in their needs and wants, however, their lives become greatly enriched: fulfillment of physical needs and wants is ample yet not excessive; relationships bring respect, support, love, and joy; honesty, courage, faithfulness, fairness, generosity, wisdom, and creativity flourish; and the human spirit becomes noble, compassionate, and good.

The flowering of our growth
brings aliveness, effortlessness,
individuality, playfulness,
completion, richness.

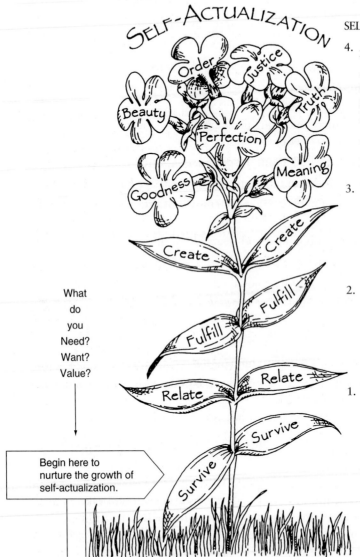

SELF-ACTUALIZATION

4. **ALTRUISTIC NEEDS:**
   We all must interact with
   others to survive, but to
   live life fully is to have that
   generous, loving spirit that
   promotes truth, goodness,
   beauty, justice, perfection,
   order, meaning, and all that
   is noble and good in the
   world.

3. **INTELLECTUAL NEEDS:**
   A degree of knowledge
   and understanding is
   necessary for survival, but
   a truly developed mind is
   one in which wisdom and
   creativity flourish.

2. **EMOTIONAL NEEDS:**
   Basic caring from others is
   necessary for our growth.
   Rich relationships bring us
   joy and the courage that
   comes from emotional support, love, and respect.

1. **PHYSICAL NEEDS:** We all
   have needs for food, clothing, shelter, safety—the
   things that keep us alive.
   Our carefully chosen wants
   enrich us and enable us to
   simplify our lives and feel
   self-sufficient.

What
do
you
Need?
Want?
Value?

Begin here to
nurture the growth of
self-actualization.

Four NEED/WANT/VALUE areas lead to Personal Growth and Development.

The Flowering of Personal Growth

A study some years ago by the Stanford Research Institute found that many affluent people felt they had enough and decided to choose lives of voluntary simplicity. A Louis Harris and Associates, Inc., poll agreed, reporting that a large majority of the American public were placing importance on activities such as teaching people how to live more with basic essentials than to reach higher standards of living. These views expressed a change in our national values and aspirations, reflecting the realization that our resources are limited.[17]

Beyond Needs and Wants

When people have it all, where do they go next? The answer is that they often astound and inspire us by their incredible courage in setting aside their own wants and by their tender care for others. Heroic deeds make up the fabric of their lives as they achieve the highest form of self-actualization. At this level, a person is motivated by natural altruism or spirituality. These are the people who delight and inspire us and give us new energy and courage. Service to others becomes the primary value, and the person strives for what Jakob von Uexkull, founder of Right Livelihood Awards, called "the ability to empower, uplift, and heal the human spirit."[18]

For example, Millard and Linda Fuller wondered why so many people in rural Georgia were living in run-down shacks. Instead of getting angry, they got busy, organizing volunteers and raising money. They began to build low-cost housing in partnership with needy people who pay the cost back so that more homes can be built. The organization they founded, Habitat for Humanity, has built more than 100,000 homes worldwide since 1976.

Anita Roddick, founder of the successful company The Body Shop, leads workshops on new ways of doing business that take into account the rights of people and the planet. Pat Cane brings school supplies and teaches art and relaxation techniques to war-torn, poverty-stricken countries of Latin America, but above all, she brings love. Gradually, others are joining her in her ministry of healing for an afflicted world. She writes, "All of these communities are very poor, some in the countryside are without running water and electricity. Most of the families earn less than $10 a month. Their lives are, for the most part, simple and very humble, but very rich in love and faith and truth and many of the deep human values that matter most of all. What they have to share with us is a very different view of reality not found in the media nor in the rhetoric of the powerful and wealthy of our world. And this can lead to many awakenings within ourselves of the deeper meaning of love and justice in the world."[19]

Encouragement for helping others appears in many guises. Former U.S. Labor Secretary Robert Reich tells graduates not to retreat from the demands of the common good as many affluent people are doing. "Doing better together creates the right [best] conditions."[20] Attorney Bob Gnaizda represents the Greenlining Institute that fights institutional economic discrimination.[21]

David Suzuki talked to destitute homeless children on the streets of Brazil and found amazing altruism. One child said, "I wish I was rich. And if I were I would give all of the street children food, clothes, medicines, shelter, and love, and affection!"[22]

In every field, people are working to make a positive difference in the world. The more talents you develop and the greater your contribution to improving the world you live in, the more self-actualized you are on all levels—from physical through emotional, intellectual, and altruistic/spiritual. This world is filled with challenges. It is our work that provides many of the options and solutions.

> Hope . . . is not the same as joy that things are going well,
> or willingness to invest in enterprises that are obviously heading
> for . . . success, but rather, an ability to work for something because
> it is good, not just because it stands a chance to succeed.
> —*Vaclav Havel, former president of Czechoslovakia*[23]

THE WORK ETHIC: A PERSONAL VIEW

An integral part of our value system and a reflection of our personal growth is our attitude toward work—our *work ethic*. Is work really necessary? Is it valuable? Demeaning? Enhancing? Often we are ambivalent. While necessary, work is viewed differently by various cultures. In the modern technical world, people are expected to work hard and achieve much, leaving enjoyment and fun for ever-shrinking leisure hours.

The American work ethic has its roots in early colonial days when the maxim "Idleness is the devil's workshop" was a basic belief, along with Ben Franklin's dictum, "Time is money." Americans value those who have "made it" and often look down on people who haven't. People should work hard for their just rewards. Thus, by and large, we are work addicts—striving, struggling, sometimes becoming ruthless and immoral to succeed. (Work itself sometimes becomes the devil's workshop!)

The backlash from our national policies and attitudes was vividly described in *Work in America*, a special task force report to the secretary of Health, Education, and Welfare that is still relevant today.

> Because work is central to the lives of most Americans, either the absence of work or employment in meaningless work is creating an increasingly intolerable situation. The human costs of this state of affairs are manifested in worker alienation, alcoholism, drug addiction, and other symptoms of

poor mental health. Moreover, much of our tax money is expended in an effort to compensate for problems with at least a part of their genesis in the world of work. A great part of the staggering national bill in the areas of crime and delinquency, mental and physical health, manpower and welfare are generated in our national policies and attitudes toward work.[24]

Not everyone subscribes to the American work ethic. Senator Edward Kennedy recounts how, during his first campaign for the U.S. Senate, his opponent said scornfully in a debate, "This man has never worked a day in his life!" Kennedy says that the next morning as he was shaking hands at a factory gate, one worker leaned toward him and confided, "You ain't missed a goddamned thing."[25]

Somewhere between these two extremes of workaholism and alienation you will develop your personal work ethic, your personal perspective on the meaning of work for you.

JUST A JOB, OR A CAREER?

Your career choice will more completely match your values when you clarify your work ethic and decide on the degree of commitment you are willing to make to your work. Do you want a career or just a job? A job might be defined as something one does to earn money, requiring little involvement beyond one's physical and mental presence. Many people of all levels of intelligence and creativity approach work this way: some, because their job is the only work they want or can get; others, to support hobbies and creative activities for which there seem to be no work opportunities.

In contrast to a job, a career can be seen as a series of work experiences that represents progression in a field. This kind of work usually absorbs much of a person's energy. A career is often planned for and trained for, and it often involves dedication of time and talent beyond the minimum required.

Two people may do identical work, yet one may view the work as "just a job" whereas the other sees it as "my career." Sometimes a person trains and sacrifices to achieve a career only to face disillusionment and end up just putting in time. Conversely, some people have been known to perform what society calls "menial" work with a level of dedication worthy of a career professional.

A demanding career may cause a loss of family, health, friendship, and leisure. How much are you willing to sacrifice? How much involvement is enough for you? Keep the question of commitment in mind, as well as your other values, as you consider your career choice. When you find work that matches your needs, wants, values, interests, and abilities and see that it brings you many rewards, your respect for your workplace and colleagues

And thanks to you, Linda, I got a great job,
fantastic salary, wonderful boss, super company . . .

will grow. You will be eager to put forth your best effort, and you will enjoy the challenges that each day brings. What began as a job may become your career.

We seem to be in a period of rising expectations about ourselves and about work, even in a frequently shaky job market. As T. George Harris, former editor of *Psychology Today*, once said, "We were doing all right until some idiot raised the ante on what it takes to be a person and the rest of us accepted it without noticing."[26] Well, why not? Why not expand our vision? To paraphrase nineteenth-century feminist Elizabeth Cady Stanton, the true person is as yet a dream of the future.[27] Why keep that idea forever in the future? Why not begin to make it a present reality? The premise of this manual is that people can find joy in work and life and be more than they thought possible. For the first time in history we can allow ourselves the luxury of thinking of work as both fulfilling and a responsible way to provide good things for ourselves and others. And each person will find that fulfillment in a unique way. A carpenter will fit each piece of wood more tightly; a secretary will prepare reports with extra-special care. We can all contribute in some way to the well-being of others as well as to ourselves as responsible, productive, and contented workers. If we can find a place where we feel some measure of success, some value, we will find new energy to put into our work.

We have many resources of mind and spirit. Can we move to a place of greater joy in work and in life? Harvard researchers Bartolomé and Evans tell us, "You will fit your job/life activity, and we can say, be more successful if you feel confident, enjoy the work and if your moral values coincide with your work."[28] Reflecting on what success means to you, what your values are, is essential and may be quite surprising and different from what you have expected.

As you go about the process of choosing a career, your image of success will sharpen. May your career choice contribute to *your* dream of a successful future.

SUMMARY

Success to one person is not necessarily the same to another. Some people look at success as making a lot of money, having fancy cars and big houses. Others look at success as discovering a cure for cancer or building a streamlined space vehicle. Still others see success as helping others and making a difference in people's lives. With success can also come failure, but the ability to learn from your mistakes can move you toward your goals. Understanding your *needs,* what you really need in your life; your *wants,* those things that will make your life better; and your *values,* what is of utmost importance to you; leads to a successful career search. The *shoulds* in life can hold you back from achieving your goals, and they need to be evaluated carefully. A successful career search takes persistence and determination, so you can achieve success and live a fulfilling and satisfying life. You are the one at the helm to achieve success in your life, whatever success means to you.

SELF-ASSESSMENT EXERCISES

Self-assessment exercises throughout the text are designed to help you with your career search. Each set will prove helpful for the chapters ahead. Use *only the ones that are useful to you. You may not need to do them all.* In Chapter 9, "Work Affects the Soul: The Final Analysis," you will find a place to summarize all the exercises.

1. Needs and Wants: Dream Your Goals

a. Survival needs plus: Your enriched wants reflect your values

What lifestyle is important to you? Dream—let your imagination soar; describe your ideals in the following areas and what you expect from each, or write a paragraph or two about those most important to you:

Your home_____

Your clothing _____

Your food _____

Your family _____

Your friends _____

Your associates _____

Your transportation _____

Your pets or plants_____

Your gadgets and playthings_____

Your activities_____

Other _____

b. Fulfillment needs and wants

Dream again! If you could instantly be in your ideal career/lifestyle, already skilled and trained, what would it be?

- To delight yourself and amaze your family and friends?

  _____

  _____

- To improve the world?

  _____

  _____

c. Life balance

What do you do, over and above absolute need, to contribute to your well-being on each of the following four levels?

Physical _____

Emotional _____

Intellectual_____

Altruistic/Spiritual _____

2. Tapping into Feelings and Shoulds

What seems to block your effectiveness? It's easier to make career/life decisions if problems are not getting in the way.

a. Life problems checklist

Identify the factors that you feel are a problem for you. Rate the items listed by checking the appropriate columns: I am happy with; I am managing with; I am having trouble with. Year + = this problem has been going on for a year or more; Chronic = this problem has been present for a great deal of my life. Then go back and circle the items you would like to change.

	Happy	Managing	Trouble	Year+	Chronic
Parents/brothers/sisters					
Spouse/children					
Family closeness					
Friends/relationships/love					
Privacy/freedom					
Dwelling					
Work					
Finances					
Personal achievements/success					
Confidence					
Health					
Diet/drugs/drinking/smoking					
Exercise					
Physical appearance					
Physical well-being					
Time/leisure					
Recreation/hobbies					
Emotional/mental well-being					
Status					
Intellectual ability					
Artistic ability					
Education					
Social concern					
Political concern					
Spiritual/religious well-being					

b. Feelings checkpoints

Check (✓) any of the following feeling responses that often create problems for you. Mark with a plus (+) those areas you'd like to improve.

_____ Anger	_____ Fear	_____ Pessimism
_____ Apathy	_____ Frenzy	_____ Resentment
_____ Boredom	_____ Frustration	_____ Skepticism
_____ Confusion	_____ Hostility	_____ Violence
_____ Depression	_____ Hurt	_____ Worry
_____ Discouragement		

c. Shoulds

List and examine the *shoulds* that hold you back. Can you drop them or change them to *wants*? Answer below.

_____

_____

_____

_____

3. What is Success to YOU?

When you are ninety-nine-and-a-half years old and you look back on your life, what do you want to be able to say about the success of your life?

_____

_____

_____

How will you know? _____

_____

_____

4. Identifying Your Values

The following will help you identify the values that are important to you personally and for your career. Put a check next to those values that are very important to you. If a value is missing, add it to the list.

a. What are the core values that truly make you who you are?

_____ Achievement	✓ Environmental awareness	_____ Knowledge
_____ Balance	✓ Family	_____ Power
_____ Belonging	✓ Honesty	_____ Self-respect
✓ Commitment	_____ Independence	✓ Spirituality
_____ Contribution	✓ Integrity	_____ Status

Other core values? _____

b. What values are important to you in your career?

_____ Adventurousness	_____ Fast paced
_____ Advocacy	_____ Flexible
_____ Aesthetically pleasing	_____ Friendships
_____ Analytical	_____ Fun
_____ Autonomous	_____ Harmony
_____ Benefits	✓ Helping
✓ Caring	_____ High earnings
✓ Challenging	_____ Individualism
_____ Competitive	_____ Initiating
_____ Conceptualizing	✓ Leadership
_____ Cooperation	_____ Leading edge
_____ Creative	_____ Learning
_____ Decision making	✓ Loyalty
✓ Detailed	_____ Management
_____ Diversity	_____ Open communication
✓ Excitement	✓ Organizing

_____ Physical   _____ Security

_____ Predictable   _____ Sense of community

_____ Problem solving   _____ Structured

_____ Public contact   _____ Support

_____ Quiet   _____ Teamwork

_____ Recognition   _____ Time freedom

_____ Relaxed   _____ Trust

_____ Research   _____ Variety

_____ Risk taking

Other career values: _____

c. **Now go back and review your list. Choose your top ten and write the values below in order of importance and define what the value means to you.**

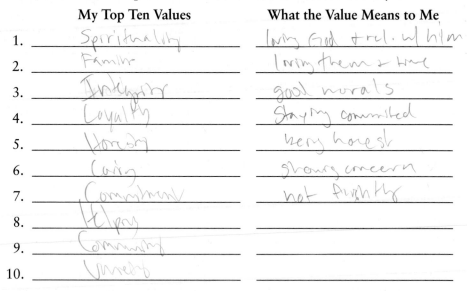

	My Top Ten Values	What the Value Means to Me
1.	Spirituality	loving God + rel. w/ him
2.	Family	loving them + time
3.	Integrity	good morals
4.	Loyalty	Staying committed
5.	Honesty	very honest
6.	Caring	strong concern
7.	Commitment	not flighty
8.	Helping	
9.	Community	
10.	Variety	

5. Goal Setting

Set goals! Go back over the preceding exercises and pick one area for improvement. Write down a key word and post it someplace where you can see it, perhaps on the bathroom mirror. What specific steps, little or big, can you take to improve your life? Perhaps see a counselor to talk over such issues as problem areas, strong feelings, or values conflicts.

I'd like to improve: _____

Steps to take: _____

_____

_____

6. Your Expectations

At this point, do you feel that you want a career or "just a job"? Explain.

_____

_____

_____

7. Candid Camera—3-D

Each activity you've chosen to do contains important clues about you, your skills, and your interests. This exercise will be one of the first steps on the road to career decision making. It is also the first step toward preparing a résumé and getting ready for an interview. Your life in 3-D will help you discover who you are, decide your goals, design your strategies. Spend an intense hour doing this exercise as outlined here. Use scratch paper. Then save it and add to it, refine it, and organize it according to the exercises that follow.

- **Loves:** Make a list of ten to twenty activities you love to do, not *like* or *should* but *love*. Don't *think* too much; just list whatever comes to mind first.
- **Jobs:** List five to ten or more of the jobs most important to you that you've done for pay, way back to baby-sitting or lawn mowing.
- **Other:** List five to ten of your most important extracurricular activities, community volunteer jobs, hobbies done at home or on vacation, sports, anything that gave you confidence and good energy.
- Then take a separate sheet of scratch paper for two or three of the most important items above and begin to list in detail what you did to accomplish each activity. For example, if skiing is on your list, you might write buying/organizing equipment, doing fitness exercises, choosing a slope, making reservations, trying new techniques, teaching friends, what else?
- **Data, People, Things:** Using your lists, note when you deal with people or things. Notice when you are dealing with ideas and information alone as, for example, when reading, analyzing, and organizing material—just what this exercise requires. You will see that in dealing with people and things, you always need ideas and information (data). Then code each activity D, P, or T. We will use this code later to help you sort out various types of job qualities.

P = activities when you deal directly with people (some use of data always implied)

T = activities when you deal directly with things (some use of data always implied)

D = activities when you deal just with ideas and information, called *data* (there is little or no interaction with people or things)

8. Drawing a Self-Portrait: Your Autobiography

You may wish to choose one of the following to use as a basis for writing the story of your life. Some people may find doing more than one useful as background for their history.

a.   Briefly write the story of your life.

b.   Use the value words in Exercise 4 to describe your values and how they have evolved over the years.

c.   Using pictures from magazines or old photos, make a poster or collage that illustrates you.

d.   Create a personal "I Wheel" like the one on page 37.

GROUP DISCUSSION QUESTIONS

1. Discuss success and failure.
   a. Define success and failure for yourself.
   b. Try substituting the word *happiness* for *success*. Is there a difference?
   c. Name some of the many life roles you have played as you grew up. Describe your surroundings; tell what you were doing.
   d. Do stereotypes about the roles you see yourself in now limit your chances for success? Explain.
2. What is the connection between our needs and wants and the work we and others do?
3. Give as many answers as you can to this question: Why do we work?

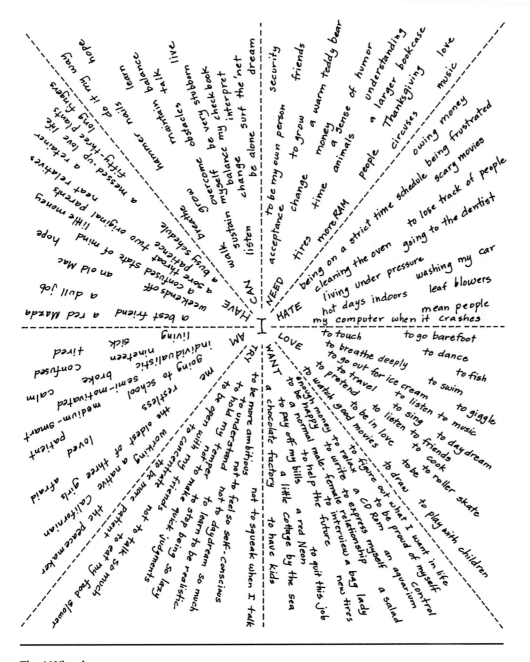

The I Wheel

2/

Personality and Performance

Pieces of the Puzzle

 GOALS

- Assess your Personality Mosaic.

- Identify your career interests.

- Pinpoint your relationship to data, people, things, and work qualities.

- Identify your skills trio.

- Determine your personal style.

A personality can be likened to a stained glass window—a mosaic of light and color. A stained glass window is an enduring object of carefully chosen colors, yet it changes with the changing sun. In darkness it seems to disappear, but in the light it comes alive with color.

> It takes
> its life from light
>   it sleeps at night
>   and comes ablaze at dawn
>   it holds the day
>   'til shadows fade,
>   its brilliance strangely gone.
>   —*Michelozzi*

You have surveyed your needs, wants, values, and important activities. You've begun to gather pieces of your own one-of-a-kind mosaic to create a portrait of a special person—*you*. The activities you've enjoyed so far will give you clues to the interests unique to your personality. These in turn will help you discover your skills. You'll be ready to relate the assembled information to satisfying positions in the world of work. When you enter the workplace, you may have had to make some compromises, but the ideal is to minimize the compromises and maximize the match.

AREAS OF INTEREST: THE PERSONALITY MOSAIC

Psychologist and vocational counselor John Holland says that one of six major personality types—or perhaps a combination of two or more types—plays a highly important role in an individual's career choice.[1] We become interested in some areas more than others early in life. These areas become focal points, largely because of choices we make that stem from our needs, wants, and values.

Notice what interests draw individuals when family or friends get together. Sports and cars are a magnet to some; the lives and loves of people are a concern to others; participating in mind-bending discussions, plotting a financial move, or sharing creative endeavors can keep some members of a group going until all hours. Because every person notices and experiences things differently, *you* are unique in the combination of things that interest *you*. Those interests make up your predominant personality characteristics and are keys to your career satisfaction.

Becoming aware of your "lesser lights" can also provide some illumination and enrichment. We are all born with innumerable possibilities. Some of our talents may remain undeveloped for half a lifetime only to surface in the middle and senior years. Personal growth leads to the discovery of new dimensions of ourselves. Then there is that rare "Renaissance person" who seems able to be and to do all things with apparently equal ease, who is at home in all settings and with all people.

In this chapter, you can identify the predominant orientation of your personality with an inventory called the Personality Mosaic. It's important to take this inventory before reading the interpretation that follows. Then you can analyze the kinds of activities you've been enjoying all your life. Having reminded yourself of your interests, you will be ready to tie these data into the Job Chart in Chapter 3.

◎ PERSONALITY MOSAIC

Circle the numbers of statements that clearly sound like something you might say or do or think—something that feels like *you*. Don't stop to analyze your responses too much. If you wish, put question marks (?) in front of doubtful items and X's on the numbers of statements that feel very unlike you.

1. It's important for me to have a strong, agile body.
2. I need to understand things thoroughly.
3. Music, color, writing, beauty of any kind can really affect my moods.
4. Relationships with people enrich my life and give it meaning.
5. I am confident that I'll be successful.
6. I need clear directions so I know exactly what to do.
7. I can usually carry/build/fix things myself.
8. I can get absorbed for hours in thinking something out.
9. I appreciate beautiful surroundings; color and design mean a lot to me.
10. I'll spend time finding ways to help people through personal crises.
11. I enjoy competing.
12. I prefer getting carefully organized before I start a project.
13. I enjoy making things with my hands.
14. It's satisfying to explore new ideas.
15. I always seem to be looking for new ways to express my creativity.
16. I value being able to share personal concerns with people.
17. Being a key person in a group is very stimulating to me.
18. I take pride in being very careful about all the details of my work.
19. I don't mind getting my hands dirty.
20. I see education as a lifelong process of developing and sharpening my mind.
21. I like to dress in unusual ways, try new colors and styles.
22. I can often sense when a person needs to talk to someone.

23. I enjoy getting people organized and on the move.
24. I'd rather be safe than adventurous in making decisions.
25. I like to buy sensible things I can make or work on myself.
26. Sometimes I can sit for long periods of time and work on problems or puzzles or read or just think.
27. I have a great imagination.
28. I like to help people develop their talents and abilities.
29. I like to be in charge of getting the job done.
30. I usually prepare carefully ahead of time if I have to handle a new situation.
31. I'd rather be on my own doing practical, hands-on activities.
32. I'm eager to read or think about any subject that arouses my curiosity.
33. I love to try creative new ideas.
34. If I have a problem with someone, I'll keep trying to resolve it peacefully.
35. To be successful, it's important to aim high.
36. I don't like to take responsibility for making big decisions.
37. I say what's on my mind and don't beat around the bush.
38. I need to analyze a problem pretty thoroughly before I act on it.
39. I like to rearrange my surroundings to make them unique and different.
40. I often solve my personal problems by talking them out with someone.
41. I get projects started and let others take care of details.
42. Being on time is very important to me.
43. I enjoy doing vigorous outdoor activities.
44. I keep asking, "Why?"
45. I like my work to be an expression of my moods and feelings.
46. I like to help people find ways to care more for each other.
47. It's exciting to take part in important decisions.
48. I am usually neat and orderly.
49. I like my surroundings to be plain and practical.
50. I need to stay with a problem until I figure out an answer.
51. The beauty of nature touches something deep inside me.
52. Close personal relationships are valuable to me.
53. Promotion and advancement are important to me.
54. I feel more secure when my day is well planned.
55. I'm not afraid of heavy physical work and usually know what needs to be done.
56. I enjoy books that make me think and give me new ideas.
57. I look forward to seeing art shows, plays, and good films.
58. I am very sensitive to people who are experiencing emotional upsets.
59. It's exciting for me to influence people.
60. When I say I'll do it, I do my best to follow through on every detail.
61. Good, hard manual labor never hurt anyone.
62. I'd like to learn all there is to know about subjects that interest me.
63. I don't want to be like everyone else; I like to do things differently.

64. I'll go out of my way to be caring of people with problems.
65. I'm willing to take some risks to get ahead.
66. I feel more secure when I follow rules.
67. One of the first things I look for in a car is a well-built engine.
68. I like a conversation to be intellectually stimulating/challenging.
69. When I'm creating, I tend to let everything else go.
70. I feel concerned that so many people in our society need help.
71. It's challenging to persuade people to follow a plan.
72. I'm very good about checking details.
73. I usually know how to take care of things in an emergency.
74. Reading about new discoveries is exciting.
75. I appreciate beautiful and unusual things.
76. I take time to pay attention to people who seem lonely and friendless.
77. I love to bargain.
78. I like to be very careful about spending money.
79. Exercise or sports are important to me in building a strong body.
80. I've always been curious about the way nature works.
81. It's fun to be in a mood to try something unusual.
82. I am a good listener when people talk about personal problems.
83. If I don't make it the first time, I usually bounce back with energy and enthusiasm.
84. I need to know exactly what people expect me to do.
85. I like to take things apart to see whether I can fix them.
86. I like to study all the facts and decide logically.
87. It would be hard to imagine my life without beauty around me.
88. People often seem to tell me their problems.
89. I can usually connect with people who get me in touch with a network of resources.
90. It's very satisfying to do a task carefully and completely.

Scoring Your Answers

To score, use the table on the following page and circle the same numbers that you circled on the Personality Mosaic.

Count the number of circles in each column and write the total number of circles in the spaces, 15 being the highest possible score:

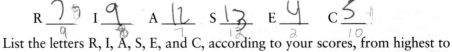

R __7__ I __9__ A __12__ S __13__ E __4__ C __5__

List the letters R, I, A, S, E, and C, according to your scores, from highest to lowest:

1st __S__   2nd __A__   3rd __I__   4th __R__   5th __C__   6th __E__

R	I	A	S	E	C
1	2?	3	4	5	6
7	8	9	10	11	12
13	14	15	16	17 X	18
19	20	21 X	22	23 X	24
25	26	27	28	29	30
31	32?	33	34	35 X	36
37	38	39	40	41	42
43	44	45	46	47	48
49	50	51	52	53 X	54
55	56	57	58	59	60
61	62	63?	64	65	66
67	68	69	70	71	72
73	74	75	76	77 X	78
79	80	81	82	83	84
85	86	87	88	89	90

Handwritten totals above columns: R 9, I 8, A 7, S 12, E 2, C 10

Number of question marks:

R __1__ I __2?__ A __11__ S _____ E _____ C _____

Number of X's:

R __2__ I __6__ A __3__ S __2__ E __10__ C __10__

If you put question marks on the inventory, does adding them in change the order? __NO__ How? _____

Which areas have the most X's? __E & C   E + A__

_____

In which areas do you have the most "unlike you" scores (X's)? __E__

_____A_____

Were you aware at any time of responding according to "shoulds"? __Yes__ NO

In what cases? ____service + responsibility____

Do you have a tie score in two more or columns? If so, the remainder of this chapter will help you to decide which type is closest to the "real you."

To get more in touch with yourself, read aloud some of the statements for each orientation from the Personality Mosaic. *Be* that kind of person. Embellish and dramatize the statements to see how that kind of behavior feels. You may want to role-play this activity in a group.

Interpreting the Personality Mosaic

The inventory you have just taken is based on the six personality orientations identified by John Holland. As you can see from your score, you are not just one personality type—that is, you are not a person with fifteen circles in one area and no circles in any of the others. In most people, one or two characteristics are dominant, two or three are of medium intensity, and one or two may be of low intensity. A few people score high in each category because they have many interests. Others, who don't have many strong interests, score rather low in all areas.

Sometimes people experiencing emotional stress in their lives find it difficult to do this inventory. Finding a counselor or another trusted person to talk to may help before you continue your career exploration.

Here is an overview and discussion of the six personality types and their relationship to each other. Try to find yourself in the following descriptions.

Realistic Personality

Hands-on people who enjoy exploring things, fixing things, making things with their hands

Express themselves and achieve primarily through their bodies rather than through words, thoughts, feelings

Are usually independent, practical-minded, strong, well coordinated, aggressive, conservative, rugged individualists

Like the challenge of physical risk, being outdoors, using tools and machinery

Prefer concrete problems to abstract ones

Solve problems by doing something physical

Realistic individuals are capable and confident when using their bodies to relate to the physical world. They focus on *things*, learn through their hands, and have little need for conversation. Because they are at ease with material objects, they are often good in physical emergencies. Their ability to deal with the material world often makes them very independent. Because these characteristics describe the stereotypical male, many women shrink from displaying any capability in this area, and even in this enlightened age, women may be discouraged from doing so. However, women are increasingly participating in traditionally male-dominated activities.

Investigative Personality

People who live very much "in their minds"

Are unconventional and independent thinkers, intellectually curious, very insightful, logical, persistent

Express themselves and achieve primarily through their minds rather than through association with people or involvement with things

Like to explore ideas through reading, discussing .

Enjoy complex and abstract mental challenges

Solve problems by thinking and analyzing

The investigative type deals with the "real world" of things but at a distance. These individuals prefer to read, study, use books, charts, and other data instead of getting their hands on *things*. When involved with people, they tend to focus on ideas. Wherever they are, they collect information and analyze the situation before making a decision. If they enjoy the outdoors, it's because they are curious, not because they enjoy rugged, heavy, physical work.

Artistic Personality

People who are creative, sensitive, aesthetic, introspective, intuitive, visionary

See new possibilities and want to express them in creative ways

Are especially attuned to perception of color, form, sound, feeling

Prefer to work alone and independently rather than with others

Enjoy beauty, variety, the unusual in sight, sound, texture, people

Need a fairly unstructured environment to provide opportunities for creative expression

Solve problems by creating something new

Artistic people express creativity not only with paint and canvas but with ideas and systems as well. Those sensitive to sight, sound, and touch will be drawn to the fine arts such as art, drama, music, and literature. The weaver designs and makes fabric; the poet creates with words; the choreographer arranges dancers in flowing patterns; the architect creates with space; and the technically gifted create captivating Web sites. But the industrialist creates systems for the flow of goods; the program planner creates better delivery of services. Others will be content just to enjoy aesthetic experience.

Artistic types often love the beauty and power of the outdoors to inspire their creativity—but not its ability to make them perspire with heavy work. They would rather create ideas than study them. They like variety and are not afraid to experiment, often disregarding rules. Their ideas don't always please others, but opposition doesn't discourage them for long. Their irrepressible spirits and enthusiasm can often keep them focused on a creative project to the exclusion of all else, though plowing new ground can be lonely and agonizing. Not producing up to standard (their own) can plunge them to the depths of misery.

Social Personality

People persons who "live" primarily in their feelings

Are sensitive to others, genuine, humanistic, supportive, responsible, tactful, perceptive

Focus on people and their concerns rather than on things or intellectual activity

Enjoy closeness with others, sharing feelings, being in groups and in unstructured settings that allow for flexibility and caring

Solve problems primarily by feeling and intuition, by helping others

The social personality focuses on people and their concerns. Sensitive to people's moods and feelings, these individuals may often enjoy company and make friends easily but not necessarily. Some, with a concern for people, may be shy individuals and even introverts who need time alone, although they focus on people's needs. Their level of caring may range from one person to the entire planet. Their relationships with people depend on their ability to communicate both verbally and nonverbally, listening as well as speaking and writing. Their empathy and ability to intuit emotional cues help them to solve people problems sometimes before others are even aware of them. They can pull people together and generate positive energy for the sake of others, but not for themselves. Because the social orientation seems to describe the "typical female," many men shrink from expressing or dealing with deep feelings. The social personality types sometimes focus on people concerns to the exclusion of all else. They sometimes appear "impractical," especially to the realistic types.

Enterprising Personality

Project people who are thoroughly absorbed in their strategies

Are energetic, enthusiastic, confident, dominant, political, verbal, assertive, quick decision makers

Are self-motivated leaders who are talented at organizing, persuading, managing

Achieve primarily by using these skills in dealing with people and projects

Enjoy money, power, status, being in charge

Solve problems by taking risks

The enterprising person is a leader who initiates projects but often gets others to carry them out. Instead of doing research, these people rely on hunches about what will work. They may strike an observer as restless and irresponsible because they often move on after a job is under way, but many activities would never get off the ground without their energizing influence. They need to be a leader of the "in crowd," but because their relationships center around tasks, they may focus so dynamically on the project that the personal concerns of others, and even their own, go unnoticed.

Conventional Personality

People who "live" primarily in their orderliness

Are quiet, careful, accurate, responsible, practical, persevering, well organized, task oriented

Have a strong need to feel secure and certain, get things finished, attend to every detail, follow a routine

Prefer to work for someone of power and status rather than be in such a position themselves

Solve problems by appealing to and following rules

The conventional person also is task oriented but prefers to carry out tasks initiated by others. Because these individuals are careful of detail, they keep the world's records and transmit its messages on time and accurately. They obey rules, and they value order in the world of data. They like to be well prepared ahead of time and prefer minimal changes. Getting tasks finished gives them immense satisfaction. Their sense of responsibility keeps the world going as they focus on details of the tasks at hand to the exclusion of all else.

The Personality Hexagon

The six personality types can be arranged in a hexagon. In the figure, "Personality Types: Similarities and Differences," the types next to one another are most similar. The words linking them indicate their shared traits or interests. For example, realistic and investigative people focus on things. The R person does something to or with the thing; the I person analyzes it. Investigative and artistic types are both "idea" people. The I explores and may develop ideas logically; the A invents them intuitively. Artistic and social people like to be in tune with their feelings—the A person with feelings about

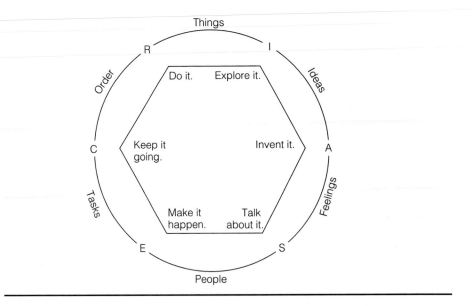

Personality Types: Similarities and Differences SOURCE: Reproduced by special permission of the publisher, Psychological Assessment Resources, Inc., from *Making Vocational Choices,* Third Edition. Copyright © 1973, 1985, 1992, 1997 by Psychological Assessment Resources, Inc. All rights reserved.

surroundings, the S person with feelings about people. Social and enterprising people are people leaders: the S person is concerned about people; the E person wants to get people motivated to undertake a task. The conventional person will carry out the details of the task to the last dot. Thus the E and C are both task oriented in different ways—the E person initiating and leading, and the C type carrying through to completion with the utmost responsibility. Both C and R types value order: the C values data/paper order; the R values physical order. People seek out work activities that enable them to be with others of like personality. Workplaces, too, tend to gather similar types and reflect the style of these workers.

The types opposite each other on the hexagon are most unlike. For example, the artistic personality is independent, doesn't mind disorder, and likes to try new things. The conventional person depends more on other people, likes order, and would prefer things to stay the same.

Two people who are strongly opposite in personality can improve their relationship by understanding the differences between them. A realistic person doesn't deal much with people's feelings, whereas a social person sees much of life through feelings. The introspective I person is amazed at the outgoing E person's ability to act without doing much research. Because opposites complement each other, it can be advantageous to see a radically different personality as a potential source of support and enrichment. Wise

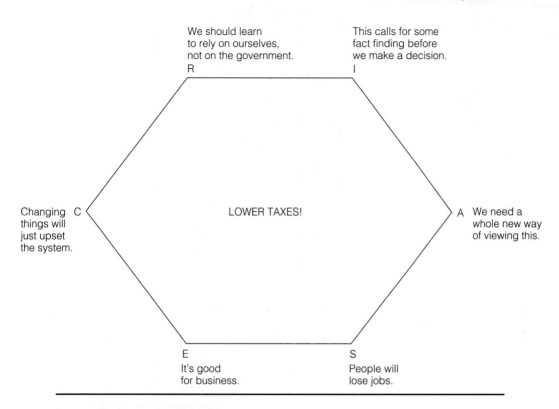

We should learn
to rely on ourselves,
not on the government.
R

This calls for some
fact finding before
we make a decision.
I

Changing   C
things will
just upset
the system.

LOWER TAXES!

A   We need a
whole new way
of viewing this.

E
It's good
for business.

S
People will
lose jobs.

Personality Types: Typical Talk

employers will hire those whose personality orientation is appropriate for the work to be done.

The strengths of each type can be weaknesses if taken to excess, giving each personality type a "down side." People who focus too narrowly may miss the nuances, the ways in which others' views and ways of doing things fit together to bring perspective to a situation. For example, attention to detail is a plus but can lead to such an extreme desire for perfection that a person can't finish a job lest it have a flaw, can't make a decision lest it be a mistake.

Imagine six people sitting around the hexagon. Each person is a strong representative of a personality type. Give the group an issue to discuss (such as lower taxes, in the figure "Personality Types: Typical Talk") and each person will look at it in a different way. A, I, R, C, and E types focus mainly on the tasks they do, whereas the social personality is the one who focuses on the impact these tasks will have on people.

Sometimes we have personality conflicts within ourselves. We'd like to be creative and try something different, but our conventional nature tells us that's a "no-no." We'd like to take an enterprising risk, but our investigative side

PERSONALITY TYPES: AN EYE OPENER

An engineering manager is orienting a group of older women exploring careers in his company. The conversation turns to personal matters, and he shares with them his early difficulties in communicating with his wife. He found it hard to understand her continued wish that he would *talk* to her. When a divorce threatened, he sought some communications training and struggled with this strange new activity: sharing feelings he never knew he had. The women related well to this story. After a tour of the plant, they agreed that working with electronic circuits wasn't for them. Then the engineer replied that it would be as hard for them to work in his more realistic/investigative area as it was for him to learn the social skills of dealing with people and their feelings!

wants to gather all the facts before deciding. Realistic folks who mostly like to be alone dealing with physical objects need some people interaction, too. All personality types are surprised to learn that the characteristics of an opposite type can help make their own lives work better. The social personality may need to learn a certain amount of independence from people; the enterprising one, to find out facts before acting; the artistic, to be careful of detail; the realistic person, to stay in touch with other people and their feelings; the investigative person, to take a risk; and the conventional person, to try something new!

You will likely find a job difficult if it lies in an area very different from the interests of your personality type. An engineer with thirteen years' experience in the field admitted that he had thought engineering would involve his hands and now wished to become a technician. An industrial arts teacher wished that his job didn't involve motivating people all the time. His industrial specialty was also "too clerical" because it dealt with safety and time studies. Both these people would have been more content with work that let them use machines and tools in some way.

A woman who works as an audiologist confides that after she obtained her degree in speech pathology and audiology she did remedial speech in a school setting. She felt that results were not very clear and successes difficult to pin down. She now finds that administering hearing tests and fitting people with hearing aids gives her a sense of definite accomplishment, enables her to use her hands, and gives her just the right amount of social interaction.

Rose Marie Dunphy, a realistic/artistic woman, illustrates what it feels like to be doing "what you are fitted for," as Maslow says. She says about her sewing, "Each time I touch a piece of fabric, magic occurs. I don't see corduroy or cotton but a dress, a shirt, curtains with tiebacks. Each time I sit on my chair facing the sewing machine, I disappear. I've gone into my hands . . . fabric, foot, and needle join hands to perform one function. In the process, they become one, and as in a chemical reaction, a totally different thing emerges. Not just a dress or curtain, but a new me."[2]

Wynne Busby describes the same sensation she observes happening in a young carpenter who puts in a window for her. "I could sense all the skill, years of experience, of loving handling of tools and wood, which was available to him even for such a simple task as this." And she sees the same absorption, the same intimacy of hand, mind, tool, materials in her calligraphy teacher. "Her hand remembers the shape of the pen. The ink flows and the letters curve, black and clean on the page. All the skill which her hand remembers is available for her work of creation."[3]

On a whimsical note that illustrates the differing approach of the investigative/idea, not-always-practical people and the realistic pragmatic ones, an old "Down-easter" said, "One of the things that struck me and other Maine people [was that] the bright young people had all the ideas about the way things should happen. The Maine people were more used to getting the hay in before it rained."[4]

At first you may not see yourself clearly in the results of the Personality Mosaic. One woman told her class that she was certain she was not investigative. Then she admitted to the delight of the group that her next thought was, "I wonder *why* it turned out that way!" Take time to study and understand each personality type, and only then accept the data that really seem to fit you well.

Understanding your personality can help you make a good career decision. Understanding the personalities of others can improve your human relationships and ease your acceptance of the choices that others make. And note that we may act in each of these six modes more than we realize. They represent activities that we need and want to do.

Realistic: Physical Mode
Running on the beach
Eating a pizza
Cleaning the sink

Social: People Mode
Laughing with a friend
Hugging the baby
Listening to an aging person

Investigative: Mind Mode
Discussing politics
Reading *War and Peace*
Planning a trip to Europe

Enterprising: Accomplishment Mode
Organizing a party
Saying "Hello" first
Applying for a job

Artistic: Aesthetic Mode
Enjoying a sunset
Wearing complementary colors
Decorating a cake

Conventional: Structure Mode
Stopping at a stop sign
Straightening your closet
Finishing a paper on time

Well, what have we here?

Does growth mean allowing all these dimensions to surface and actualizing them to the best of your ability? Albert Einstein was not only a great scientist but also a creative visionary with concern for people. As you grow, will you feel more comfortable in all these areas? Your career decision may fall within the area of your highest personality type; it may reflect a blend of several types. Stop and take a good look at your personality; then discuss your dominant personality characteristics with someone and explain why they feel right to you.

DEALING WITH DATA, PEOPLE, AND THINGS

The world around you has only three areas your personality can relate to: data (ideas and information), people, and things. We have organized much of the decision-making material that follows into these three areas.

Data

The human mind can take in and give out great quantities of information, or data, in the form of words, numbers, and symbols. All day long the mind clicks away, taking in and expressing thoughts and ideas, often creatively and always in a way unique to the individual. When you notice you are out of bread and jot it down on the grocery list, you've just processed some data. Reading, writing, speaking, and listening all deal with data. Every activity deals with data to some extent, from simple to complex. The cry of the newborn gives us data about how the baby feels. Lights blinking on your car dashboard can be saying, "Stop and get oil—now!" Some people think of data as complex numbers and computer spreadsheets. But data include all kinds of ideas and information: the words you speak, read, hear; the music you enjoy; the smiles of your friends; the colors of the sunset. Anything that is not a person or a concrete object is called data, and we deal with it on various levels of complexity, from just noticing it to copying it to developing or creating it.

People

Another kind of activity depends on interaction with people. We deal with people at various levels of complexity, from greeting and waiting on them to dealing with their long-term personal growth. A rent-a-car clerk in an airport observed that she liked working with people, but not with the public. Conversely, a person who thought she wanted to be a counselor found the less-involved people contact she experienced as a bank teller to be just right. *We use a great deal of data when we deal with other humans.* We involve all sorts of body/mind perceptions and linguistic skills. The emotions, which are physical responses to sensory information, permeate our mental processes and influence our behavior and relationships with others. For example, managers find that people generally respond better to the people skills of genuine respect and affection, the basis for good human interaction, rather than to competition and control.

Things

We relate to physical objects in any number of ways: building, repairing, carrying, making things, running machines; tinkering with gadgets from food processors to power saws. The physical object that we use may be our bodies in such activities as sports and dance. Involvement with things can range from simple activities (putting up a picture) to complex ones (repairing a satellite). The body skills used require various degrees of strength, agility, and coordination in relating to other physical objects. The way the body fixes and builds things often requires creative ability. And, of course, we need the data required to deal with those things.

You learned to deal with data, people, and things at all levels early in life. Look again at your Candid Camera 3-D lists from Chapter 1. How many times have you planned events, organized people, or repaired objects in your lifetime? Using data, people, and/or things, individuals do tasks that range from repairing cars and computers to creating music, art, literature, and scientific and technical wonders. And amazingly, every day—using your body, emotions, mind, and spirit—*you* create your life.

Activity Analysis

In the Candid Camera 3-D exercise in Chapter 1, you listed every activity you could think of that you've done in your life: jobs, community and extracurricular activities, education, and other projects, along with all the things you had to do to accomplish each activity. This expanded activity list gave you background that helped you determine your personality orientation. Now you will use it to choose satisfying life activities.

It's important to analyze activities in detail. A woman says she is realistic because she likes to garden. Her notebook shows that she obviously loves collecting, organizing, and analyzing data, as she had a list of seeds, a planting schedule, a layout of her garden. Asked how her garden was, she said, "Not so good!" She didn't get out there very much. Her personality type and then her activity analysis showed that she was much more investigative than realistic and that data were more interesting than things. So study your lists to be sure that you have broken down each activity into as many specific component activities as possible. And check to be sure that you have coded them D, P, and/or T for their involvement with data, people, or things. These lists will be important for the skills identification exercises that follow.

Skills

If you had actually listed all the activities you've ever done, your list would be enormous. Now here is one of the most important connections for you to make. When you've *done* any activity, that means you *can* do it! You've shown you have the ability, and that ability is a *skill!* Many people think they have no skills because they can't play the oboe or dance up a storm. But in reality they have been accomplishing things successfully for many years and have the capacity to accomplish much more. One factor is confidence. If you *think* you can, then you are well on the way to accomplishment. At least you can probably do something that has some of the satisfiers of your dream job.

For example, a teacher completed an interest inventory that suggested a career in the performing arts. Acting seemed intriguing, but not likely to provide much income for a beginner. It suddenly dawned on the teacher how much she loved "appearing" in a class or workshop, making people laugh and appreciate her. When she first became a teacher, she found teaching difficult and, as a result, tended either to over- or under-discipline her classes. Her confidence grew with her realization that she could teach and have fun doing it. Now she rarely misses a chance to talk with a group.

So instead of groaning at your "lack of talent," think of all the talents you've used in a life filled with data, people, and things. And because the majority of workers have only average skills—most workers can do *many* jobs. And that includes you! Part of using skills effectively is having confidence in yourself. The question is, then, of all the skills you possess, which do you enjoy using? And more important, which would you like to use in a work setting? For having skills is only one part of the puzzle. Do you prefer to work primarily with data, people, or things? Of all the jobs you *can* do, which would you *like* to do? Then knowing when and where to use those skills wisely takes growth.

> If you like what you are doing,
> you will likely excel at it!
> —*Ironworker Clif Signor*

The interests you have been listing are usually a good clue to your skills. Most people acquire skills in areas they enjoy, and they tend to neglect other areas. If you like something, you spend time doing it, get better at it and like it more, and spend more time doing it.

We came into this world already well equipped for action. Unless a serious defect exists, human growth and potential for growth are phenomenal. Look at a six-month-old and be amazed at the complexity of skills he or she has acquired compared with those of a newborn infant. Compare with a six-year-old and be further astounded! Educator and author Peter Kline says that we are all budding "everyday geniuses" when we are born. But we express that genius in different ways.[5] Sometimes, somewhere along the line, confidence and energy may begin to lag. Brain researcher Jean Houston says that by age seventeen we are using only 17 percent of our body's potential for flexible movement, compared to what we used at age three. She says that as the body goes, so does the mind. Houston finds that even the very elderly, with correct exercise, can "remake" their bodies in six months, and their mental and emotional powers are greatly enhanced at the same time.[6]

Dividing the self into "mind" and "body" is only an exercise about concepts that are very difficult to define. Because our educational system stresses mental activities, we sometimes infer that men and women who work with their hands are not "using their heads." In reality, the two cannot be separated; they can only be examined separately as two different modes of living and learning. Life experiences help us develop innumerable skills of both mind and body.

The Skills Trio

There are three kinds of skills: transferable, work-specific, and personal responsibility skills.[7] *Transferable skills* are used in many kinds of activities and are transferred from one job to another. For example, planning can involve the following steps: (1) determine/establish objectives for a program; (2) set policies, procedures; (3) do long- and short-range forecasts; (4) schedule strategies; and (5) evaluate/revise the program. We take steps like these almost unconsciously as we learn to make decisions and plan to accomplish some task.

Every job requires transferable skills, with communications skills in writing and speaking highly important to many positions and often the key to getting a job and advancement on the job. For example, engineers find they must often write up and present proposals for projects and then report their results. Perhaps 80 to 90 percent of the content of most jobs require transferable skills—those you already have *to some degree.* Employers usually look to hire people who have broad transferable skill sets that enable them to master their new job quickly, "fit in" with their coworkers, and contribute to the company's success.

Work-specific skills, the other 10 to 20 percent, may require on-the-job training (OJT), further formal education, or both. A salesperson, for example, depends largely on transferable skills and can learn quickly. More and more jobs require special training, especially in science, technical fields, and the arts. This training develops work-specific skills, such as those used by electronics technicians, business managers, doctors, and ballerinas. For example, job seekers who are knowledgeable and at ease with computers will have a major advantage over those who are not.

Personal responsibility skills reflect the ways you manage *yourself* in relation to data, people, and things; they reflect the ways you express your transferable and work-specific skills. They are the traits that parents and teachers often stress: common sense; responsibility; dedication; willingness to learn, to work hard, and to finish what you begin; careful use of others' property; working well with people; working without undue anxiety; acceptance of criticism; good grooming; courtesy; kindness; honesty; humor; optimism; promptness. Every skill area is greatly enhanced by personal responsibility skills.

The ability to deal well with oneself in relationship to other people is an aspect of personal responsibility skills that is a strong predictor of success. You may have noticed that the brainiest kids in your class may not always be the most adept at getting along with people. Now researchers are beginning to measure this important area of ability, which they call emotional intelligence (EQ—Emotional Quotient); it is quite distinct from intelligence (measured in the past by IQ—Intelligence Quotient.)[8] Some people develop such skills at an early age, often independent of formal education. Others must learn them by encountering and solving difficulties in their interpersonal relationships. Review the statements and the qualities of the social personality from the Personality Mosaic to gain more insights about emotional intelligence.

Negative interpersonal habits *can* be changed by taking an unprejudiced look at the "trouble spots" you experience with others. Assess how much of the problem is your responsibility without unduly blaming yourself. Learn to sense what you and other people are feeling and don't blame them for what you experience. For example, no one can *make* you angry, even though it seems that way. To improve his or her EQ, a person can work at being sensitive, caring, and kind to others; to see the positive side of events; to be persistent and enthusiastic; to learn to delay gratification; to give credit to others when it is due.

Employee recruiters often remark that the ability to get along with people is one skill they look for above all others. In management positions, the ability to motivate, encourage, and respect others is a giant plus. Acquiring all the personal responsibility skills is more vital than ever for career and life success as workplaces downsize, require more education of new hires, and use more technology, depending on each employee to "self-manage"—that is, take more responsibility on the job. This is especially true in small entrepreneurial companies that require everyone to wear many hats.

It's great to be intelligent, to be proficient with data and things, but without good people skills, success is often hard to achieve. Using well-developed interrelational skills can even help return "civility to our streets and caring to our communal life," says Harvard psychobiologist Daniel Goleman, author of *Emotional Intelligence*.[9] Generally, we would much rather work with, play with, and marry someone with good people skills.

You have survived modern life so far. Your physical, mental, emotional, social, and financial well-being have depended on your abilities. You *must* possess a good measure of skills in all areas *and be able to build on this foundation.*

GETTING AN EDGE ON THE JOB HUNT PROCESS

People often underestimate what they have done in life. Both career searching and job hunting require that you know what you have done so you can apply it to what you want to do. When a high school graduate was asked to make a list of her job activities in a drive-in, she replied that she had done nothing of importance. "All I did was make hamburgers." But speaking informally, she was able to describe what she did in more detail. She then coded each activity with a P (dealing directly with people), T (dealing directly with things or material objects), or D (dealing with data): she noticed when supplies were running low, and ordered (D) and put them away (T). She took charge when the owners were away (D). She showed new clerks what to do (P, D). Sometimes she did minor repairs on kitchen equipment (T). She made all the sauces (T). She settled disagreements about orders (P). She could always tell when a new clerk wasn't going to work out (D).

After a great deal of polishing, her list looked like this:

Human Relations (People, Data)

Worked well with customers/employers, coworkers (good teamwork)

Oriented, trained, evaluated employees

Settled customer/employee disagreements

Materials Maintenance (Things, Data)

Inventoried, ordered, stored, prepared materials

Did maintenance/repair

Opened and closed business

Handled cash/cash register

Data Without People or Things

Organized/scheduled work

Her work had a great deal of variety, also. Knowing what she had done enabled her to make a better career decision.

A section of her résumé, developed for a management trainee position in a small restaurant, summarized her experience as a supervisor/cook:

Inventoried, ordered, prepared, and stocked food supplies.
Settled employee and customer problems and complaints.
Oriented/trained new employees, informally evaluated performance.
Did minor repairs/maintenance.
As occasional acting manager, opened and closed shop, handled cash/cash register.

She also included a summary of her qualifications that pointed out her personal responsibility skills.

Demonstrates good teamwork with customers, employees, and coworkers.
Notices and takes care of details.
Reliable with excellent time management skills.

Reprinted with permission from Mal Hancock.

With her additional training in food and restaurant management, she was qualified for the position she was seeking.

Observe yourself. What skills do you want to acquire and develop to get where you would like to be? In what ways would you like to focus your transferable skills to gain those that are more work specific? If you have good finger dexterity, for example, would you prefer to become adept at the guitar, the computer keyboard, brain surgery, or all three? Are you willing to devote some time to further training and education to acquire these work-specific skills? Which personal responsibility skills are your strengths? Which will you work to improve? These are important questions to answer when you are making career decisions.

A Look at Your Personal Style and Careers

Each of us has preferences for the *way* we focus our attention, gather information, make decisions, and interact with the world around us. The work of Swiss psychologist Carl Jung indicated that behavior that seemed unpredictable could in fact be anticipated if one understood the underlying mental functions and attitudes people preferred. The Myers-Briggs Type Indicator (MBTI®), developed by the mother-and-daughter team of Katherine Briggs and Isabel Briggs-Myers, is a contemporary assessment tool that is widely used to help identify personal preferences and the kinds of careers and work environments that are a good fit for each personality type.

Understanding your personal style can be important in finding the career of your dreams. Ask yourself these four questions:

1. Where do you focus your attention—externally, with people and things, or internally, with contemplating thoughts and reflections?
2. How do you gather information—from actual data and information or from "hunches" or intuition?
3. How do you make decisions—from objective considerations or from personal feelings?
4. What type of lifestyle do you like—one that is planned or one that is more spontaneous?

You may be saying to yourself that it depends on the situation what your preference will be, and you are absolutely right. We all act differently in different situations. Say you know your boss is coming to your office at noon to talk to you. Usually your office has papers all over and things cluttered on your desk—this is your preferred work environment—*but,* you clean things up knowing that you want to make a good impression. Your preferred style is the more natural and comfortable one for you and is usually reflected in your career choice.

Understanding your personal style helps you to recognize and appreciate your unique talents; to capitalize on them to build stronger working relationships; to make good decisions; and to contribute your best work. It also helps you to evaluate your current work situation and plan for future career options. For example, a thirty-year-old computer programmer who is dismayed because he does not have enough interaction with people finds himself talking "around the water cooler" or sending personal e-mails rather than doing his work. In his performance review, the computer programmer explained that he liked being around people, "shooting the breeze" rather than programming, helping others solve their technical problems. He also enjoyed the compliments he received for his assistance. It seemed that he was more of a "people person," receiving his energy from others. Luckily, he had an astute manager who understood the programmer's unique talents and made an appropriate work reassignment. Within six months, the once unproductive computer programmer became a successful technical assistance expert, combining his technical expertise with his ability to communicate with others.

To explore personal style further, David Keirsey, who wrote the book *Please Understand Me*[10] offers a free online assessment similar to the MBTI® (www.keirsey.com). Two other excellent resources and Web sites that explain personal style, using the MBTI® as a basis and in relation to careers, are *Do What You Are: Discover the Personality Career for You Through the Secrets of Personality Type*[11] by Paul Tieger and Barbara Tieger (www.personalitytype.com); and *What's Your Type of Career? Unlock the Secrets of Your Personality to Find Your Perfect Career Path*[12] by Donna Dunning (www.dunning.ca/whattype.html).

You can find additional career assessments online. Online assessments can be a good beginning **but,** they do not replace the value of discussing your career search with a professional. Many of the services are free. If you decide to purchase an online assessment, make sure that it is from a reliable source and that you will receive what you are paying for.

The Princeton Review Career Quiz is a brief questionnaire of career interests and personal work style. It takes about five to ten minutes to complete and gives you a short summary of your results. In addition, if you register at their Web site, you will receive a list of careers that match with your results (http://www.princetonreview.com/cte/).

Career Storm (http://www.careerstorm.com/stormnavigator) is a Finnish site that offers free online assessments in several foreign languages. It is one of the best sites to quickly evaluate your personal style, skills, interests, and values.

The Career Key helps you choose a career or a college major; change a career; and focus your career planning (http://www.careerkey.org/english/yo).

The Career Center at Missouri University (http://career.missouri.edu/holland/) offers an online simplified career interests assessment based on John Holland's RIASEC personality types.

SUMMARY

In this chapter, you have discovered your Personality Mosaic. You have examined the six major personality types—Realistic, Investigative, Artistic, Social, Enterprising, and Conventional—and identified which type or combination of types interests you most. There are three areas your personality can relate to: data (information), people (interactions with others), and things (activities). You relate to all three areas, but you may tend to gravitate toward one area over the others. There are three kinds of skills: transferable/motivated, work-specific, and personal responsibility skills. You have identified skills that have motivated you successfully in the past and will carry you into your future. Each person has a personal style preference for our ideal interactions with the world around us. The diagnostic tools in this chapter have enabled you to identify your personal style and learn the importance of understanding your style when searching for a career. You are putting together some extremely valuable pieces of the career decision puzzle. By better understanding who you are and how you work best, you are beginning down the road to finding a satisfying and fulfilling work life.

◉ SELF-ASSESSMENT EXERCISES

1. Six Personality Types

Social, Conventional, Realistic, artistic, Investigative, Enterprising

a. Circle the personality types that describe you best: ~realistic~, investigative, ~artistic~, ~social~, enterprising, conventional.

b. Discuss the strengths and weaknesses of your top interest personality types. *My strengths are that im personable, weakness — Its hard for me to slow down the shit.*

2. Data, People, Things Indicator

To determine your most important orientations in regard to data, people, and things, consult the Activity Lists you have been working on from Chapter 1, Candid Camera 3-D. Be sure that the lists are as long as you can make them, that you have broken down your activities into specific component activities, and that you have coded all these activities with a P, T, or D as follows:

P = interacting directly with people

T = interacting directly with things

D = using ideas and information (data) without interacting with people or things

Now, check the following: (No check means "little or no involvement.")

Data: I want to get involved with data on my job:

_✓_ At a modest level with data that are easy to learn or that I simply keep track of while others direct my work.

_____ At a high level by putting ideas and information together to plan/organize work and perhaps develop new ideas and ways to do things.

People: I want to get involved with people on my job:

_____ At a modest level by being friendly and cooperative, greeting and serving them, discussing simple problems with them.

__✓__ At a high level by leading/influencing/organizing/motivating them, teaching/entertaining them, negotiating, or exchanging ideas with them, counseling them.

Things: I want to get involved with things on my job:

__✓__ At a modest level by following simple procedures set up by others.

_____ At a high level by working with more complex procedures/equipment that allow my own input.

3. Identifying Your Transferable/Motivated Skills

These are the skills you use naturally, those you enjoy using and that give you energy to do your best work. Transferable skills are very important in generating career options. There are hundreds and hundreds of transferable skills. The list on the following page will help you begin to identify those transferable skills that support your best work. After each skill is a (D) for data, a (P) for people, or a (T) for things, indicating the specific area where the skill is typically used. Some skills can be used in more than one area. For example, you can organize data, things, or people. What is your choice? Feel free to change the (D), (P), or (T) if it differs from how you perceive the skill. In the blank boxes at the end of the list, add other skills relevant to you that were not mentioned. In the spaces preceding each skill, complete each of the four instructions below, finishing each instruction before going to the next:

1. Check column number 1 if you feel competent using that skill.

2. Check column number 2 if you enjoy using that skill and want to continue to use it in your daily work.

3. Check column number 3 if you do not feel competent using that skill but want to develop your proficiency using it.

4. Check column number 4 if you feel competent using that skill *but* do not like or want to continue using it.

1	2	3	4	Skills	1	2	3	4	Skills	1	2	3	4	Skills
✓	✓			Act as liaison (P)	✓	✓			Drive (T)					Operate (T)
	✓	✓		Advise (P)	✓	✓			Encourage (P)					Order (D)
	✓			Analyze (D)	✓	✓			Entertain (P)					Organize (D)
✓				Appoint (P)	✓				Evaluate (D)					Perform (P)
				Assemble (T)					Explain (P)					Persuade (P)
				Audit (D)					Facilitate (P)					Plan (D)
				Body coordination (T)					Fit (T)					Process (D)
				Budget (D)					Forecast (D)					Program (D)
				Build (T)					Guard (T)					Read (D)
		✓		Calculate (D)			✓		Hand dexterity (T)					Record (D)
	✓			Clean (T)	✓				Hire (P)					Refer (P)
		✓		Coach (P)			✓		Illustrate (D)					Repair (T)
	✓			Communicate (P)	✓				Influence (P)					Represent (P)
				Compare (D)					Innovate (D)					Research (D)
		✓		Compile (D)					Inspect (T)					Restore (T)
✓				Compute (D)			✓		Install (T)					Schedule (D)
		✓		Conceptualize (D)	✓	✓			Interview (P)					Sell (P)
✓				Configure (T)	✓				Lead (P)					Serve (P)
✓				Construct (T)					Learn (D)					Set up (T)
		✓		Coordinate (P)					Lift (T)					Spatial relations (T)
✓	✓			Counsel (P)			✓		Listen (P)					Stimulate (P)
	✓			Create (D)	✓				Manage (P)					Supervise (P)
				Cut (T)			✓		Measure (T)					Synthesize (D)
		✓		Debug (T)	✓	✓			Mediate (P)					Teach (P)
				Decide (D)	✓				Mentor (P)					Tend (T)
	✓			Decorate (T)					Monitor (T)					Test (T)
✓				Delegate (P)	✓				Motivate (P)					Troubleshoot (T)
	✓			Demonstrate (T)					Move (T)					Visualize (D)
✓				Design (D)					Negotiate (P)					Work outdoors (T)
				Direct (P)					Numerical reason (D)					Write (D)

- Write each skill for which you checked spaces 1 and 2 in the appropriate columns following: Data (D), People (P), and Things (T). Do you find a concentration of skills in one column or an equal distribution across columns? Do the skills interrelate with each other within each column and across columns? If so how? Is there a theme emerging about how you want to use your skills? If so, what is it? What do you discover about yourself when you rank order the skills you have selected in terms of importance to you from most to least important? All of these are your truly motivated skills, ones that you feel competent in and enjoy using. These skills should be a major part of your work!

Data	People	Things
_____	_____	_____
_____	_____	_____
_____	_____	_____
_____	_____	_____
_____	_____	_____
_____	_____	_____
_____	_____	_____
_____	_____	_____
_____	_____	_____
_____	_____	_____

- Now what skills do you want to develop? Write down those skills for which you checked space 3. These are the skills that you want to develop further so that they can become a part of your motivated skills. Jobs that require these skills may be very attractive to you.

Data	People	Things
_____	_____	_____
_____	_____	_____
_____	_____	_____
_____	_____	_____
_____	_____	_____
_____	_____	_____
_____	_____	_____
_____	_____	_____
_____	_____	_____

- Now, do you have any skills for which only spaces 1 and 4 were checked? If so, write them below. These are your burnout skills. These skills can get you a job because you are good at them. *But:* If you are currently using them extensively in your job, you may have grown or will soon grow tired of using these skills, feel stuck and unable to grow professionally, and you could even start resenting your job, which will negatively impact your performance and job satisfaction. Try to avoid having to use these skills as a major part of your work, if possible; otherwise, you will soon get discouraged and will begin looking for jobs elsewhere.

Data	People	Things
_____	_____	_____
_____	_____	_____
_____	_____	_____
_____	_____	_____
_____	_____	_____
_____	_____	_____
_____	_____	_____
_____	_____	_____
_____	_____	_____
_____	_____	_____

4. Personal Responsibility Skills

Evaluate yourself and your ability to handle data, people, and things. Check (✓) "Good" or "Could Improve" after each statement.

- Evaluate YOURSELF

I usually:	Good	Could Improve
Work hard, with persistence	_____	_____
Use common sense	_____	_____
Show enthusiasm	_____	_____
Have a sense of humor	_____	_____
Am aware of and handle my feelings and moods well	_____	_____

Dress appropriately for work   _____   _____

- Evaluate your interaction with PEOPLE

I usually:

Balance my needs and wants with those   _____   _____
of others

Respond with tact and courtesy   _____   _____

Accept criticism without anger and learn   _____   _____
from others

Communicate assertively without attacking   _____   _____
or blaming others

Admit mistakes; apologize   _____   _____

Respect and compliment the ideas and good   _____   _____
work of others

Share with and assist others; enjoy teamwork   _____   _____

- Evaluate your interaction with DATA and THINGS

I usually:

Follow rules and also work to make them   _____   _____
more reasonable

Am willing to learn, asking for help only   _____   _____
when necessary

Am flexible, willing to try new and unfamiliar   _____   _____
tasks

Carry through with difficult or pressured   _____   _____
work on time, without excuses

Take care of property and equipment   _____   _____

5. Work-Specific Skills

List your work-specific skills—those acquired by education or training—
to do a particular job:

_____   _____

_____   _____

_____   _____

6. A Quick Look at Personal Style

In the four boxes following you will see a pair of personal style descriptions, one in each column. Read each description and decide which one sounds most like you. In your everyday activities you will exhibit characteristics of all eight of the personal styles, but you tend to have a preference for one over the other in each of the four pairs. After you have read the descriptions in each preference pair, circle the letter in parenthesis of the preference you prefer. Write that letter on the line following.

WHERE YOU FOCUS YOUR ATTENTION

EXTROVERSION (E)	INTROVERSION (I)
"Talk to me."	"I've got to think about this."
■ Gets energy interacting with others	■ Gets energy by introspective reflection
■ Likes ideas and information from others or outside resources	■ Likes to think things over independently
■ Prefers having others around when working	■ Prefers working alone to complete tasks
■ Learns best through outside interactions	■ Learns best by independent analysis

---

HOW YOU GATHER INFORMATION

SENSING (S)	INTUITION (N)
"I need the relevant facts and data."	"I can see the big picture."
■ Likes to have all of the facts and details before forming opinions	■ Doesn't like to get bogged down with details
■ Likes to process information sequentially from beginning to end in work and learning situations	■ Can easily see the relationships between ideas and concepts to form opinions
■ Enjoys using all of their senses for work or learning	■ Jumps around different ideas or tasks to process information, learn, or work
■ Likes being grounded in the "here and now"	■ Enjoys looking at the "what if" possibilities in work or learning situations

HOW YOU MAKE DECISIONS

THINKING (T)	FEELING (F)
"I only use logic."	"I am concerned how others will react."

- Makes logical decisions based on the evidence at hand through a systematized analysis
- May appear "cold" and "aloof" in learning or work environments when discussing people
- Likes interactions to be rational and objective
- Makes plans using impersonal logic

- Has concern that decisions may affect others negatively or cause discomfort
- Is sensitive to others in the group or workplace and how they will react
- Is comfortable discussing the social implications of actions or performance
- Likes a supportive, pleasant work or learning environment

HOW YOU ORIENT YOURSELF TO THE OUTSIDE WORLD

JUDGING (J)	PERCEIVING (P)
"I need to get it done now."	"I want to look at all my options first."

- Likes things done in a precise order according to detailed plans
- Is punctual and prefers clearly defined work hours
- Is task oriented, moving sequentially from one to another, on time
- Likes unambiguous requirements and objectives

- Takes things as they come and enjoys deviating from the plan
- Is not a slave to the clock and enjoys coming and going freely
- Can start projects but lacks follow-through to completion, often running up against deadlines
- Easily distracted

Which did you choose?	E or I	S or N	T or F	J or P
Write your four-letter style here:	_E_	_N_	_F_	_P_

This is just the beginning of understanding your personal style and how it relates to career satisfaction. Refer to the Web sites and resource materials in this chapter to understand more about your own style and careers best suited for you. Or talk to a professional who is certified to administer the MBTI®, and take the actual assessment. Be sure to have someone interpret it for you.

7. Sharing Your Discoveries

In the space that follows (or on a separate sheet of paper), you may find it helpful to write an enthusiastic paragraph or letter about yourself and your abilities to a potential employer (or friend). Use as many of the skill words as possible from this chapter to describe yourself and show that you would be an effective worker. Later you will be able to use the data gathered in this chapter to write an effective résumé.

I am an extroverted person that loves people and enjoys consistent, daily interaction with them. I love to listen and help solve people's problems. I would be affective at counseling people and helping them with their problems and concerns and at the end of the day I would feel valuable and fulfilled.

 GROUP DISCUSSION QUESTIONS

1. Looking at past accomplishments or positive experiences in your life is one of the best ways to identify how your transferable/motivated skills, values, interests, and personal style all work together. Think back on your life and identify three positive experiences or accomplishments that you found satisfying and enjoyable. For each situation, discuss your role, what you did, who else if anyone was involved, and what made the experience so enjoyable and satisfying. Are there any themes or patterns that emerge? What skills did you use? What was it about each accomplishment or experience that made it so important to you?

2. Discuss the personal responsibility skills that make you the unique individual you are. How will these skills be important in your future work?

3. Discuss how you want to spend your time in your future work, working with data, people, and/or things. Which is most dominant and why?

3/

The Career Connection

Finding Your Job Satisfiers

◎ GOALS

- Identify your satisfying job areas.
- Survey the U.S. job market.
- Learn to research jobs.

MAKING THE CAREER CONNECTION

In the previous two chapters you spent time discovering your needs, wants, values, interests, personal style, and skills. All of this information has helped you discover how you work best. Are there common threads among your interests, personal style, motivated skills, and values? If so, you are ready to begin to make the connection between *your* best work and the world of work.

Chapter 3 is designed to help dispel some of the mysteries of the work world and to guide you to discover career areas that you will want to explore further. Many people get overwhelmed at this point and are tempted to stop and take any job so they don't have to go through the hassle of career searching. Unfortunately, those who quit looking for their ideal job usually have unfulfilling work lives.

Persistence is important. Keep searching, and you will have a great chance to learn more about yourself and the work world. All in all, the career search process is exciting, challenging, and a real confidence builder. The more you know about yourself and the career areas that would suit you, the better chance you have to make the right connection for the perfect job.

Occupational Information 101

The career self-assessments you did in Chapters 1 and 2 will provide important background information as you explore the job market. Understanding occupational information is time consuming. The better you understand who you are and what your wants and needs are, the easier it will be to find the occupation that's right for you. Occupational information provides job descriptions, employment qualifications, wage information, employment projections, labor market trends, and other pertinent data that will help you in your career search.

Occupational information can be found in many places: publications, videos, Web sites, pamphlets, newspapers, magazines, professional associations, and on the Internet. Public libraries, school and college career centers, and your local employment office should have the resources available for your review, along with Internet access. Usually these resources are found in a reference section and may not be available for check-out. Allow yourself plenty of time to research, keep your information organized, take notes, and if possible, verify the information by talking with people in the field. You may even want to start a notebook or file for each area you research, write down your reactions to what you find out, and see if what you discover is a match to your career self-assessment. Your diligence will ensure that you pursue training and careers where there is market demand.

It is your work in life that is the ultimate seduction.
—*Pablo Picasso*

The U.S. Department of Labor (DOL) (**www.dol.gov**) is the primary resource for labor market information (LMI) at the national level. In addition, each state has its own version of the LMI system. Some are more comprehensive and easier to use than others. State and local labor market information is sometimes considered more relevant than nationwide information, because state or local industry patterns and trends can be very different from those at the nationwide level. For example, an occupation may be growing rapidly in one state, but it may be declining in another state due to specific industry patterns and trends.

Two companion agencies to the DOL that provide important access to sources of information are the Bureau of Labor Statistics (BLS) (**http://stats. bls.gov**) and the Employment and Training Administration (ETA) (**www. doleta.gov**). The Bureau of Labor Statistics offers several publications and resources on the national labor market. The most useful and best known nationally is the *Occupational Outlook Handbook*[1] (OOH) (**www.bls.gov/ oco/**). The OOH provides valuable career profiles for approximately 250 occupational groups that together represent about 75 percent of all jobs. Each profile follows the same basic format: nature of the work, working conditions, employment, training, qualifications and advancement, job outlook, earnings, related occupations, and sources for additional information. Its comprehensive information is very useful in assisting individuals in making decisions about their future work lives. The OOH is revised every two years. Later in this chapter, you will review and compare your results from the Personality Mosaic to the job families in the OOH.

The Employment and Training Administration, the companion agency to the BLS, provides a number of important career and labor market information resources under the name America's Labor Market Information System (ALMIS) (**www.acinet.org**). The purpose of the system is to bring public employment and training services under one umbrella through the One-Stop Career Centers. The One-Stop Centers (**www.careeronestop.org**) are publicly funded career resource facilities for job seekers in cities throughout the United States.

The most up-to-date information for jobs and careers is on the O*NET —Occupational Information Network[2] (**http://online.onetcenter.org**). It is the DOL's replacement for the outdated *Dictionary of Occupational Titles*[3] (DOT) and integrates the ALMIS resources and Web sites, thus becoming the nation's primary source of occupational information. The new standard occupational classification system contained in the O*NET database is comprehensive and is easily updated regularly. It is the new standard used for

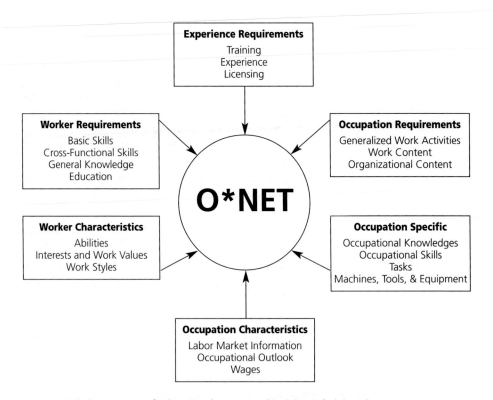

SOURCE: *U.S. Department of Labor, Employment and Training Administration*

collecting and organizing job information nationwide. The database has updated information on more than 1,000 job titles covering nearly 100 percent of the job market, and it provides a much better reflection of the American economy than did the DOT. The content model shown above forms the foundation for the O*NET database.

The O*Net database uses twenty-three major job families to classify occupations. Each job family breaks out further into more detailed groups and occupations. You will review these job families later in this chapter.

Another resource that you will review is the *Guide for Occupational Exploration*[4] (GOE). First published by the U.S. Department of Labor (DOL), it was used as a standard reference to explore career and learning options. Now revised by Jist Publishing, the well-liked GOE reflects today's workplace, incorporates information from the O*NET database, and makes the resource readily available to the public in printed form. The GOE has fourteen job families that relate to interest areas; it has new data and detailed narratives about jobs and careers. It has a wealth of information and is easy to use. The third edition is the most recent and useful.

On the following pages you will find some specific career-related exercises and information and questions about the RIASEC Holland personalities, followed by charts of the three major resources described—the O*NET database, GOE, and OOH—organized by the RIASEC Holland personalities. Each resource is grouped by the job families that fit that particular RIASEC personality. The job family is divided further into subgroups. You will notice that the O*NET database and GOE job families begin with a set of numbers. These numbers serve as references to be used to find the information in the specific resource document. You will also notice that there are many similarities among the three resources in wording and nomenclature for selected job families.

The questions on the next few pages will help you confirm your RIASEC scores and interest areas and possibly tempt you with new areas to explore more fully. Read the information about each personality carefully, and answer the questions. If it appears that you have an interest in the area, go to the resource chart for the personality, read the information, and circle the job families and subgroups that sound interesting to you. Enjoy the search!

CAREER FOCUS: JOB CHART INVENTORY

Find satisfying job families by answering these questions about personality types in the job market.

Realistic Personality Type: Things/Body

Y N   Do Do you like using your hands, e.g., to make, repair, "tinker with" physical objects?
Y N   Do you like being physically active?
Y (N)   Do you generally prefer working with physical objects rather than people?
Y N   Do you like practical hands-on work and problem solving?

If you answered Yes to any of these questions, read further and find out more about Realistic and Realistic/Social interests. If you answered No to all of the questions, then go on to the Investigative and Investigative/Social interest category.

People in the *Realistic* interest category typically work with things, from simple to complex; they require little contact with people unless it involves supervising, teaching, or managing; use of data depends on complexity of the job. Some of the job skills that are needed include good body coordination, operating, debugging, inspecting, monitoring, and installing, and the ability to construct, build, and repair. The world of things is associated with the realistic personality, which gravitates toward jobs that deal with mechanical systems; factory or production jobs; extensive outdoor work with nature; police work, firefighting, or other protective types of employment.

Realistic Interest Areas

Farming, Fishing, & Forestry (O*NET & OOH); Plants & Animals (GOE)
Y N   Do you like physical, outdoor work?
Y (N)   Do you like working with plants and animals?

Installation, Maintenance, & Repair (O*NET & OOH); Mechanics, Installers & Repairers (GOE)
Y N   Do you like large mechanical systems?
Y N   Do you like working with machines and tools?
Y N   Do you like to build or repair things?

Construction & Extraction (O*NET & OOH); Construction, Mining & Drilling (GOE)
Y (N)   Would you like work where you build large or small structures?
Y N   Do you like to operate powerful equipment?
Y N   Would you like to do the final detail work on a building?

Transportation & Material Moving (O*NET & OOH); Transportation (GOE)
(Y) N   Would you like to move people or materials from one place to another?
Y (N)   Would you like to guide or direct vehicles from one destination to another?

Production (O*NET & OOH); Industrial Production (GOE)
Y N   Do you like to do manual work using your hands or tools?
Y N   Do you like to do repetitive, concrete activities?

Building & Grounds Cleaning & Maintenance (O*NET); Service (OOH)
Y (N)   Do you like to maintain grounds and structures to make sure they are usable and attractive?
Y (N)   Do you like to clean and maintain things?

Realistic/Social Interest Area

Legal, Protective Services (O*NET); Law, Law Enforcement, & Public Safety (GOE); Professional—Legal and Service—Protective Service (OOH)
Y N   Does protecting people's lives and properties interest you?
Y N   Would you enjoy work that involves physical risk, such as law enforcement or firefighting?

Did any one job family or subgroup stand out for you above the others or did you have "Yes" answers in more than one? If you answered Yes to any of the questions, explore the Realistic or the Realistic/Social job chart and highlight the job family and subgroups that interest you. Are any of the job skills mentioned similar to the ones you chose?

If you answered No to all the questions, then move on to the Investigative and Investigative/Social interest categories.

REALISTIC

O*NET	GOE	OOH
45 Farming, Fishing, & Forestry • Supervisors, Farming, Fishing, & Forestry Workers • Agricultural Workers • Fishing & Hunting Workers • Forest, Conservation, & Logging Workers	**03 Plants & Animals** • Managerial Work in Plants & Animals • Animal Care & Training • Hands-on Work in Plants & Animals	**Farming, Fishing, & Forestry**
49 Installation, Maintenance, & Repair • Supervisors of Installation, Maintenance, & Repair Workers • Electrical & Electronic Equipment Mechanics, Installers, & Repairers • Vehicle & Mobile Equipment Mechanics, Installers, & Repairers • Other Installation, Maintenance, & Repair Occupations	**05 Mechanics, Installers & Repairers** • Managerial Work in Mechanics, Installers & Repairers • Electrical & Electronic Systems • Mechanical Work • Hands-on Work with Mechanics, Installers & Repairers	**Installation, Maintenance, & Repair** • Electrical & Electronic Equipment, Mechanics, Installers & Repairers • Vehicle & Mobile Equipment Mechanics, Installers & Repairers • Other Installation Maintenance & Repair
47 Construction & Extraction • Supervisors, Construction & Extraction Workers • Construction Trades Workers • Helpers, Construction Trades • Other Construction & Related Workers • Extraction Workers	**06 Construction, Mining & Drilling** • Managerial Work in Construction, Mining & Drilling • Construction • Mining & Drilling • Hands-on Work in Construction, Extraction & Maintenance	**Construction & Extraction**
53 Transportation & Material Moving • Supervisors, Transportation & Material Moving Workers • Air Transportation Workers • Motor Vehicle Operators • Rail Transportation Workers • Water Transportation Workers • Other Transportation Workers • Material Moving Workers	**07 Transportation** • Managerial Work in Transportation • Vehicle Expediting & Coordinating • Air Vehicle Operation • Water Vehicle Operation • Truck Driving • Rail Vehicle Operation • Other Services Requiring Driving • Support Work in Transportation	**Transportation & Material Moving** • Air Transportation • Material Moving • Motor Vehicle Operators • Rail Transportation • Water Transportation
51 Production • Supervisors, Production Workers • Assemblers & Fabricators • Food Processing Workers • Metal Workers & Plastic Workers • Printing Workers • Textile, Apparel, & Furnishings Workers • Woodworkers • Plant & System Operators • Other Production Occupations	**08 Industrial Production** • Managerial Work in Industrial Production • Production Technology • Production Work • Metal & Plastics Machining Technology • Woodworking Technology • Systems Operations • Hands-on Work: Loading, Moving, Hoisting & Conveying	**Production** • Assemblers & Fabricators • Food Processing • Metal & Plastic Workers • Plant & System Operators • Printing Occupations • Textile, Apparel & Furnishings • Woodworkers • Other Production Occupations
37 Building & Grounds Cleaning & Maintenance • Supervisors, Building & Grounds Cleaning & Maintenance Workers • Building Cleaning & Pest Control Workers • Grounds Maintenance Workers		**Service** • Building & Grounds Maintenance

Realistic/Social

O*NET	GOE	OOH
23 Legal • Lawyers, Judges, & Related Workers • Legal Support Workers **33 Protective Service** • First-Line Supervisors/Managers, Protective Service Workers • Firefighting & Prevention Workers • Law Enforcement Workers • Other Protective Service Workers	**04 Law, Law Enforcement, & Public Safety** • Managerial Work in Law, Law Enforcement, & Public Safety • Law • Law Enforcement • Public Safety • Military	**Professional** • Legal Occupations **Service** • Protective Service

Job Chart: Realistic, Realistic/Social

Investigative—Ideas/Intellect

Y **N** Do you like solving problems and puzzles?
Y **N** Do you like to do research and probe deeply into a problem?
Y **N** Do you like to work alone?
Y **N** Do you like to think or read about or discuss new ideas?

If you answered Yes to any of these questions, read further and find out more about Investigative and Investigative/Social interests. If you answered No to all of the questions, then go on to the Artistic interest category.

People in the *Investigative* interest category are typically scientific/investigative types with logical/rational personalities, who like to explore ideas. Jobs usually involve high to medium use of data and little involvement with people (except in medicine). Some of the job skills that are needed include researching, calculating, analyzing, synthesizing, forecasting, compiling, and conceptualizing. Those investigative types that pursue the physical or biological sciences or engineering need to have some sense of the realistic world. Purely investigative people with little interest in the physical world usually take their inquiring minds into areas such as theoretical math, or they may research people, the arts, industry, or business—any area that requires little direct interaction with things or people.

Investigative Interest Areas

Computer & Mathematical, Architecture & Engineering, Life, Physical, & Social Science (O*NET); Science, Math & Engineering (GOE); Professional—Technical (OOH)

Y N Do you enjoy using your mind to solve various kinds of problems?
Y **N** Do you enjoy working with scientific principles, formulas, and mathematical equations?
Y **N** Do you enjoy research and exploring the physical world?
Y **N** Do you enjoy working alone for long periods of time?

Investigative/Social Interest Area

Healthcare Practitioners & Technical (O*NET); Medical & Health Services (GOE); Professional—Health (OOH)

Y N Do you have an interest in helping others stay healthy?
Y **N** Would you enjoy working as part of a team to solve a medical issue?
Y **N** Would you like to discover a cure for a life-threatening disease?

Did any one job family or subgroup stand out for you above the others, or did you have "Yes" answers in more than one? If you answered Yes to any of the questions, explore the Investigative and Investigative/Social job chart and highlight the job family and subgroups that interest you. Are any of the job skills mentioned similar to the ones you chose?

If you answered No to all the questions, move on to the Artistic interest category.

Artistic: Ideas/Intellect

Y N Do you like to create new things?
Y N Do you like to work independently and at your own pace?
Y N Do you have an imaginative mind and have good ideas to solve problems?
Y N Do you enjoy the fine arts: art, drama, dance, music, or literature?

If you answered Yes to any of these questions, read further and find out more about Artistic interests. If you answered No to all of the questions, then go on to the Social and Social/Conventional interest category.

People in the *Artistic* interest category typically like to create things and explore ideas. Some skills needed include design, innovation, illustration, and performance. Artistic people are generally very intuitive and may find satisfaction in painting, sculpture, or crafts if they have a facility with things. The more investigative artistic types deal with music and writing. Some artistic people with little specific "talent" give creative expression to their many ideas in a variety of other environments; e.g., the innovative side of engineering or the innovative worlds of the classroom or business operations.

Artistic Interest Areas

Arts, Design, Entertainment, Sports, & Media (O*NET); Arts, Entertainment & Media (GOE); Professional—The Arts (OOH)

Y N   Do you enjoy expressing your feelings and ideas in innovative and creative ways?

Y N   Would you like to perform and entertain people?

Y N   Do you enjoy sports and would like to coach or play on a sports team?

Did the Artistic job family or subgroups stand out for you? If you answered Yes to any of the questions, explore the Artistic job chart. Are any of the job skills mentioned similar to the ones you chose?

   If you answered No to all the questions, move on to the Social and Social/Conventional interest categories.

INVESTIGATIVE

O*NET	GOE	OOH
15 Computer & Mathematical • Computer Specialists • Mathematical Science Occupations **17 Architecture & Engineering** • Architects, Surveyors, & Cartographers • Engineers • Drafters, Engineering & Mapping Technicians **19 Life, Physical, & Social Science** • Life Scientists • Physical Scientists • Social Scientists & Related Workers • Life, Physical, & Social Science Technicians	**02 Science, Math & Engineering** • Managerial Work in Science, Math & Engineering • Physical Sciences • Life Sciences • Social Sciences • Laboratory Technology • Mathematics & Computers • Engineering • Engineering Technology	**Professional** • Architects, Surveyors, & Cartographers • Drafters & Engineering Technicians • Engineers • Computer & Mathematics • Life Scientists • Physical Scientists • Social Scientists

Investigative/Social

O*NET	GOE	OOH
29 Healthcare Practitioners & Technical • Health Diagnosing & Treating Practitioners • Health Technologists & Technicians • Other Healthcare Practitioners & Technical Occupations **31 Healthcare Support** • Nursing, Psychiatric, & Home Health Aides • Occupational & Physical Therapist Assistants & Aides • Other Healthcare Support Occupations	**14 Medical & Health Services** • Managerial Work in Medical & Health Services • Medicine & Surgery • Dentistry • Health Specialists • Medical Technology • Medical Therapy • Patient Care and Assistance	**Professional** • Health Diagnosing & Treating & Technologists **Service** • Healthcare Support

ARTISTIC

O*NET	GOE	OOH
27 Arts, Design, Entertainment, Sports, & Media • Art & Design Workers • Entertainers & Performers, Sports & Related Workers • Media & Communication Workers • Media & Communication Equipment Workers	**01 Arts, Entertainment & Media** • Managerial Work in Arts, Entertainment & Media • Writing & Editing • News, Broadcasting & Public Relations • Visual Arts • Performing Arts • Craft Arts • Graphic Arts • Media Technology • Modeling & Personal Appearance • Sports: Coaching, Instructing, Officiating & Performing	**Professional** • Art & Design • Entertainers & Performers • Media & Communication

Job Chart: Investigative, Investigative/Social; Artistic

Social—Helping and Assisting: The World of People

Y N   Are you concerned about the welfare of others?
Y N   Do you enjoy working with people on a common cause?
Y N   Do you enjoy listening to people's problems and helping them discover solutions?

If you answered Yes to any of these questions, read further and find out more about Social and Social/Conventional interests. If you answered No to all of the questions, then go on to the Enterprising and Enterprising/Social interest categories.

People in the *Social* interest category typically require ongoing involvement with people; the level of data increases with complexity of the work; there is usually little or no involvement with things except in jobs requiring physical contact. Skills important to the social personality type include ability to communicate effectively with people, good listening skills, teaching, explaining, facilitating, and counseling. Jobs involve helping and assisting others to obtain information or reach a goal. For career seekers who would love to work helping people, opportunities are numerous, ranging from teacher to minister, social worker to probation officer, counselor to waitress, and chef to hotel manager.

Social Interest Areas

Community & Social Services, Education, Training & Library (O*NET); Education & Social Service (GOE); Professional—Social Service & Education (OOH)

Y N   Do you want to deal with people's personal concerns, their personal growth and/or education?
Y N   Do you like fairly steady involvement with people who have problems or needs?
Y N   Do you like to teach others?

Social/Conventional Interest Areas

Food Preparation & Serving Related and Personal Care & Service (O*NET); Recreation, Travel, & Other Personal Services (GOE); Service—Food & Personal Care (OOH)

Y N   Do you enjoy waiting on people and serving them in some way?
Y N   Do you enjoy working in a job where others are relaxing and enjoying your service?
Y N   Do you like to prepare food for others to enjoy?

Did any one job family or subgroup stand out for you above the others? If you answered Yes to any of these questions, explore the Social and Social/Conventional interest job chart and highlight the job family and subgroups that interest you. Are any of the job skills mentioned similar to the ones you chose?

If you answered No to all the questions, move on to the Enterprising and Enterprising/Social interest category.

Enterprising—Selling and Leading

Y N   Do you like to talk people into doing a project and get them organized?
Y N   Do you enjoy persuading people to accept an idea, service, or product?
Y N   Do you like to influence people and their opinions?

If you answered Yes to any of these questions, read further and find out more about Enterprising and Enterprising/Social interests. If you answered No to all of the questions, then go on to the Conventional interests category.

People in the *Enterprising* interest category typically require leadership roles. They search for ways to be leaders, organize groups, show people what to do, direct projects, and solve business problems. Enterprising types who wish to work with people at a high level should consider earning a degree in business or one in the behavioral sciences. Skills that are important to enterprising people include communicating, managing, directing, persuading, selling, negotiating, and creativity.

Enterprising Interest Areas

Sales & Related Occupations (O*NET & OOH); Sales & Marketing (GOE)

Y N   Are you confident and persistent, with enough energy to get things done?
Y N   Do you enjoy persuading people to accept an idea, service, or product?

Enterprising/Social Interest Areas

Management (O*NET & OOH); General Management & Support (GOE)

Y N Do you like to be a key person in a group?

Y N Do you enjoy encouraging people to try new ways of thinking or doing things?

If you answered Yes to any of the questions, explore the Enterprising and Enterprising/Social job chart and highlight the job family and subgroups that interest you. Are any of the job skills mentioned similar to the ones you chose?

If you answered No to all the questions, move on to the Conventional interests category.

SOCIAL

O*NET	GOE	OOH
21 Community & Social Services • Counselors, Social Workers, & Other Community & Social Service Specialists • Religious Workers **25 Education, Training, & Library** • Postsecondary Teachers • Primary, Secondary, & Special Education School Teachers • Other Teachers & Instructors • Librarians, Curators, & Archivists • Other	**12 Education & Social Service** • Managerial Work in Education & Social Service • Social Services • Educational Services	Professional • Community & Social Service • Education, Training, Library & Museum

Social/Conventional

O*NET	GOE	OOH
35 Food Preparation & Serving Related • Supervisors, Food Preparation & Serving Workers • Cooks & Food Preparation Workers • Food & Beverage Serving Workers • Other Food Preparation & Serving Related **39 Personal Care & Service** • Supervisors, Personal Care & Service Workers • Animal Care & Service Workers • Entertainment Attendants & Related Workers • Funeral Service Workers • Personal Appearance Workers • Transportation, Tourism, & Lodging Attendants • Other Personal Care & Service Workers	**11 Recreation, Travel, & Other Personal Services** • Managerial Work in Recreation, Travel, & Other Personal Services • Recreational Services • Transportation & Lodging Services • Barber & Beauty Services • Food & Beverage Services • Apparel, Shoes, Leather & Fabric Care • Cleaning & Building Services • Other Personal Services	Service • Food Preparation & Serving • Personal Care

ENTERPRISING

O*NET	GOE	OOH
41 Sales & Related Occupations • Supervisors, Sales Workers • Retail Sales Workers • Sales Representatives, Services • Sales Representatives, Wholesale & Manufacturing • Other Sales & Related Workers	**10 Sales & Marketing** • Managerial Work In Sales & Marketing • Sales Technology • General Sales • Personal Soliciting	Sales & Related Occupations

Enterprising/Social

O*NET	GOE	OOH
11 Management • Top Executives • Advertising, Marketing, Promotions, Public Relations, & Sales Managers • Operations Specialties Managers • Other Management Occupations	**13 General Management & Support** • General Management Work & Management Support Functions • Management Support	Management

Job Chart: Social, Social/Conventional; Enterprising, Enterprising/Social

Conventional—Words/Numbers/Symbols

Y ⊗ Do you enjoy organizing and keeping information in an orderly matter?

Y ⊗ Do you like to work with numbers and manage systems and data?

People in the *Conventional* interest category require work that involves consistent use of data or business detail: words, numbers, and symbols; there is usually little involvement with people beyond what is required to process business details or other tasks; things dealt with are often office machines. Skills that are important include computing, compiling, analyzing, organizing, recording, processing, and researching. Conventional personalities who are careful about detail are valued for their contribution in keeping track of the many transactions that go on in the work setting. If your interests lie in the conventional type and your present job does not include this, look for ways to handle the data of your work environment.

Conventional Interest Areas

Office & Administrative Support (O*NET & OOH); Business & Financial Operations (O*NET); Business Detail (GOE)

Ⓨ Ⓝ Do you enjoy using the computer to organize data and information for business?

Ⓨ Ⓝ Do you enjoy working with office machines?

Ⓨ N Are you generally prompt and very accurate?

Y Ⓝ Do you prefer to follow a set routine with established guidelines?

If you answered Yes to any of the questions, explore the Conventional job chart and highlight the job family and subgroups that interest you. Are any of the job skills mentioned similar to the ones you chose?

If you answered No to all the questions, move on to the next section in this chapter to explore combinations of personality types and other considerations.

CONVENTIONAL

O*NET		GOE		OOH
13 **Business & Financial Operations** • Business Operations Specialists • Financial Specialists 43 **Office & Administrative Support** • Supervisors, Office & Administrative Support Workers • Communications Equipment Operators • Financial Clerks • Information and Record Clerks • Material Recording, Scheduling, Dispatching, & Distributing Workers • Secretaries & Administrative Assistants • Other Office & Administrative Support Workers		09 **Business Detail** • Managerial Work in Business Detail • Administrative Detail • Bookkeeping, Auditing & Accounting • Material Control • Customer Service • Communications • Records Processing • Records & Material Processing • Clerical Machine Operation		**Management–Business & Financial** **Office & Administrative Support**

Job Chart: Conventional

Some Combinations and Other Considerations

People are attracted to jobs for all sorts of reasons besides interest in the job itself. They want people to like them. They'd like to feel important. They want to avoid competition, to please parents, to look like the stereotypical successful male or female, to earn more money. We are all influenced by the convenience and availability of jobs. All these reasons tap into our value system. But can you find long-term satisfaction in a career field that doesn't interest you? This all-important question must be answered in a way that is consistent with your values. If you pay attention to your strong interests, you will probably find that you have fewer conflicts with your value system. Also, people often have an interest in more than one area and would like a career that will use those interests. Although many jobs tend to reflect a single interest, most jobs, just like people, will have significant qualities of more than one interest area.

A person who enjoys physical activity and doesn't mind working with mechanical systems but would also like to work with people and follow set guidelines (the realistic, social, and conventional personality) may enjoy one of the many careers in health care. A person who is mechanically adept and enjoys persuading people about a product may find technical sales or service an interesting area (the realistic, enterprising, conventional personality), whereas the mechanically inclined person with an investigative bent may like research and development in industry (realistic and investigative personality). The realistic and conventional personality would find satisfiers in safety and time studies and other data-keeping tasks as well as with data processing equipment; the more creative person may enjoy product/process design, crafts, model building, or graphics (realistic and artistic personality).

The investigative person can also research and analyze people, the arts, and business—in fact, this individual can find satisfiers in almost any workplace. Likewise artistic/creative people can innovate new systems in many job settings that are flexible enough to allow for their creativity. And social personalities can find people to supervise, manage, train, and develop in almost any place they work.

Remember, many social, investigative, artistic persons enjoy working with people to solve problems by creating new systems. This is important in just about every workplace.

Understanding these interests can sometimes save people from jobs where they will feel quite uncomfortable. For example, realistic personalities with few social characteristics often find that a promotion to management status brings headaches they'd rather do without. And an artistic person may feel stifled doing routine work all day.

Perhaps none of those combinations and considerations interests you right now. For the present, you feel you simply want to consider a job in an

"Your son has made a career choice, Mildred. He's going to win the lottery and travel a lot."

© 1998. Reprinted courtesy of Bill Hoest and Parade Magazine.

enjoyable place that will allow for advancement. But as you travel on through the career search process, you will have the opportunity to look at a variety of creative as well as traditional career ideas that could expand your view of what is available down the road. You will see how alternative work schedules, a change of work environment, an involvement with a different product or service, or a new slant on an old challenge may be the trick that will turn the tide toward satisfaction in your present career or even launch you in an entirely new direction. You may want to review this career focus material with a career counselor or career specialist if you still feel uncertain about which interest area is of greatest importance to you.

Exploring Further: Researching Your Options Using the O*NET Database, GOE, and OOH

Research using the O*NET database, GOE, and/or the OOH enables you to survey the entire job market and eliminate those areas not right for you while you zero in on those that are important. Let's look at how the O*NET database, GOE, and OOH can help make research easier.

The Department of Labor has focused its attention on developing the O*NET database. The easiest way to use the database is to go to the Web site (http://online.onetcenter.org). Here you will find various ways that you can sort for occupational information. Select "Find Occupations," and select a job family that you circled on the charts on pages 77, 79, 81, and 82, and you will see a list of the related occupations in the O*NET database. Select an occupation that sounds interesting and review its "summary." This will give you an overview of the occupation, key skills needed, expected work activities, interest areas based on the RIASEC, work styles including values, work context, organizational context, and the required experience and training. If you select "details," it will rank all of the factors in relationship to the occupation in percentage of importance, a handy way to understand how much the factors affect the job. Another way to search for occupations is go to the O*NET database and select "Skill Search." Here you have an opportunity to select a variety of skills that you are competent in using or want to acquire, similar to the transferable/motivated skills you selected in Chapter 2. You can search the O*NET database for occupations that use those skills. You may find that the forty-six O*NET skills that you can choose from may limit you in some interest areas, such as artistic. There is also a link that allows you to get information by state for a particular occupation, including wages and employment. Overall, the information is very useful; you need to pick and choose what information best fits you.

The *Occupational Outlook Handbook* (OOH) is updated every two years and puts occupational information in an easy-to-read text format, describing significant points about each occupation. It can be reviewed in hard copy or online at **www.bls.gov/oco/.** Whether you are searching by specific occupations or job families, the OOH is easy to use and gives you a good description of what it would be like to work in a specific occupation. It provides additional information and resources for each occupation and also provides a cross-reference to the O*NET database. The OOH is a good place to start your research, but be reminded that it is a national publication. State and local wage and employment outlooks might be different.

The *Guide for Occupational Exploration* GOE, third edition, cross-references the O*NET database and OOH and gives detailed information for more than 1,000 occupations. It is produced by a national publishing company and at this point does not have a Web site, but it does have some very useful information about careers.

America's Career InfoNet (**www.acinet.org**) is an extensive Web site where you can find information about particular occupations, what training is needed, market demand, potential earnings, and much more. There are also more than 300 short career videos that you can review online.

University career centers often have marvelous Web sites that offer a wealth of career information. The career center at University of Wisconsin in Oshkosh has a good Web site for those looking to explore the question "What can I do with a major in . . . ?" Find it at **http://www.uwosh.edu/ career/whatcanidowithamajorin.**

Quintessential Careers (**http://www.quintcareers.com/career_exploration .html**) is a valuable Web site for many aspects of the career search. It provides links and resources for assessment, career exploration, training, and education, as well as useful articles and tips on how to manage your career search.

It's great to be able to sample until you find the one you really want.

Once you have narrowed your search down to a few career areas, check out related professional associations for more information, and talk to people working in the field to get their firsthand experiences. Keep notes about what you learn, and examine your needs, wants, values, interests, motivated skills, and personal style with the information you have acquired. Whenever many of your likes and skills point toward the same area or areas, you've hit the bull's-eye on your career target.

At this point you might be feeling a little scared, anxious, or confused. These are all normal feelings for anyone on the verge of a *great discovery!* Keep going! Don't be overwhelmed if you find that several career areas look good to you. Some people are comfortable in more than one. Sometimes a person needs more work experience before making a decision. Give yourself more time if you need it. Don't decide to decide without seeing clearly.

There are still other activities that will help you zero in on a career. The next chapter will lead you to reflect on major societal challenges and the ways people are dealing with them as part of their work. This will give you perspective when you take the next step—researching workplaces. After an in-depth study of companies and alternative workplaces and workstyles, you will be ready to look at the elements necessary for the job hunt. Although you will have been making many decisions throughout the process, you will then have a chance to review a structured decision-making process. Making a

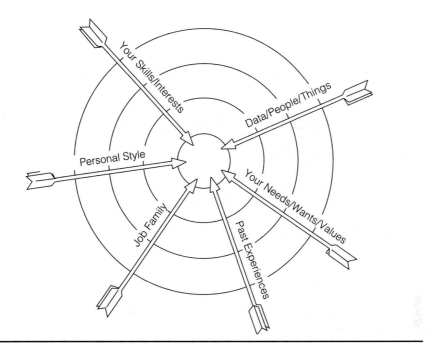

The Career Target

good career decision is a growth process, and growth takes patience. You can't make a flower grow by pulling on it!

SUMMARY

Making the connection between the world of work and where you might find a satisfying career can be a huge task. It is important to be persistent and organized so you don't become tempted to stop the process and take any job. The closer your work is aligned with your needs, wants, values, interests, motivated skills, and personal style, the greater the opportunity for career satisfaction. Understanding your personality interests based on the RIASEC in relationship to occupations and job families narrows down the possible career options. Understanding occupational information can be a time-consuming task. Your school or college career center, public library, or one-stop career center has the resources and professionals available to help you make sense of the information. The Internet is also a valuable tool to use to explore occupations. Three resources that you will find valuable to begin your search are the O*NET database, the *Guide to Occupational Exploration* (GOE), and the *Occupational Outlook Handbook* (OOH). When reviewing the resources, keep a file or notebook on the various occupations you explore;

write down your thoughts and perceptions as they relate to you and your career assessment results. Talk to people who are in your field of interest and find out more, check out professional associations for information, and talk with career specialists who can give you additional insights.

◉ SELF-ASSESSMENT EXERCISES

1. Research Your Options

a. Go to the job chart. From each resource select up to three job families that you would like to research further. Indicate the RIASEC area each is from.

O*NET Database	RIASEC Area
_____	_____
_____	_____
_____	_____

GOE	RIASEC Area
_____	_____
_____	_____
_____	_____

OOH	RIASEC Area
_____	_____
_____	_____
_____	_____

b. Why are these areas interesting to you?

_____

_____

_____

_____

c. Does your RIASEC code match with the job families you have chosen?

d. Select one of the resources (O*NET database, GOE, OOH) either online or in hard copy, and choose one of the job families from that resource that you wrote down in (a). Review the occupations in that job family. If you find one that sounds interesting to you, begin your research and answer the following questions. If none of the occupations sounds interesting, then go to another job family until you find one you want to research.

Occupation Title: _____

■ Summarize the kind of work you would do.

_____

_____

_____

_____

_____

■ Summarize the skills and abilities needed for this kind of work.

_____

_____

_____

_____

■ Which of these skills and abilities do you have and feel competent using? Which ones do you need to learn?

_____

_____

_____

■ Summarize clues that tell whether you would like or could learn this work.

_____

_____

_____

_____

_____

- Summarize the training needed and the methods of entry into this field.

  _____

  _____

  _____

  _____

- Do you have the necessary training? If not, what training do you need to acquire? Where can you get this training?

  _____

  _____

  _____

- List related job titles that you might like to explore further.

  _____

  _____

  _____

- Identify three people you could talk to about this occupation.

  _____

  _____

  _____

e. Now that you have researched one occupation, continue on and explore others using the questions listed as a framework to discover important information about possible jobs or careers of interest.

2. Confirm Career Choice

- Have you decided on a career choice? If so, what is it and why is it a good choice for you?

  Yes, vocational ministry and I chose it because I love the Lord, want to serve him and care about people + want to invest in them.

- Is this clearly your own choice? Why? Who else may have influenced your decision? Why?

  Yes. Mentors previously. b/c they made a huge difference in my life.

- Are there things keeping you from looking over alternatives? Are you making a decision too quickly?

  No, No.

- What other important factors exist that may change your decision? Are you open to exploring them?

  Money, yes.

- How can you support your choice with facts about your skills, interests, and values? Write a paragraph explaining why your career choice is a good decision for you.

  Because I am a relational being & I love people and investing in them & carry on them.

3. Identify Blocks and Barriers

At this point, what could be holding you back from completing the career search process?

___ In too much of a hurry to take time to explore

___ Have done some exercises (or pieces of the puzzle) but left others out

___ Experiencing personal/painful traumas

___ Afraid to look at myself; low/no self-confidence

___ Afraid to make a commitment

_X_ What else? ___ *none*

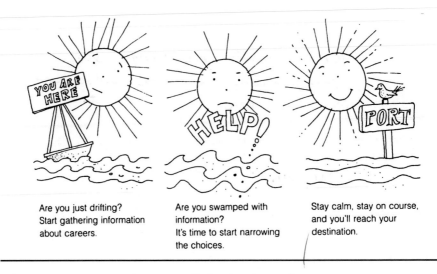

Are you just drifting? Start gathering information about careers.

Are you swamped with information? It's time to start narrowing the choices.

Stay calm, stay on course, and you'll reach your destination.

Where are you now on the Career Choice Continuum?

 GROUP DISCUSSION QUESTIONS

1. Which of the three resources was most helpful to you? Why?

2. What did you discover about some interesting career or occupation through your research?

3. What are the pros and cons of these three career resources (O*NET database, GOE, OOH)?

4. How have or will you use the Internet in your career research?

5. What decisions have you made so far in regard to your career or life choices and how do they feel to you?

4

Work

Challenges, Options, and Opportunities

 **GOALS**

- Reflect on the meaning of work.

- Explore challenges and options for the twenty-first century.

- Relate personality types to job market opportunities.

Yᵒu have assessed your needs, wants, and most cherished values. You know your personality orientation and your interests and abilities. You have identified qualities that represent the unique person you are. And you have seen how, by identifying these qualities, you can find your satisfiers in the job market. By now, you may also have an inkling that self-discovery is a lifetime process.

Next, either to firm up or to facilitate a career decision, wise career searchers will do well to acquire a broader, deeper understanding of work in the global village. This chapter considers the meaning of work and looks at some of the many positive and hopeful options and opportunities we have for responding to the societal challenges we face. You will look at ways people with your personality type can relate to the job market of the future. As you continue deepening your understanding of work, you'll also realize your need for a set of enduring values and a hopeful outlook that will enable you to maintain a broad sense of direction without being swept away by fads or predictions of gloom and doom. In short, you'll be ready to face the fast-paced, fast-changing world of the twenty-first century.

> The trouble with the future
> is that it arrives before we're ready for it.
> —*Andy Capp*

CHARTING THE FUTURE:
A GLOBAL PHILOSOPHIC VIEW OF WORK

The Time of No Time

The pace of change seems to accelerate daily. This speed is captured by John Peers, founder of Silicon Valley's Robotics Institute, who said, "We live three days in a day compared to the 1950s. We do in one day what couldn't be done in a week in 1900, in a lifetime in the 1600s."[1] As this is being written, California bulldozers can literally be seen moving mountains to repair the state's coast highway, which was damaged by El Niño storms—a task that couldn't be done in the 1600s.

In an instant, with a process unknown a few years ago, we can e-mail our computer thoughts to Guam or Guatemala and overnight see them turn into prototypes or procedures. Like a riddle, we save time, yet have none of the time we saved.

> We live in the time of no room . . .
> when everyone is obsessed with lack of time,

> with saving time, conquering space, projecting into time and space
> the anguish produced in them by the technological furies
> of size, volume, quantity, speed, number, price,
> power, and acceleration.
> —*Thomas Merton*[2]

Such speed and its attendant decisions affect both the economy and the environment and have an ethical impact on the lives of individuals and communities, often in far-reaching and unforeseen ways. As the twentieth century ended, the economy and the federal budget were booming, largely because of growth in the technology sector. Yet as the twenty-first century began, the corporate theft of billions of dollars, with the complicity of public accounting firms was revealed, and the overvaluation of stocks in the technology sector sank the economy into red-ink shock, and ordinary Americans looked ahead with trepidation as unemployment rose and investments slid down. A United States relatively at peace was attacked on September 11, 2001, and terrorists and the possibility of war loomed large on the horizon.

Although all of this has made choosing a career and finding a job an extra-large challenge, it simply demands an extra-large dedication to moving with and adapting to the times, as rapidly as they are changing, while moving with care at one's own pace.

Jeremy Rifkin suggests as a motto for the twenty-first century: "Slow is beautiful."[3] It seems that we need to slow down and reflect very seriously and creatively on the future and how our choices can contribute in a positive way to that great adventure called life.

Work Past and Present

We can roughly divide jobs into two categories: those that produce goods and those that supply services. From the beginning of time until very recently, most work produced goods that supplied basic needs: farming, construction, mining, and manufacturing. As late as the early 1900s, more than one-third of the workers in the U.S. labor force were still farmers.[4] Such work was often brutally hard, done at or close to home. As the industrial revolution accelerated, it brought dramatic change to many of the slow-paced, self-sufficient communities of the world; the entire goods-producing world changed.

The Global Panorama

Picture the entire world at work. Day and night it hums with the sounds of people and machines producing goods for one another. Mines and forests, oceans and fields yield raw substances to make mountains of *things*. Wood and metal, coal and cotton, giant and motley masses of materials are baked and baled, pounded and pummeled, mixed and milled, cut and checked, piled and packed for delivery to the world. Trucks and trains, ships and planes move endlessly, huffing and hauling it all to factories and farms, stores, and homes. Things! They are bought, sold, used, recycled, worn out, and finally discarded to become heaps of debris—some of it to return to the earth, some of it to pollute and plague us.

Today fewer than one-fifth of U.S. workers are employed in product-oriented industries. For example, the farming population has decreased markedly in this past half-century—fewer than 2 percent still live on farms.

The other four-fifths of the job world includes transactions, interactions, communications, deals, those intangible "services rendered," which mingle with the flow of goods.[5] Orders are taken, food served, children taught, cases tried, patients treated. Many services that used to be done with modest training and common sense now require more and more education and a continuous supply of information. For example, firefighters have became explosives and toxics experts, bomb defusers, and structural engineers. They get degrees in fire science, chemistry, engineering, and human relations.

We are all becoming *information* mills. We create it, collect it, evaluate it, manipulate it, control it, and pass it on to the twenty-four-hour-a-day world. Screens glow, faxes beep, copiers click, computers talk to computers, and modems squeak and squawk to each other while we sleep. Vast webs of information "technet" around the world at the stroke of a key, bringing us online and in line. The piles of data grow too fast to be absorbed and comprehended. Bombarded with so much information, we feel that we know less and less. Even so, we need to respond more quickly than ever. In the cyber world, information is called the product and power of the future.

Information is like a child's riddle: it's not only renewable, it's also expandable; it's never scarce, uses few resources, and takes little energy to produce; it can be kept while being given away. It has changed the way we live and work in ways we have barely begun to understand. We call all this *work!*

Once a mysterious shuffling of papers, work is now an even more mysterious shuffling of electronic impulses. The silicon chip is king, computers reign, and robots rule. James Burke, host of the PBS series *Connections,* noted years ago we are rushing into a technology trap.[6] When the power goes out or your computer crashes, you understand what he means. We feel lost and left more and more to our own devices to find our way through the techno thicket.

Futurist and author Alvin Toffler called this feeling "future shock." José Ortega y Gassett wrote in *The Revolt of the Masses,* "Modern man is becoming more primitive. He understands as little about the technology that serves him as primitive people understood about lightning and air."[7] Most people facing a new computer know just what he means!

Stephen J. Kline defines technology as a sociotechnical system in which people meld with machines, resources, processes, and legal, economic, political, and physical environments. He says that without this system, we humans now might not exist as a species, and if we did we should be relatively powerless, few in number, and of little import on the planet.[8]

Though most of the world, and indeed many people in the United States, have not gone high tech, the assumption is that everyone must do so or be left behind. Some people question that assumption. Nevertheless, schools "tech" up. Students plunge in; they e-mail their professors, listen to lectures, observe intricate science experiments, and solve problems via videos and the Internet. Sometimes they spend more time in their dorm rooms or at home in front of a computer monitor than in a lecture hall or lab.

Jeremy Rifkin's book, *The End of Work,* predicted a trend toward highly skilled "knowledge workers" with fewer low-skilled, low-paid, easily replaced workers, mostly due to automation, and reduced production time for goods. A bike can be ordered and made in three hours. In Italy, a factory churns out 150,000 metal broom handles a day, with only four people monitoring two shifts. Priscilla Enriquez of the Food Institute feels that there is an unnecessary trend toward the "downgrading of work." With automation, fast-food clerks, for example, hardly need to know any math or even how to read.[9]

In a humorous vein, a University of Miami aeronautics professor described an aircraft of the future to the International Airline Pilots Association: "The crew will consist of one pilot and one dog. The pilot's job will be to nurture, care for, and feed the dog. The dog's job will be to bite the pilot if he tries to touch anything."[10]

In the tech world, this service/information sector with its four-fifths of all workers includes federal/state/local government, education, health services, law, entertainment and the arts, and repair services as well as wholesale/retail trade, finance/banking, insurance, real estate, management, and marketing. Service/information continues to grow rapidly.

Although this new world can be seen as a world of hazards, it is also one of possibilities and hopes. In newly technological societies of this past half-century, and in the United States in particular, work and life choices have multiplied beyond anything our elders could have dreamed. A cornucopia of abundance has spilled forth, and the "good life" has become a reality for countless numbers of people.

Despite the view in the United States from the top of the tech heap, most of the world's people still make their living at low-tech, goods-producing activities, as well as some service enterprises so small as to be unnoticed. In tiny courtyards and on dusty country roads and city streets, people from little children to the elderly work in this informal sector. They are marginalized people, often displaced from their land and their villages

Reprinted with permission of Mal Hancock.

by large-scale enterprises such as logging, mining, and agribusiness. Their work is not counted, taxed, or noted in important statistics. They do small-scale farming; shuck and grind corn; cook; care for children; make small items by hand such as clay pots, straw mats, belts, and twine; do piecework for apparel makers; weave fabric. In public squares, they squeeze oranges, make tortillas, roast chickens, sell apparel and any other salable object, buy in bulk and sell to villagers, and guide tourists. They carry products to market—vegetables, fruit, chickens, pigs, and articles of clothing—on buses or trucks or on foot over many miles, untouched by the virtual technology world.

We see increasing contrasts between a small, highly sophisticated work force and an increasingly, marginalized global majority. Former Soviet President Mikhail Gorbachev said,

We are facing a sweeping crisis that challenges our entire civilization. It has expended most of its resources, its patterns of life are fading. We are in dire need of redefining the parameters of our society's economic, political, and social development. . . . [T]he conflict between man and the rest of nature carries the risk of truly catastrophic consequences. We are seeing a crisis in public life, in international relations, and in the loss of fundamental spiritual values, the anchors that are indispensable for normal life worthy of human nature . . . and finally a crisis of ideas. The prevailing ideologies have proven to be incapable of either clarifying this situation or offering ways of dealing with it.[11]

Work impacts not only your own life but the planet as well. It can be rewarding, exciting, fulfilling, exasperating, enriching, exhausting, and dreadful—sometimes all at once. Work is often hard work, and in this time, it presents considerable challenges as well!

SOCIAL PERSPECTIVES: CHALLENGES AND OPTIONS

As a career seeker, you are told to find a need and fill it. Finding the need is the easy part. The media are filled with overwhelming problems. But seeing these problems as *challenges* can be invigorating, especially when we begin to see that there are innumerable, real, hopeful, *and* socially responsible *options* for every challenge, not just *a* solution to *a* problem. Stop here for a moment and brainstorm or list the global challenges that you see happening.

The areas of major challenges we will consider—economics, environment, and ethics—are all closely connected to work and lifestyle choices. The hopeful options that follow are only the tip of the iceberg of thousands of socially responsible activities being developed and actually being done as paid work around the globe. As you read about the challenges of today's work world, think about your values and your job satisfiers. Ask yourself, "Which of these challenges challenge *me?*"

ECONOMICS OVERSIMPLIFIED

The word *economy,* from the ancient Greek word for *household,* means the system by which we exchange goods and services with each other. Paul Reynolds, Coleman Foundation chair holder in entrepreneurial studies at Marquette University, says, "The major objective [of economics] is to have a livable, just society with an acceptable level of economic efficiency and adaptability."[12] As simple as this sounds, the challenges facing us in the new global economy are formidable.

Work, in the economies of the industrial/technical nations, is tightly connected to the dramatic science/technological explosion of the twentieth century and the globalization of business. All career areas—including such human service fields as health care and education as well as the arts—have increasingly become businesses that are oriented toward and dependent on technology, looking to the bottom line for value.

As this partnership among science, technology, industry, and business creates marvels, it creates monsters as well. It saves us from disease, it creates disease; it creates jobs, it eliminates jobs; it rescues us from tedious and boring work, it generates work that is tedious and boring; it makes wealth, it leaves many people behind in poverty; it preserves life, it destroys life; it has given us better, warmer, healthier shelters and abundant food and medicine as it destroys farmland and draws down resources to do so; it increases longevity and shortens lives; it both cleans and pollutes; it saves time and consumes time; it brings us education, it entertains us with trivia; it brings us new information, but not always truth and wisdom.

The challenges that face us indeed seem formidable. As the economy heats up and goes global, using Earth resources in increasing amounts, the environment seems to be increasingly threatened and ethical decisions hard to come by. Renowned "world watchers" Lester R. Brown, Christopher Flavin, and Sandra Postel write in "A Planet in Jeopardy" that we are as slow to come to grips with the potential disaster in earth functions as were passengers on the *Titanic*.[13]

State of the Ark People: Worldwide

Although the poverty level of the world's poor has improved slightly, 23 percent still live on less than $1 a day, and the richest people continue to see their wealth increase dramatically (**www.worldbank.org/poverty/data /trendsincome.html**). As many as half the world's population live on less than $2 a day; the global economy barely touches them.[14] In addition, 2.5 percent of the world—increasingly women as single parents, the elderly, and children—do not have housing, clean water, health care, or education. Between 6 million and 7 million children die every year from malnutrition, leaving millions more stunted both physically and intellectually.[15] The Poverty Site (**www.povertyfighters.com**) urges people to "click" every day to donate to the world's poor.

For example, the Hunger Web site (**www.thehungersite.com**) tells us that as many as 24,000 people die daily of hunger, mostly because they are too poor to buy food, not because of famine or war, which causes 10 percent of these deaths. They urge a "click" each day to donate food to the hungry of the world. You will also find other sites where you can donate and find information about the world's people. For example, at Give Water (**www. givewater.org**), you can provide water for others. For more information on hunger, visit: //**www.bread.org**.

State of the Ark People: United States

There are people and places in the United States that are equally poor. 11.7 percent of families in this country live below the poverty level, which for a family of four in 2001 meant an income of less than $18,000 per year.

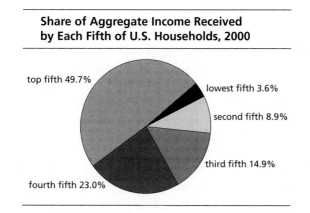

**Share of Aggregate Income Received
by Each Fifth of U.S. Households, 2000**

top fifth 49.7%

lowest fifth 3.6%

second fifth 8.9%

third fifth 14.9%

fourth fifth 23.0%

SOURCE: *http://www.census.gov/hhes/www/img/incpov00/fig12.jpg*

With a minimum wage of $7.25 per hour, a full-time worker earns $14,500. In many parts of the country, more than double that is necessary to rent or own a home. Where affordable housing is scarce, finding a place to live may mean living in overcrowded conditions. Full-time workers can be found in large numbers among the homeless. Many of them have children. Single mothers, especially minority mothers, are among the poorest people in our midst.

Although workers' wages have increased during the past two decades, corporate profits and executive compensation have vastly outpaced them. The wealth of the top 1 percent of U.S. households grew to equal the bottom 95 percent. From 1997 to 2000, the wealth of the richest people grew at a rate of 6,602 times the daily minimum wage. CEO pay increased from 96 times the average worker's pay in 1990 to 458 times in 2000.[16] In 1999—a good economic year—31 million Americans were food insecure, meaning they were either hungry or unsure of where their next meal would come from. Of these Americans, 12 million were children.

It is very difficult for the average American to fathom the plight of most of the world's people, yet some question whether democracy and social stability can flourish when so many people are excluded from the global economy. Some feel that this disparity makes the United States the target of disaffected people who espouse terrorism in their frustration.

There is enough
for everyone's need;
But not enough
for everyone's greed.
—*Gandhi*

BUY NOW, PAY LATER:
THE CONSUMER SOCIETY GOES GLOBAL

After World War II, retailers followed the thinking of retailing analyst Victor Lebow, who declared, "Our enormously productive economy . . . demands that we make consumption our way of life, that we convert the buying and use of goods into rituals, that we seek our spiritual and ego satisfaction in consumption. . . . We need things consumed, burned up, worn out, replaced, and discarded at an ever-increasing rate."[17]

The values expressed by the electronic media—television and computers—are often the values we "learn" from repeated exposure. As competition in the marketplace overheats, the urge to urge people to consume grows apace. Media messages are so strong that young people who live in the most remote villages of the world, who do not even have enough to eat or shoes to wear, will buy U.S. consumer goods that do not always represent the healthiest aspects of our society. Technology in this information age is a mixed bag —it has extraordinary value in bringing the wonders of the world to the world; it can also bring messages that are harmful to our long-term welfare.

To keep the affluent supplied with consumer goods, poor people in developing countries, many of them children, subsidize us by their labor: They struggle to survive on low wages in inhumane working conditions, making brand-name products that sell in the United States for many times the workers' earnings. Famous athletes earn millions advertising these products. The poor often live in inadequate shelters, and sometimes go without food and medicine for themselves and their children as they work for us.

By now we've heard the statistics: The United States, with fewer than 6 percent of the world's population, uses a third of the world's resources and causes almost half of its industrial pollution. If everyone lived an American lifestyle, we would need two or more planets the size of Earth to live sustainably.

We have enough retail stores to service a population far greater than ours. Often large chains cause small businesses to close, create low-wage, low-skill jobs, increase the need for such city services as roads and fire and police protection, and send revenues out of the local economy. A survey found that one well-known superstore adds 140 low-paying jobs in a town and destroys 230 higher-paying jobs.[18]

In the United States, advertisers spend hundreds of dollars per person each year for ads, so that our waking hours are bombarded by more and more ads. An eighteen-year-old will have spent 20,000 hours watching TV, compared to 11,000 hours in a classroom and much less on homework and reading. In a lifetime, the average American spends thirteen years as a couch potato. Many people would argue that ads do not influence them, but 89 percent of women and 79 percent of men admit to buying more than they need,[19] with the ratio of nonjunk to junk in the typical American household estimated at roughly 1:10.[20] The natural resources consumed would fill 300 shopping bags per week for each American.[21] Lance Morrow once wrote in *Time* magazine that "whole nations could live comfortably on [our] leftovers."[22]

Megacorporations amass more power and money than many governments. The Fortune 500 firms control 70 percent of world trade and 25 percent of the world's economic output, yet they employ only one-twentieth of 1 percent of the world's population.[23]

> We often forget that the price of never-ending economic growth and material prosperity has been spiritual and social impoverishment, psychological insecurity, and the loss of cultural vitality.
> —*Helena Norberg-Hodge*[24]

Energy Fires Up the Industrial/Technical World

Just about everything we use involves energy—in production, use, and maintenance. Despite severe pollution, the specter of global warming, and threats that "the oil is running out," energy use is increasing in developing countries as well as in affluent countries, as everyone struggles to obtain many of the amenities they see others enjoying. Energy consumption still grows yearly by leaps and bounds.

Think of all the ways you use energy. How does the United States as a whole use it? As much as 25 percent of U.S. energy goes to maintain buildings.[25] Cars, giant energy guzzlers, leave no part of the environment untouched from the materials they use; the land for roads and parking they take up; the earth, air, water they pollute; to the huge amounts of fuel they consume every day.

Nuclear power, once thought to be the key to unlimited energy, has not lived up to expectations; its waste products are dangerous for centuries, and states are unwilling to provide a storage place for them. Even though it is becoming clearer that their time is running out, fossil fuel interests are unwilling to lose profits to alternative fuels.

Military Security

Wars are fought for many reasons, but often over wealth-producing resources, including land and energy, and of course over personal and political power. More than any other activity, war costs billions of dollars and destroys infrastructure. Then millions of dollars and many years are required to repair the results of its devastation on lives, property, and the environment.

The tools of war become more deadly; violence at home, school, and the workplace seems to escalate. The United States, at last count, was moving away from controlling its own array of weapons while urging others to do so with theirs. The world arms trade is a huge money-maker, with merchants selling to anyone who will buy, regardless of the causes they espouse.

> Every gun that is made, every warship launched, every rocket fired,
> signifies in a final sense, a theft from those who hunger and are not fed,
> those who are cold and not clothed.
> —*Former U.S. president and general Dwight Eisenhower*[26]

Our economy—ever expanding and heating up and needing protection—is affecting the environment in ways that seem to threaten life on the planet. Without question, economics meets the environment at the factory gate and the office door.

ECONOMY MEETS THE ENVIRONMENT

Spotted owls! Who needs them? In reality, we all do. The truth is that we are all environmentalists—at least, those of us who breathe, eat and drink, wear clothing, live in shelters. We all depend on the Earth. The loss of the spotted owl signals the loss of an entire ecosystem and the irreparable loss of old-growth forests that house a vast array of plant and animal species. We often destroy a system before we understand it. Lt. Dick Lawrence, director of a wildlife program that dealt with alligators in Florida, asked, "Why do we always kill what we do not understand?"[27]

Prominent zoologist Jane Lubchenco says, "[M]ore and more ecologists . . . are becoming convinced that the systems they have known and loved and studied for years are changing . . . in ways they wouldn't have believed possible. And they are feeling . . . frustrated that the information that they think they have to share has not been heard or sought."[28]

> Trees can live without people,
> but people cannot live without trees.[29]

As these words fall on the page, a nearby tree is slowly dying—one of many Monterey pines in the Monterey Bay area being attacked by a disease. Why it should happen is a mystery. We still understand very little about our fragile and interconnected ecosystems. Many species keep other destructive species in check. Slight changes in overall temperature bring new predator insects to vulnerable plants. Many magnificent examples of species that are strong, graceful, and beautiful as well as those that are lowly, cumbersome, and ugly—though useful—are becoming scarce.

Our Basic Needs

Air: Breathing Life   We know now that damage to the ozone layer has gone global. Pollution chokes cities, threatening health and causing the shutdown of many activities.

Climate: A Closed System   Emissions of greenhouse gases into the atmosphere include 6 billion tons of carbon dioxide per year (the main greenhouse gas), largely from burning fossil fuels.[30] Burning just one gallon of gasoline releases twenty pounds of carbon dioxide into the atmosphere.[31] Many elements make up the world's climate, but global warming does seem to be increasing. Storms are growing in frequency and force. The insurance industry is alarmed because this increase is overwhelming them with natural disaster claims. They have begun to work against the burning of fossil fuels.[32] Our economic activities seem to be having many unforeseen effects on the environment. A computer simulation of the Sahel in Africa showed that activities such as clearing forests reduce humidity, favorable winds, cloud formation, and rainfall.[33]

Fresh Water: Drinking Life   After air, water is our most important basic need. Like the Earth with its oceans, our bodies largely consist of water, which keeps our systems running. In times past, outside cities, fresh clear water was abundant. Today, few people would dare to drink out of a stream in the wilderness. One-fifth of Americans are said to be drinking dangerous, dirty tap water.[34] Worldwide, water wars are already in process, notably in the Middle East, where oil flows. The world is slated to live in countries facing moderate or severe water stress.[35] California, the country's largest grower of produce, is a prime example. Easily available pure water is a luxury for most of the world. While we struggle with shortages, we still do not fully understand how water works in earth/air systems.

Earth Systems: Land's End   A nation's ultimate health—physical, economic, emotional, and spiritual—is said to depend on the health of its land. In the United States, we lose 6 billion acres of soil a year through erosion and by building roads and shopping malls, often on prime agricultural land.[36] Soil erosion has exceeded soil formation by 26 billion tons worldwide.[37] We are told that artificial fertilizers, pesticides, and their overuse are depleting soil fertility. Soil is the source of most of our food and fiber as well as countless other products necessary for life.

Forests: Earth's Lungs   Worldwide we are losing 168 square kilometers of forests per year.[38] Deforestation takes more than 17 million hectares through clearing, burning, and cutting, an area about the size of Arkansas.[39] As of 1993, 55 percent of the world's richest species habitat, the tropical forest, had already been destroyed.[40]

Species: Our Companion Creatures   Most people are intrigued by a trip to an aquarium or a zoo. When no one is looking, many of us may find ourselves conversing with a brightly colored parrot, a cat, or a dog if one is in the vicinity. Like the earth under our feet, we take these companion creatures for granted, too. Species have always disappeared, as the dinosaurs tell us. But in the 68 million years prior to the industrial age, it took 10,000 years for 50,000 species to disappear.[41] Today, an estimated 50,000 plant and animal species are lost *each year*.[42] The numbers of bees are decreasing rapidly, a fact that may not move you until you realize that bees are a vital link in the food chain. The waters of the Earth, especially oceans, also a symbol of mystery and abundance, are at risk. Sixty percent of fish stocks, once a low-cost food for millions, especially the poor, are being overfished or are depleted, while an estimated 100,000 fishers have been put out of work.[43] Pollution is found in the most distant parts of the oceans. As bodies of water such as the huge Aral Sea dry up, fish are left high and dry, the environment a desert.

Food/Farming: The Most Basic of Needs   We might think that famine is due solely to food shortages, but in reality, poverty, poor farming methods, bad weather, military buildups, war, inadequate transportation, politics, and ecological devastation are more likely the causes. In many cases, land has been taken over for luxury crops for export, leaving the poor without the place to grow food they have used for centuries. Cheap food imports and the patenting of such for sale further undercut the livelihood of many of the world's poor.

Americans consume very expensive food, shipped an average of 1,300 miles before it reaches them, processed and packaged, using great amounts of energy.[44] It may not be fresh; its vitality, nutrients, minerals, and vitamins are often reduced; frequently, it is treated with pesticides, covered with wax, and picked before it is ripe.[45] Some 20 percent of all the food produced in the United States each year is wasted or lost, enough to feed all the country's hungry people.[46]

Overall, unsustainable food systems can cause more harm than good. Once thought to be the answer to food shortages, factory farms that breed and feed livestock are accused of animal cruelty and massive pollution. Tropical biologist Christopher Uhl of Pennsylvania State University calculates that every hamburger imported to the United States requires the clearing of 5 square meters of jungle. A pound of U.S. feedlot steak costs five pounds of grain, 2,500 gallons of water, and about thirty-five pounds of eroded topsoil.[47]

Health   It's often pointed out that no amount of money can buy good health, but access to help in a health crisis can go a long way toward that goal. In the United States, about 41.7 million people lack health coverage,[48] and many people do not take advantage of the abundant information available that would lead to improved health. The excellent U.S. health care systems are threatened by shrinking dollars. New diseases stalk us, transmitted through rapid global transportation.

Pollution   A pollution stew of pesticides, toxic and hazardous wastes, and just plain junk mix with air, water, soil, and the products of these in ways we do not understand.

Population: Planet People Increasing and Multiplying   As many species disappear, there seems to be no shortage of people on the planet, their numbers increasing dramatically every day. The world population has now passed the 6 billion mark. Whereas fertility rates are decreasing more than expected, population is still increasing faster than some believe we have resources to support. People, especially the poor, are crowding into the world's cities, outpacing services and employment.[49]

Years Needed for Human Population to Reach Successive Billions[50]

First billion = 2,000,000 years

Second billion = 105 years

Third billion = 30 years

Fourth billion = 15 years

Fifth billion = 12 years

Sixth billion = 11 years

Although its strictly economic implications
have still not been worked out,
it should be clear:
an exhausted planet is an exhausted economy.
—*Thomas Berry*

OPTIONS BANISH GLOOM AND DOOM

By now, you may be having nightmares over the formidable challenges that face us, but there are many more reasons to be positive. We may feel helpless, but author and monk Brother David Steindl-Rast said, "We know enough." We know enough to bring health and beauty to the Earth and its people. Designer Buckminster Fuller realized very early that we were the first generation to be aware that we are affecting the universe with our every act. He saw by the 1970s that we had the capability to produce and sustain, within ten years' time, a higher standard of living than ever imagined for all humanity, using fewer resources and already existing technologies.[51] We *do* know what to do.

As the technological revolution has taken root, our global consciousness, or awareness of the interconnectedness of life on this planet, has grown. Viewing the earth from space, astronaut Russell Schweickart said:

> It is so small and so fragile, such a precious little spot in the universe . . . you realize that everything that means anything to you—all of history and art and death and birth and love, tears and joys, all of it—is on that little blue and white spot out there, which you can cover with your thumb.[52]

The challenge, rather than getting discouraged or looking for another planet, is to catch the options that put us on the side of change.

There *is* a growing consciousness that we can tame science and technology for human need. We understand the necessity for pure air and water and for systems that do not pollute; for renewable energy; for healthy, vigorous soil and environmentally friendly food production; for biodegradable products and packaging; for hazardous waste cleanup; for shelter and clothing made of alternative or recycled materials. We already know many ways to use technology without causing undue harm to the planet.

Many government and private groups have identified hundreds of Earth-friendly options in every area of challenge, including those involving buildings, transportation, manufacturing, electricity generation, forestry, and food. Although these options are sometimes expensive in initial outlay, they require no major technological breakthroughs. Their long-run savings far outweigh the expense. For example, with technologies and methods available today, industry and agriculture could cut air and water pollution significantly. Farmers could cut water needs 10 percent to 50 percent, industries by 40 percent to 90 percent, and cities by 33 percent—with no sacrifice of economic output or quality of life.[53] We are learning to live in harmony with nature.

As the new millennium begins, some people are seeing a different kind of economy. Sharron Cordaro of *Yes! The Journal of Positive Futures,* says, "Hopefully, with the growing interest in voluntary simplicity, more people are choosing to ignore the commercial clamor of the media and are opting out of this lifestyle. They have discovered not only financial relief, but a sense of freedom, joy, and harmony with the earth, with others, and within themselves."[54] In the first century B.C., the Roman poet Horace said, "This was what I prayed for: a piece of land, not so very large where there would be a garden, and near the house a spring of ever-flowing water, and besides these a bit of woodland . . . more and better than this have the gods done for me. I am content."[55]

SUSTAINABLE SYSTEMS DEFINED

In the past, the systems that supplied basic necessities were sustainable—that is, they were largely self-renewing. For example, if we grow tomatoes, save the seeds, fertilize the soil with vegetable and other plant scraps and mulch the soil so that we use little water, and sometimes let the soil rest, we can continue growing tomatoes with little outside input for a very long time. Because fresh food is fragile, selling locally minimizes transportation and storage costs and increases the sustainability of the process. Land has been farmed this way by indigenous people for many centuries. The Worldwatch Institute provides a yearly report on progress toward a sustainable society, and their research shows innumerable ways of charting a path to a sustainable future.

If people indigenous to tropical rainforests are left to harvest the products of their lands and if they are encouraged by new markets, they *and* the forests can survive well in sustainable harmony. Harvesting quick-growing and sturdy parts of rainforest cactus for twine and domesticating animals for food—thus saving the wild variety—are just two examples of viable businesses that can help save the natural environment.[56] People produce, market, and use jewelry, art, and furniture that does not exploit forests or wildlife. Rubber tapper Chico Mendes, who was murdered for working to preserve an area of rainforests in Brazil, said, "A rubber tree can live up to one hundred years if you tap it right, *affectionately.*"[57]

Mining metals and other products to make cars, computers, plastic gadgets and toys, and then discarding them when they are too old to use—these are nonsustainable processes. Recycling, using sunlight for energy, using alternative transportation like bicycles and mass transit are a few examples of systems that come closer to being sustainable. There are many viable options to help create a healthy planet. Solutions will come, often slowly, drop by drop. For example, a project in Chile uses huge nets to catch enough "fog drops" to provide a nearby village of 450 people with twenty liters of water per day for each person.[58] A group of inventors and visionaries have created a sustainable community called Gaviotas in one of the most barren and difficult places in Colombia.[59]

How Do They Work?

Air and Water: Cleansing the Systems   Many industries as well as individuals are cleaning up and polluting less, recycling more, trying to create user-friendly products. CO-OP America's *Green Pages* directory highlights these businesses. Some cities are saving valuable nutrients, using partially purified wastewater as fertilizer instead of chemical materials. John and Nancy Todd, founders of the Center for the Restoration of Waters at Ocean

Arks International, use sewage-eating plants or bacteria they call "living machines" to bring sewage water back to pristine purity; it can then be used to produce food and fish as well as nonfood items.[60]

Swampy wetlands, now rightly seen as powerful water cleansers as well as rich wildlife habitats, are being protected and restored. Use of drip irrigation, delivering tiny amounts of water where it is needed, is increasing. Mulching and conditioning soil is recognized as lessening its need for water. Low-flow showers and toilets are mandated in some places to conserve water and the energy used in purifying and pumping it. "Composting" toilets that compost waste using little or no water are viable water and resource savers. Research on oceans, aquifers, and other water systems is still in its infancy.

Trees Support Life   We are beginning to understand more clearly that trees refresh and cool the air as well as bring beauty to a landscape. Trees supply us with many resources such as building materials, food, and medicine. Beyond that, one tree will eventually remove twenty-six pounds of carbon dioxide from the air every year.[61] Urban trees also save Americans an estimated $4 billion a year in air conditioning expenses.[62]

Rogue Community College in Oregon has a "Jobs in the Woods" program to teach former loggers environmental restoration of the forests.[63] Eco-Timber sells thousands of board feet of "certified" lumber—that is, lumber logged in an environmentally sound and sustainable way.[64] Many jobs are opening up that bring people to better appreciation of natural and beautiful areas as they also work to preserve and restore them or lead groups on eco-vacations.

Food/Farming: Planting the Planet   New and old food systems are coming online. A giant food processor, seeing the demand for more natural food, calls people to make one of the nation's most productive agricultural areas totally organic. Rodale Research Institute in Pennsylvania, promoters of organic food production, have shown that crops grow better and are pest-free in healthy soil using organic compost and natural fertilizers. Natural pest control is being used successfully to grow organic crops. The number of certified organic farms continues to grow across the country. Some companies are researching, developing, and selling organic pesticides. Here are some examples of these systems:

- Dennis Tamura, a graduate of the Agricology Program at the University of California, Santa Cruz, grows and sells elegant produce throughout the San Francisco Bay Area on land called Blue Heron Farms "never touched by pesticides."
- Eliot Coleman finds that one-half to five acres is a highly productive scale for organic vegetable growing, using simple tools and no chemicals.[65]

- Rooftop gardens, driveway gardens, prosperous greenhouses in the ghetto, gardening without soil, gardening in hay bales, gardening in gravel, or even gardening in a bed of crushed soft drink cans—it's all been done successfully.

- At least 40 percent of Americans are gardeners,[66] supplying a great deal of their own food, saving energy and water, and lessening or eliminating pesticide use.

- Urban agriculture is a growing phenomenon and the best way to ensure fresh food with the least cost of resources; about 15 percent of food is grown in cities, according to the United Nations Development Program.[67]

- Farmers' markets are growing everywhere, many of them featuring organic produce.

- Gray Bears, a volunteer organization, gleans food left over in fields after harvesting to provide meals for poor elderly people.

- People reduce meat consumption when they realize that every 10 percent reduction in consumption of grain-fed livestock products frees up 64 million tons of grain for direct human consumption—and this diet is healthier.

- Farmer Bob Cannard grows gourmet, organic vegetables for upscale restaurants in Berkeley, California, and they in turn send back their food waste for compost on his farm, forming a circle of community.[68]

- Seeds of Change company founder Kenny Ausubel says, "It's taken the planet millions of years to slowly assemble and evolve its intricate cellular opera and there are still at least 50,000 known edible plants still left on earth. Yet only three of those—rice, corn, and wheat—account for half of everything we eat."[69] Groups are saving heirloom/heritage seeds to preserve genetic diversity. Food specialists are discovering easily grown, nutritious food plants and developing alternative diets; health and environmentally conscious restaurants and supermarkets are increasing.

- Alida Stevens, founder/owner of Smith and Vandiver, manufactures personal care products using such natural substances as almond meal, apricots, honey, sea salt, sesame oil, and mint, and she prefers local, agricultural products. Her firm employs ninety people, markets to 6,000 stores in fourteen countries, and recorded $8.5 million in sales in 1993.

- Planting wind breaks, multicropping, using mulch, planting marginal land with grass or trees or letting it return to a native state, and contour plowing all greatly reduce erosion and nourish the soil.

Preserving Planet People   We are appalled when we hear of population control methods that use force to make people limit their families. Population control is a contentious issue, as it touches on people's deepest religious, social, and personal values. Yet statistics show that one of the best means of cutting population is educating women. There is "no social indicator that correlates more closely with the shift to smaller families than the level of female education," and this holds across all cultures.[70] Educated women marry later; often involved in careers, they opt to have fewer children. It helps also to educate men to realize that women are still worthwhile even though they may have fewer children. People can be taught systems of birth control that fit even the strictest ideologies. It's possible that in a few decades the world could have a population that's heading downward to a number the Earth can support comfortably.

Looking simply at the population's well-being, the United States has some of the best and most abundant food sources in the world and some of the healthiest living/working spaces. We are aware of the need to exercise, avoid drugs and alcohol, and eat a healthy diet. We have the latest technology and pharmaceuticals and research facilities seeking to combat new diseases that arise. People are questioning their doctors, asking for second opinions, and spending billions on alternative health care like relaxation techniques, herbal medicine, chiropractic, acupuncture, and homeopathy—more than they spend on primary care physicians.[71] Health food stores have become upscale markets with upscale profits as the food industry races to keep up with people's desire for good, toxin-free food.

People consult with businesses to develop cost-containing health plans; others are becoming ombudspersons and inspectors to ensure proper care for patients in health care institutions; still others are opening health care centers. Fitness spas and recreational sports centers flourish. In-home health care, including hospice, grows, a comfortable, viable, money-saving alternative to hospitals. People are taking more and more advantage of education, including lifelong learning, to create a sense of well-being as well as career enhancement.

Safety/Security   Although threats like 9/11 are still possible, we also have many hopeful signs that safety and security are increasing. New methods of law enforcement, firefighting, and military strategy are being developed continually to protect our lives and property. Community policing cuts crime and strengthens neighborhoods. The protection of civil rights and human rights spreads slowly across the globe with focus on reducing child and spousal abuse and prosecuting war crimes and other violent practices against humanity. Former U.S. President Jimmy Carter won the Nobel Peace Prize in 2002 for his decades-long, painstaking work to find peaceful solutions to international conflict based on social and economic development and cooperation rather than force.

How much more delightful to an undebauched mind
is the task of making improvements on the earth,
than all the vain glory which can be acquired from ravaging it.
—*George Washington, shortly after the Revolutionary War*[72]

Mediation, a nonviolent reconciliation of conflict, is being taught in schools and has been used successfully to negotiate conflict; observers often see ways that many wars could have been avoided. The editor of *Sojourners,* Jim Wallis, urges us to foster a "culture of nonviolence." Professor Emeritus Michael Nagler of the University of California, Berkeley, has been researching and teaching nonviolence for many years. In his latest book, *Is There No Other Way?,* he gives numerous examples of nonviolent mediation efforts that seldom make the headlines but nonetheless have proven effective time and time again. We hear voices raised asking us to redefine national security as a state when people's basic needs and enriching wants are sufficient. Congressman Dennis Kucinich of Ohio urges the creation of a national cabinet-level department of peace to use the methods at our disposal to avoid conflict and war.

Cooling the Planet: Energy Savings   The stores of renewable and safe energy resources in the United States and globally are enormous. Here are some specifics.

The sun shines everywhere, in some places over long periods of time. Researchers at the U.S. Department of Energy estimate that if PV (photovoltaic) panels—panels that produce electricity from light—were mounted atop 5,000 square kilometers of roof space, they could generate 25 percent of the electricity used in the United States.[73] Globally, sunlight on rooftop solar panels/collectors could supply much needed electricity and heat for residential and business buildings. Homes in the coldest parts of the country can be heated by the sun and kept within 5 degrees plus or minus of 70 degrees all year long without a furnace or woodstove.[74] Such simple technologies as super insulation and thermal-pane windows and draperies can save energy. Straw-bale or rammed earth homes can both heat shelters and keep them cool.[75] Construction oriented to the sun, thermal mass heat collectors such as stone floors and walls, containers of water (either glass or black-coated) as well as attached greenhouses (which can also provide food) keep or release heat into shelters. Solar power can run water pumps and other small machines. Solar water heaters provide hot water. Solar ovens as well as more efficient stoves are usable, especially in developing countries, for cooking, heating, and purifying water.[76]

The sun produces the temperature differential that creates wind. Wind power, especially in California and the Midwest, has been the fastest growing energy market since the 1990s.[77] In 1993, the school district in Spirit Lake,

Iowa, powered its schools with a wind turbine that now generates about $25,000 of electrical energy annually.[78]

Plants also grow by sun power. Biomass—vegetable and animal by-products such as manure, corn husks, bagasse from sugar cane, and other decaying biological materials—is being converted into clean-burning fuels such as methane and alcohol.

Heat generated from copiers and other machinery and even bodies is being recycled and used in commercial buildings. Cogeneration recycles heat from industrial processes to heat homes, offices, and other industrial sites instead of letting it escape.

Transportation   New developments have multiplied the speed and ease of movement in the past century. Automakers now produce affordable "hybrid cars" that can run alternately on electricity or gasoline. They have developed electric cars with motors four and five times as efficient as internal combustion engines with lower battery weight, shorter recharging time, and longer drive range.[79] Cars have been run successfully with both hydrogen fuel cells and solar cells with no pollution. Slowing down can help. A car that consumes 5 liters at 80 kilometers per hour will need 20 liters to go 160 kilometers an hour.[80] Add conservation by using mass transit, van pooling, car pooling, and many energy conserving devices and systems, and the results can be impressive.

Bicycles are used mostly for utilitarian purposes by many of the world's people and are the principal means of transport other than walking.[81] Some cities have developed safe bike lanes and encourage the use of bikes to haul and deliver goods.[82] Many more bicycles are produced worldwide than cars each year, and their production is increasing.[83] For some people in developing countries, having a bike is a giant step up to an easier and profitable lifestyle.

Efficient, comfortable, affordable, flexible mass transit is being developed with community input. Municipalities explore clean, comfortable, efficient rail service: per passenger mile, trains use one-third the energy of an airplane and one-sixth that of a driver-only auto and cost as little as 10 percent of the price of freeway construction.[84] A two-track right of way for a rail system can carry as much traffic as sixteen lanes of highway.

Cooling the Planet: Energy Savings   For the past three decades, Amory and Hunter Lovins, founders of the Rocky Mountain Institute, have been teaching us how to have abundant energy without using fossil fuels. In 2000, America used 40 percent less energy and 49 percent less oil to produce each dollar of gross domestic product (GDP) than in 1975 simply by conserving and using efficient technologies.[85] The Lovins have told U.S. officials, "America's energy bill could shed $300 billion a year using conservation with existing technologies rather than building and maintaining traditional energy systems, that are profitable at today's prices." This can be done with no sacrifice in our present lifestyle or standard of living.[86]

If all U.S. households replaced their regular bulbs with fluorescent bulbs, we would save $30 billion a year, use 20 percent to 25 percent less electricity, and shut down 120 thousand-megawatt nuclear power plants.

Energy can be saved in innumerable ways from large to small. One family practices energy efficiency and has a utility bill at least 75 percent lower than those of its neighbors with little or no sacrifice of comfort. They turn off lights, TVs, and other appliances when not in use. They use heat only when and where necessary; their lights are compact fluorescent; they use a solar clothes dryer, otherwise known as a clothes line.

Shelter/Community   From cabins to condos, people have managed to create a wondrous array of shelters. Whether it's a home or a workplace, the best structure is a beautiful one that gives its inhabitants a sense of belonging and a sense of safety, at reasonable cost in a human-scale community integrated carefully into the natural surroundings. Bob Berkebile, a principal in one of Kansas City's leading architectural firms, says that "we are waking up to the fact that our buildings and our communities are part of nature rather than an environment apart."[87] Oberlin College has recently developed a sustainable environmental studies building that aims to show just that and to educate by its very design. It incorporates state-of-the-art technologies in water, energy, and resource use.[88] The savings will be considerable.

Former mayor of Davis, California, Michael Corbett not only wrote about a new "village" concept but he also developed one at Village Homes.[89] More such villages, even within cities, are on the drawing boards, creating, as Sarah van Gelder calls them, cities of exuberance.[90] In these communities, trees and gardens flourish. Rainwater can be preserved in cisterns and also moves naturally along streambeds to nourish the groundwater. The automobile is deemphasized; walking and biking are encouraged. Shops and other workplaces are nearby. Community is strengthened.

Many abandoned inner cities are finding new life. Old, well-built housing stock is being remodeled for energy efficiency. Transportation and cultural, social, and educational amenities are being developed in convenient locations. Locally owned and operated stores flourish, as do their support staff and suppliers. This generally ensures that money is recycled over and over right in town, not hundreds of miles away. Urban gardens can be used to provide organic food, save energy, and strengthen community. When urban development takes place, outlying open space and farmland are preserved. Wherever a sense of community develops, crime and pollution are lessened.

Another innovative approach to living is called co-housing, which saves resources by blending private space with shared facilities. Some groups including municipalities are using community land trusts to keep land costs from escalating; here, the land is not sold but only rented for a small yearly fee.

Robert Rodale of Rodale Press pioneered the concept of regenerating towns that have failing economies. By working with the forces of nature instead of trying to overcome them, restoring nature instead of destroying it, and avoiding centralization and monopolization, a regenerated community uses local renewable resources and energy sources so that they do not need to be transported from far away. Cleaner, healthier, prosperous networks of caring neighborhoods develop. The arts as well as businesses flourish. The local economy becomes both self-generating and self-improving; the worker base is kept intact, and people's health and welfare count more than monetary wealth as a measure of success.[91] Income is spent locally, energy is saved, health and the environment are enhanced, and people get involved with each other and have time to celebrate.

> The concerns for man and his destiny must always be
> the chief interest of all technical efforts.
> Never forget this among your diagrams and equations.
> —*Albert Einstein*

Recycling: A Sustainable Option   At the time of the first Earth Day in April 1970, did *anyone* know *anyone* who recycled? At that time someone posed the question, "What if you had to keep all your discards on your own property?" It brought the problem home at once: there *is* no "away." In a giant burst of higher consciousness, mainstream Americans began to recycle.

Now many local governments, such as those in Chicago and San Francisco, public institutions such as colleges, and private contractors are developing sustainable buildings. Some municipalities such as Los Angeles and Sacramento, California, are running their own utilities at considerable savings of money and energy. Local governments across the United States are setting up curbside pickup to recycle cans, bottles, newspapers, and cardboard. Companies are springing up to make treasures out of trash, others to find use for and market these treasures. In Naperville, Illinois, a company turns plastic milk bottles into building and fencing material that looks like wood and can be sawed and nailed. Plastic bottles turn into warm sweaters, jackets, and blankets. Recycled asphalt as well as the millions of discarded tires and even old ceramic toilets are ground up and mixed with new asphalt to become an excellent road surface. German automobile and computer makers are required to take back discarded products and reuse or recycle the parts.[92] Composting is becoming mainstream as municipalities look for ways to reduce material going into their landfills. The new motto is reduce and reuse while recycling what is left.

Sweden has inaugurated a comprehensive plan for a sustainable economy called "The Natural Step," involving everyone from the king to school children. From manufacturers to innkeepers, everyone is looking for non-polluting, energy-efficient materials and systems.[93]

HOPE ON THE ECONOMIC HORIZON:
BUSINESS AS UNUSUAL

Howell Hurst, principal of Strategic Asset Management in San Francisco, says, "We face a multitude of social problems that cry out for creative business solutions. . . . *I am interested in new businesses built on innovative concepts that contribute to the improvement of our society.*"[94]

Former Secretary of Labor Robert B. Reich urges a "new social contract between business, government, and citizens" that will help people survive global competition.[95] And *Business Week* says that "there are only two kinds of organizations: those that have embraced the global standards process, such as that found in the corporate environmental code CERES Principles, and those that will."[96]

Companies are marketing environmentally safe products, using recyclables, developing biodegradable packaging in ever-greater numbers, and creating jobs in the process. By their ecological concern, such publications as *World Watch* make us aware of the effects of business and personal activities on the planet. CO-OP America lists "Green Businesses" that support the environment by their work.[97]

Microlending: An Idea Whose Time Has Come

Economist Muhammad Yunus developed the concept of microlending to provide money to people without credit in one of the poorest countries on Earth: Bangladesh. This Grameen (or Village) Bank loaned more than $2 billion mostly to poor women in its first twenty years.[98] Microlending organizations lend amounts of money too small for traditional banks to deal with at interest rates the poor can afford. These small loans can purchase a sewing machine, a dozen chickens, equipment for a fish pond, a corn grinder, material to bake small amounts of bread, or hair clippers. They often mean the difference between a life of grinding poverty and one in which families prosper and children can be fed, clothed, educated, and given health care. Repayment rates are usually higher than those for conventional loans.

> The poor need capital, not charity;
> a hand up, not a handout.
> —*Millard Fuller*
> *Founder of Habitat for Humanity*

Microlending peer groups meet now from ghetto basements in Chicago to tiny shacks in Peru to make loan decisions, apply peer pressure for repayments, and support their members. Their businesses flourish. Since 1973, the staff of South Shore Bank in a ghetto area of Chicago has successfully financed more than 8,000 multifamily units with small loans, placed 3,500 individuals in jobs through its employment-training programs, and assisted over 156 new firms.[99] Their nonprofit housing corporation has assisted residents in rehabilitating a 265-square-block ghetto area, helping many to become homeowners.

These economic institutions range from successful cooperative businesses of Mondragon in the poor Basque section of Spain to Trickle Up (TUP) for low-income people worldwide,[100] to the Heifer Project of Arkansas, which provides food-supplying animals to poor people. Acción International says that the process of microlending is "an essential element within viable development programs";[101] U.S. banks, the World Bank, and US AID agree and are joining them.

The Real Economy

The axiom says that money makes the world go 'round, and it *is* certainly a giant motivator, but money pays for less than half of all the work that is done in society. The money part of the economy includes the private sector, which rests on and depends on the tax-generated money of the public sector. It is surprising, however, to find that more than half our production, consumption, and investment consists of unpaid activities such as volunteering, community work, family gardening, and child and elder care.

Fifty-one percent of Americans volunteer an average of 4.2 hours per week, a contribution equivalent to 9 million full-time employees and $176 billion. There are more than 1,400,000 nonprofit organizations in the United States, *many of whom do have paid staff.*[102]

This third sector encompasses all types of work; it is that group of activities that enhances the life of the community and is independent of the marketplace and the public sector. Habitat for Humanity is one such example. It is a worldwide organization that builds homes for people too poor to afford a conventional loan. Habitat keeps the house affordable by seeking donated land and materials and using volunteer labor where possible. The organization charges no interest and makes no profit. A family makes a "down payment" of as much as 500 hours of sweat equity by working on the building, then pays back such costs as building materials, permits, and fees. Everyone wins.

Futurist Hazel Henderson says this "layer cake" of private, public, and nonmonetized sectors rests and depends on Mother Nature for all its resources.[103] The economy cannot function without the environment.

Putting it all together, the White Earth Land Recovery Project in western Minnesota reclaims land that belonged to the Anishinabeg Native American reservation. The tribe's cultural and economic development now includes production of various food products, medicinal plants, and baskets. Project participants are pursuing a sustainable agricultural program, researching a wind-power project, partnering with a local financial institution in a micro-lending program, starting a reservation radio station, and developing jobs and a healthy community.[104]

THE ETHICAL PERSPECTIVE: TIME FOR A CHANGE

Both our economic and our environmental decisions have moral and ethical implications. We have access to enormous amounts of information, the best education and health care, excellent food, and stores full of wonderful gadgets; yet we must ask, Are we wiser and better people for all this—that is, are we ethical?

Workplaces are presented with ethical decisions daily. One ad urges its customers to "Play Smart, Not Fair."[105] In the next chapter, we discuss the qualities of socially responsible or ethical businesses. Needless to say, with the help of the media, the corruption of people in high and low places is brought to our attention daily. At an international conference, "The Future of Intellectual Property Protection for Biotechnology," an eminent speaker said he hoped others would not have to face "environmentalists and those who would bring ethics and other irrational considerations to the table."[106] But most people think that ethics is a very rational subject and that the Golden Rule is still a good one: "Do unto others as you would have them do unto you," or its variant, "Bring no harm to anyone." But in a complex society, the lines become blurred when people can use loopholes in laws to do what really does harm, and large institutions make decisions far from the places where the decisions will be implemented.

In the past few years, we've seen prominent organizations sinking like rocks from insider theft, lying, and cheating. With so many corporations and investors watching the star performer, Enron, the money-making flagship, one wonders how such corruption in that company could have spread in a country that prides itself on its moral and ethical principles. Downright fraud resulted in closures, loss of people's investments, government intervention, legal prosecution, and people suffering from their government's and their employers' misuse of loaned funds, losing their homes and retirements. Heads of corporations have gone to prison for disregarding public safety, and high government officials have joined them for fraud and dishonesty.

> We have seen the enemy and he is us.
> —*Pogo*

Being Good: Ethics for a New Age

> Work is the way that we tend the world,
> the way people connect.
> It is the most vigorous, vivid sign of life—
> in individuals and civilization.
> —*Lance Morrow*

In the long run, those who gain the respect and trust of others, who are most admired, are those who have lived ethically. We make many ethical choices within the borders of our own jobs and lives, and those decisions, that often seem so small and hidden, will have an impact on ourselves and on everyone whose lives we touch. In fact, they will touch many whom we will never see.

Some people are finding that ethics is good business. Some industries are hiring ethics consultants. Business schools offer ethics courses. There is a growing awareness that choices have consequences, whether they are made by private individuals or by people acting as businesses. As we have seen, actions that people think are hidden become front-page news.

Many people are longing to deal with businesses where they *know* people and feel both trusting and trusted. In rural areas, a family will sometimes leave a table with bags of fruit out by the road with a sign giving the cost and a can for buyers to drop the money in. The amounts usually tally at the end of the day! Such entrepreneurs will order items for you, trust you to pay later, and often donate to your special causes. They are friends and neighbors as well as businesspeople.

A good society, including its economy, runs on trust. Trust and ethical behavior can't be legislated. Being socially responsible, however, doesn't mean being stupid. To use good social practices does not make businesses competition-proof. Business practice must be both wise and prudent. There is no question that economics meets ethics and the environment at the factory gate and the office door.

GLOBAL CONSCIOUSNESS:
THINKING THE UNTHINKABLE, DOING THE UNDOABLE

People need time to get used to new ideas. A first reaction is often to ridicule them as unworkable. An old Chinese proverb tells us,

> Person who says it cannot be done,
> should not interrupt person doing it.

Albert Einstein wrote, "The unleashed power of the atom has changed everything except our way of thinking." And never underestimate how difficult it is for people to change the way they think. Even the "experts," positive they are right, are sometimes wrong.

- In 1865, an editorial in the *Boston Post* assured its readers that "it is impossible to transmit the voice over wires and that were it possible to do so, the thing would be of no practical value."

- Early in the 1900s, Simon Newcomb said, "No possible combination of known substances, known forms of machinery and known forms of force can be united in a practical machine by which men shall fly long distances through the air."

- Dr. Richard van der Riet Wolley, British Astronomer Royal, stated in 1956: "Space travel is utter bilge!"[107]

- Then President Grover Cleveland said in 1905, "Sensible and responsible women do not want to vote."

- Harry M. Warner of Warner Bros. Pictures said of proposed movies with sound in 1927, "Who the hell wants to hear actors talk?"[108]

We tend to resist strongly those people who give us unpleasant messages about changing our attitudes and our ways. We say they do not understand the environment or the economic systems or ethics in the real world. But such visionaries are often proven correct in the long run. People predicted all sorts of dire results to the economy if the slaves were freed or women could vote and own property and businesses. Since those events have happened, the United States has become an economic giant. The alternative: Arlene Goetze says, "The fact that everyone doesn't want to believe something doesn't mean it's not true."[109]

> The opposite of intelligence
> is not ignorance, it's denial.
> —*Brian Swimme*

People Power

Sometimes it takes years for new concepts to become trends, and the path is seldom a straight line. Someone estimated that it takes about 15 percent of the population, which they call a critical mass, to act on something for it to become mainstream. It seems that many people feel that the work they do has little meaning in the larger scheme of things, and they are looking for more meaningful alternatives to business as usual.

People *are* "voting" at the checkstand of the global marketplace, choosing socially responsible products. They seem ready to challenge companies that do not follow ethical principles in the economic and environmental areas. They are putting money in this direction. Socially responsible investing topped $1 trillion in 1997 in the United States and is growing fast.[110]

After 33,455 letters and calls prompted by Working Assets Long Distance phone service, one maker of athletic shoes agreed to pay its Asian factory workers a living wage and institute a comprehensive third-party monitoring system to interview workers and assess working conditions.[111] Students are demanding that college sweatshirts and other clothing be "sweatshop free." Apartheid fell in South Africa largely because of consumer pressure for companies to withdraw their investments and operations there. A once-invincible tobacco industry showed itself vulnerable to the public's growing awareness of the health risks of tobacco.

Oscar Arias, former president of Costa Rica and winner of the 1987 Nobel Peace Prize, says that since Costa Rica abolished its army in 1948, it has achieved a level of human development that is the envy of Latin America. In his acceptance speech for the Global Citizen Award, he suggests the unthinkable: that nations disarm and use the funds they save to address human needs.[112] Other unthinkable ideas have become reality:

- People *are* conserving water.
- Meat consumption has dropped steadily during the past decade.
- Recycling has become a mainstream activity.
- Organic produce is being sold in supermarkets, and people's demand that the definition of *organic* not be diluted was accepted.[113]
- More "green" (energy-saving) buildings are appearing.
- Insurance companies are encouraging alternative health options as well as energy-saving strategies.
- Production of ozone-depleting chemicals has fallen; the ozone hole appears to be closing.
- Energy-conserving power use is up significantly; cigarette smoking is down.[114]
- A group of wealthy people called "Responsible Wealth" urges the government to change tax laws that favor the wealthy at the expense of the poor. They suggest donating the money saved in taxes to a worthy cause or returning it to the government.[115]
- Billionaire Ted Turner gave a billion dollars to the UN for poverty programs, and others are joining him.
- Journals and books promoting a simpler, less consuming lifestyle are flourishing—for example, *Yes! A Journal of Positive Futures* and *The New Road Map Foundation Newsletter*.

- A third of mainstream medical schools are teaching meditation and other alternative forms of healing.[116]

And absolutely unthinkable is this idea: It is quite possible that a small percentage of the world's population could work—or that everyone could work a small percentage of the time—and satisfy all needs and wants for everyone, with a modest expenditure of resources, energy, and burden on the planet. Or is it?

> Never doubt that a small group of
> thoughtful committed citizens can change the world;
> indeed, it's the only thing that ever has.
> —*Margaret Mead*

Jobs Lost and Gained

One argument often presented to avoid different ways of doing things is that certain changes will take away jobs. There are, however, many arguments to refute this—like the following:

- Recycling produces more jobs per ton of solid waste than either landfills or incinerators.[117]

- Public transit and light rail investments produce 50 percent more jobs per dollar spent than new highway construction.[118]

- Increasing the recycling rate of aluminum to 75 percent would create 350,000 new jobs.[119]

- Some 2 million Americans in more than 65,000 companies earn their living doing some kind of environmental clean-up work.[120]

- Urban Ore, a recycling company in Berkeley, California, contributes more than $300,000 to the local tax base each year by salvaging, cleaning, repairing, and reselling items from the municipal waste.[121]

- Weapons industries create far fewer jobs than would the same amount of investment in other areas.[122] The U.S. Bureau of Labor Statistics says that for every 76,000 jobs created in the military versus 92,000 jobs in transport, 100,000 jobs in construction, 139,000 jobs in health, or 187,000 jobs in education could be created for the same expenditures and money.[123]

- In the area of energy, "Creating a less carbib-intensive energy system would create hundreds of billions of dollars of business, and millions of jobs—most of them in making and installing devices that cleanly and efficiently turn renewable resources into useful forms of energy."[124]

- "The Wisconsin Energy Bureau found that the use of renewable energy generates about three times more jobs, earnings, and sales than does the same level of imported fossil fuels. A 75 percent increase in the use of renewable energy would result in more than 62,000 jobs, $1.2 billion in new wages, and $4.6 billion in new sales for Wisconsin businesses."[125]

- The Organization for Economic Cooperation and Development estimates that the worldwide market for environmental goods and services is one of the world's fastest-growing sectors.

JOB MARKET OUTLOOK AND OPPORTUNITIES: REALITIES AND BALANCE

How do you fit yourself and your values into a world crowded with challenges and overflowing with options and opportunities? The best way is to be true to yourself, know your strengths, accept your limits, and find those challenges, options, and opportunities that "charge you up." Make choices that will connect you with others like yourself who are likely to hire you, or do business with you, or start a business with you. Your wise choices will definitely put you on the side of positive and hopeful change. Your good example will inspire others.

Despite images of the general affluence of this country, a major concern for most people is to make enough money to live on at any job they can live with. But ethical, satisfying work does not have to be a luxury for the lucky few, though finding work that fits their values may take extra time and persistence. Luis Samoyoa, executive director of Habitat for Humanity, Guatemala, tells of his struggle between accepting a less-well-paying job with Habitat and a very lucrative one that would involve a great deal of time away from home. At a family meeting, his younger son opted for the job that would buy more toys while his eight-year-old son said, "I want you, Daddy." His wife concurred. Today, he is making a significant difference for Guatemalan families, and for his own.

Ask yourself: Which of the challenges discussed in this chapter captures your attention, your energy, your concern? Which options seem to speak to your personality type, to your values? Remember, the content of work remains basically the same whether you are helping to create more problems for the world or finding solutions. You can produce, manage, repair, compute, sell, cure, or create in almost any type of workplace.

No matter what your career is, you will be working in an economy that affects the environment and is guided by ethics. The challenges are formidable, but the options are exciting. We need to see ourselves as dynamic pio-

You know Eric, I could have been a stock broker, jet pilot, or a master chef; but they were not careers I really wanted to pursue.

neers, looking beyond ourselves, and moving through a new century. A father used to tell his children, "The person who is all wrapped up in himself is overdressed."

We have a choice. Yes, the problems are considerable and people often act without concern for the common good. People seem to be losing confidence in established institutions. But there are also many people working for the common good and creating hopeful, positive alternatives, relying on their innate sense of what is right to do what is right. If you are trying to clarify your own beliefs and values, you may find yourself among those called "new progressives" or "cultural creatives." Estimated at about one-third of the population, they are stretching to find creative solutions to the age-old problems that face us, trying to make the world a good place for all. Some experts feel they may represent a major societal transformation.[126] They are thinking the unthinkable, doing the undoable.

PERSONALITY TYPES IN THE JOB MARKET

Realistic Type

Realistic personalities work in food, clothing, shelter, transportation, repair, and maintenance jobs. They are also at home in the world of physical performance. Careers in sports, of course, are extremely competitive and limited to the most talented athletes. Increased automation and cheap imports have cut employment for many realistic jobs. Large-scale farming, fishing, and forestry now use more technology and fewer people. Mining has decreased because of resource depletion, cheaper imports, and use of alternative materials. The employment outlook in specialized areas is good, however, especially for workers who are service-oriented or do highly skilled and specialized work. You might consider indoor or outdoor jobs in industry or with public utility companies. Vocational training, on-the-job training, or an apprenticeship in a construction union is sometimes necessary. With the increased emphasis on protecting against crime, providing security to companies, their computers, and individuals is a growing need. Government cutbacks have limited the number of outdoor jobs available to people who like to work with nature, but ecological awareness is helping to slow that trend and even create such jobs in the industrial area. Realistic people are valuable because they can handle the practical needs of any workplace.

Investigative Type

Most investigative jobs, except in some technical areas, require at least a four-year college degree. The growth of the information society, with its new ways of exploring and developing information, is tailor-made for the person who is investigative. Engineers and medical researchers who research practical problems find jobs more available and are generally well paid. The information technology world provides service jobs for multimedia content developers, services marketers, systems analysts, and software programmers. In general, the investigative job outlook is good. Investigative types who are not scientifically or technologically oriented can apply their investigative talents to other areas. Many work settings can profit from the research and analytical skills of the investigative person.

Artistic Type

Most jobs for the artistic type require special talent along with special training. They tend to be highly competitive, so the artistic person should plan alternatives. Although the work of the artistic individual enriches everyone, Americans generally do not place high value on fine arts and artists in their lives.

New developments in electronic media will provide increasing opportunities for some creative people. Packaging information using computerized layouts can be a rewarding outlet for the creative person. Technical writing would fit the scientifically minded creative person, and that area is growing. Decision makers in many businesses and industries are slowly realizing that workers on the front line often have better ideas about how to do their jobs than the people in the front offices.

Social Type

Social personality careers involve caring for people. There is great need here, especially in social service jobs, often in government, but these often are still underfunded and thus scarce. Workers in some settings are drained by responsibilities for large numbers of clients, many of whom have serious and chronic problems. With little support, few resources, and yards of red tape, a worker needs strong motivation to succeed.

The health care industry is experiencing significant restructuring, with certain careers showing promise. Fewer people are using hospitals, as outpatient care offers a cheaper and often more desirable alternative and healthier lifestyles are becoming mainstream. Although there are periodic shortages of workers, admission to training programs is often limited. With the growing population of the elderly, geriatric care managers and physical therapists should be able to find a well-paying niche. Although they are not paid well, home health aides, medical assistants, and child care workers will be in demand.

Employee assistance programs are growing as industry sees the need to help its workers with personal problems, and human resources managers guide employees through the maze of personnel demands. The desire to share some of their profits with nonprofit organizations has prompted some companies to hire "planned giving officers" who review proposals from the community and fund those that meet certain criteria. People with social concerns find that their special talents can be used in a variety of settings, however, since all employers hire people and need to solve employee and customer problems.

Enterprising Type

Enterprising personalities have the inner drive to connect with the people and events that help them get involved, and there is always a need to organize and sell goods and services in the world of things and data. Marketing financial services and providing financial planning the investors are two hot career areas. Hotel managers, tourism promoters, law firm marketers, paralegal and legal assistants, labor and employment lawyers, intellectual property lawyers, environmental attorneys, and engineers are other professionals whose jobs are likely to be satisfying to the enterprising person.

The most effective person in an enterprising job achieves a balance among courage and confidence and commitment to people's concerns. Enterprising jobs require intelligence and good verbal skills. They are readily available for the go-getter.

Conventional Type

Conventional personality careers require steadiness, order, and tolerance for data and paperwork. At times they involve business contact with people and the use of office machines. Experience may build the conventional person's confidence and the courage to advance, but generally such types prefer supportive roles. Now that we have become a nation of datakeepers and processors, jobs in this area are abundant, visible, usually easy to find, and can pay well in the right setting.

Social-Investigative-Artistic (SIAs) and Other Combinations: The Hard Cases

The realistic, conventional, and enterprising types and various combinations of these have the easiest time starting careers. But generally speaking, the SIA personalities—social, investigative, artistic, or some combination of these—have a harder time choosing and launching a career. People who work with ideas or feelings often have no tangible product to show their employers. SIA personalities gravitate toward work in which they can deal with people to solve problems by creating new systems, a need that may arise in just about any work setting. Information systems require these SIA qualities: intelligence, analytical and communication skills, autonomy, sensitivity, responsibility, commitment, flexibility, and creativity.

Satisfying jobs in this area are usually on a highly competitive, professional level, with a college education almost a must. The social and investigative person who is conventional enjoys working with people to solve problems by following established guidelines such as those in human resources, labor relations, probation and law enforcement, health care, and sales. Individuals who represent the enterprising and social combination have both drive and good people skills. Those who have or can develop both traits will usually be successful with people in business and public service administration. Often, the SIA personality has enough enterprising skills to work happily in many of the social/enterprising areas. Teachers, for example, must organize and motivate people and must serve as key figures in a group, in addition to using their investigative and creative qualities.

Realistic: Do the practical, physical work required.

Investigative: Gather information (research) and solve problems.

Artistic: Create fine arts, but also create systems in many settings.

Social: Help people resolve problems.

Enterprising: Initiate the work or project to be done.

Conventional: Follow the guidelines of others to get the work done.

People are doing positive work in all the options, responding to the challenges that face the inhabitants of planet Earth. They work in industry and business, city ghettos and upscale communities, schools, prisons, banks, hospitals, and on farms. In all these places, workers can be concerned for the well-being of the planet and its people.

BACK TO THE FUTURE:
JOB MARKET OUTLOOK AND OPPORTUNITIES

During your career search, you may often find yourself wondering, "Who needs me out there?" The truth is that there is no way to predict the future needs of the job market with absolute certainty. Fewer than 10 percent of the next generation of workers born on this planet will be born in an industrialized country.[127] So the pool of available workers in these countries seems to be shrinking—good news for young job seekers.

Discovering your personality type and interests, analyzing your transferable skills in depth and zeroing in on your personal strengths, identifying areas of the job market to explore and companies to consider are all important steps in ensuring your future. No one can guarantee you a job after you have invested many years and much money training for it. How much are you willing to risk? How motivated are you? Have you looked for ways to use your training in alternate choices?

Learning about projected job market trends for your areas of interest may be helpful. In some job classifications there are large numbers of people working, but turnover is also high, so there will be many openings even though the category is not necessarily growing. Examples are cashiers, file clerks, mail clerks, office clerks, record and bookkeeping clerks, retail sales clerks, and truck drivers.

Although change is here to stay and predictions are hard to make, those who research and weigh trends honestly will not be very surprised by the future. Listed on page 131 are some of the jobs predicted by the Department of Labor to have the fastest growth and the largest growth between 2000 and 2010. These are not always easy-to-get jobs. For example, fastest-growing job categories may employ very small numbers of workers overall and they are not always the jobs with the largest growth—that is, the largest number of jobs overall (and which tend to be lower skilled and less well paid). The *Occupational Outlook Handbook* will provide more information on the education recommended and the number and percentage of jobs available.

Every prediction of job availability carries with it a "yes, but" set of possible exceptions. The very best way to research job availability is to talk to people in your own area. A successful dentist who relocated from a busy city to a semirural place says that if he had chosen a site just five or ten miles away, he wouldn't have had enough business to sustain him.

So the availability of jobs is affected by geographical limitations, educational requirements, experience, the state of the national and even international economy, political relationships, and the personal decisions of many individuals. Jobs that have a high salary potential and few openings will always have stiff competition even though their numbers may be growing. Your state employment office can supply information on the dynamics of your local job market. Remember that even career categories that are expected to decline dramatically will no doubt still need some workers somewhere, and you could be one of those. All *you* need is that one opportunity—yours!

> We are confronted by
> insurmountable opportunities!
> —*Pogo*[128]

The world we live in depends on the input of all personality types, on all the talent that we can bring to the challenges that face us as we move along in the twenty-first century. The realistic personality can show us how to deal with the physical world capably. The investigative person will carefully explore, analyze, and critique various options. Artistic or creative individuals will keep us from staying with options that no longer work, but they will be out there way ahead of the rest of us, trying new ones. The social person will be concerned with the effects of new systems on people and will urge us to consider ways to care for the planet and its creatures. The enterprising person will take the risks necessary to begin and move enterprises that will take us through this new century. The conventional person will keep us going in the right direction and will keep track of the data, urging us not to advance too quickly lest we lose artifacts and ideas of value.

Not only do we need each personality type to contribute that group's special talents to the workplace, but we also need the diversity of gender, race, ethnic background, and age. In the next chapter, we look beyond stereotypes to see the benefit of working with a diverse mix of people in the global marketplace. You, with your special qualities, will contribute to the future.

PROJECTIONS FOR 2000–2010

FASTEST-GROWING OCCUPATIONS

- Computer Software Engineers, applications
- Computer Support Specialists
- Computer Software Engineers, systems software
- Network and Computer Systems Administrators
- Desktop Publishers
- Database Administrators
- Personal and Home Care Aides
- Computer Systems Analysts
- Social and Human Service Assistants
- Physician Assistants
- Medical Records and Health Information Technicians
- Computer and Information Systems Managers
- Home Health Aides
- Physical Therapist Aides
- Occupational Therapist Aides
- Physical Therapist Assistants
- Audiologists
- Fitness Trainers and Aerobics Instructors
- Computer and Information Scientists, research
- Occupational Therapist Assistants
- Veterinary Technologists and Technicians
- Speech-Language Pathologists

OCCUPATIONS WITH MOST OPENINGS

- Retail Salespersons
- Combined Food Preparation and Serving Workers
- Cashiers
- Waiters and Waitresses
- Registered Nurses
- Laborers and Freight, Stock, and Material Movers, hand
- Office Clerks, general
- Customer Service Representatives
- General and Operations Managers
- Janitors and Cleaners
- Stock Clerks and Order Fillers
- Security Guards
- Truck Drivers, heavy and tractor-trailer
- Teacher Assistants
- Elementary School Teachers
- Computer Support Specialists
- Nursing Aides, Orderlies, and Attendants
- Receptionists and Information Clerks
- Secondary School Teachers
- Packers and Packagers, hand
- Landscaping and Grounds-keeping Workers
- Food Preparation Workers
- Sales Representatives
- First-line Supervisors/Managers of retails sales workers
- Bookkeeping, Accounting, and Auditing Clerks

Source: Bureau of Labor Statistics, Office of Employment Projections

There are still other activities to help your decision along. One of the best ways to decide is to get some "inside information" through work experience, group tours of workplaces, and interviews of people who work in your area of interest. The following two chapters will deal with the inner workings of workplaces and workstyles. In these you'll begin to see that the career you choose will fit in many jobs and many workplaces, both old and new. You'll also begin to understand that many of the nontraditional and creative careers and lifestyles of today will be commonplace tomorrow.

Learning how to prepare for the job hunt as well as a structured decision-making process can also help you focus on where you wish to go and lead you to work that matches your values. The rest of this book deals with these concerns.

NEW PARADIGMS

We have exciting possibilities before us. It's a time, then, for all of us to make thoughtful decisions about what we wish to be and what roles we want to play and what challenges we hope to meet and what kind of world we want to live in. Growing as a person means changing, adjusting to both inner and outer reality. It means expanding into new and exciting areas of life.

Irish priest and poet John O'Donohue urges job seekers to make sure their workplaces are actually expressive of identity, dignity, and giftedness. He adds that if you sell your soul, you ultimately buy a life of misery.

> When the imagination, the force of illumination
> in the soul, is allowed to stir,
> it opens up the workplace in a completely new way.
> —*John O'Donohue in* Anam Cara[129]

Although they are a part of high-tech systems, people are feeling and relating to each other in much the same way they did in ancient times and feeling a need to be part of a human community. Many people seem to be evolving into beings who are more aware of the world around them and their interaction with it, people who have the courage to act in harmony with that world.

Stereotypes about how we *should* be hold us back from becoming fully what we *could be*. That doesn't imply that change is simple and easy but rather that it is possible for people who are open-minded and open-hearted to be caring individuals and to prosper. To paraphrase Elizabeth Cady Stanton, "The true person is as yet a dream of the future."[130]

SUMMARY

With your self-assessment well in hand, in this chapter you focused your attention outward on the state of the world in which you will be working. It's an ever-increasingly technical world going at ever-increasing speed, with great numbers of the world's people left behind.

After looking at the nature of work, you examined the challenges you will face in three major areas: economy, environment, and ethics. But rather than being discouraging, these challenges offer many hopeful options that represent just a sample of the many opportunities for socially responsible, satisfying work. A discussion followed on the bond of trust that must rest on ethical behavior in order for society to function for the benefit of all.

Work opportunities are tied into the six RIASEC personality types, enabling you to see where your unique talents will find satisfying employment.

◉ SELF-ASSESSMENT EXERCISES

1. Areas of Challenge

Circle the following areas of challenge that capture your attention. Tell which specific aspect of the challenge interests you and why.

Air and water

Earth/trees/animal species

Food/land

Planet people ??

Energy

Shelter/created environment

Transportation

Safety: Health education, military/security

Science and technology

Industry and business

Ethics

water ... necessity of life. i'm amazed by it.

2. Possible Responses

Which options might you use to respond to your most important challenge?

_____

_____

3. Possible Job Openings

Look up your first job choice in the *Occupational Outlook Handbook* and summarize what it says under "Job Outlook" about the possibility of future job openings.

_____

_____

4. Your Beliefs about the Future[131]

Circle all the items you agree with.

1. I have no control over my own future, much less the future of the world.
2. We can keep world conflicts within reasonable bounds.
3. We will be able to keep conflicts from becoming nuclear wars.
4. Conservation will become an acceptable way of life almost everywhere.
5. Luck or chance, rather than our choices, causes the outcome of events.
6. We can learn to live peacefully on Earth.
7. Enough people will learn to be careful of resources to save us from destruction.
8. The future is created, more so than not, by choices that people make.
9. We can do little about overconsumption and the waste that causes excess pollution.
10. It is possible for me to influence the direction of my future.
11. I believe that the future will be shaped by forces outside my control.
12. Soon we will not have enough of anything.
13. There are enough people making good choices to keep the world from destruction.
14. Researching and planning ahead can make my future turn out well.
15. There may be shortages, but generally we will get through the coming years well enough.
16. The world is consuming, polluting, and populating itself to death.

17. The world's resources are abundant enough to provide food, raw materials, and energy for everyone.

18. Most of our energy sources will be renewable and nonpolluting in the not-too-distant future.

19. It is largely up to people to determine the options to be taken.

20. The future will happen no matter what a person does.

21. We can rely on most people to make wise choices.

22. I look forward to the future with hope and enthusiasm.

23. People are swept along by forces over which they have little control.

24. In a few years we will begin to see declining population, rising levels of affluence, and a world of plenty.

Scoring: Circle the same numbers here that you circled in the preceding list to get an idea about how optimistic or pessimistic you feel about your future and how much control you feel you have. Where do you stand on the Pessimistic/Optimistic Spectrum?

Doomsday/Pessimistic—Little Control: 1, 5, 9, 11, 12, 16, 20, 23

Muddle Through—Some Control: 2, 3, 7, 8, 10, 13, 15, 19

Bright Future/Optimistic—Much Control: 4, 6, 14, 17, 18, 21, 22, 24

Pessimistic	Midpoint	Optimistic

 GROUP DISCUSSION QUESTIONS

1. What does John Peers mean when he says, "We live three days in one compared to the 1950s. We do in one day what couldn't be done in a week in 1900, in a lifetime in the 1600s"? Give examples. Do you feel busy? Why or why not?

2. How do you feel about keeping up with the tech world? Explain. Do you believe everyone needs to keep up to be employable?

3. How were these basic workplace functions carried out in early human societies: business, industry, education, entertainment/communication, health, government, and military? What are the major differences in the way work was carried out in those early societies and now?

4. What does it mean "to vote at the checkstand of the supermarket"? Do you choose socially responsible products? Do you live simply? Do you buy more than you need or can use? Do you ever really throw anything away completely? Explain.

5. Describe a practice that is legal but that you consider unethical. How many ethical principles can the group collect and agree on?

6. Fantasize a world in 2050 in which all robot-made products are durable and beautiful. People purchase only goods and services that enrich their lives. Many people provide some basic needs for themselves. They work only one or two days a week. Many work at home via microchip devices. How would the world be different? Would there be more unemployment or could everyone find work? What kind of work? How could people use their leisure time? What resources would be conserved? How would you feel about that world?

5

Workplaces/ Workstyles

Companies That Work

 GOALS

- Connect personality types with the seven categories of workplaces.

- Consider workplace rewards and their effects on workplace people.

- Explore and evaluate workplace values and diversity.

- Determine work/life balance.

You have looked at the ways in which your qualities can find satisfiers in the workplace. You have reviewed the trends that are likely to continue throughout the third millennium. All of this will provide background as you decide on the type of workplace and possible workstyle that will suit you best. Do you see yourself playing a role in engineering at a huge corporation or promoting your own company with your laptop from a houseboat on the bay? Here we will look at more traditional workplaces and the benefits associated with them. In the next chapter we will consider alternative workplaces and workstyles.

Workplaces can be divided into just seven categories: business, industry, education, communication/entertainment, health, government, and military. Each of these categories has hundreds of jobs, many of which have similar characteristics. If you're unable to choose a job title, just being able to pick one of these seven categories is a huge step in narrowing down your career choices.

SEVEN CATEGORIES OF WORKPLACES

Business

The category of business includes many settings, from an executive suite to a deli down the street, and includes workers from retail clerks to shipping tycoons. Business occurs when two or more people get together to trade goods and services. Labor relations, human resources, contract negotiations, accounting, marketing, consulting, and hundreds of other functions make up the work of the business world and its many support systems.

The enterprising and conventional types are most at home in business, but all types can find expression there: the social person in dealing with people and their problems, the artistic person in creating or advertising new designs, the realistic person in managing products and production, and the investigative person in research and problem solving. Choosing business, then, will narrow down your choices and still leave the door open to a variety of careers.

Facilitating the flow of goods and services in business involves both paper data and mind data. The classification *paper data* includes reading, writing, and using computers; *mind data* encompasses researching, organizing, analyzing, and teaching. General clerical skills enable you to enter the field of business as a data-entry or shipping clerk. When you feel the need for more training, you can attend workshops and seminars or take college courses at the Associate in Arts (AA) or Bachelor of Arts (BA) level in fields such as accounting or marketing. Even with a BA or an MBA degree (Master of Business Administration), most people must start near the bottom of the ladder and work up—unless a serious shortage of personnel exists or you have special expertise or experience.

Industry

Industry can be defined loosely as a concern with products and with services that involves physical objects, not with people or paper (if you exclude the business end of industry). Repairing cars, flying planes, pouring concrete, and raising wheat are industries in this sense, along with manufacturing, testing, quality control, and quality assurance of products and services. Even the artist making clay pots at home is involved in industry. Working with machines and tools and tangible materials attracts the realistic person to industries of all kinds. Individuals with an investigative bent will enjoy scientific and engineering research directed toward practical problems. The ones with a conventional side will appreciate seeing that the jobs are done correctly and with care, following all the rules; realistic people with an artistic slant will enjoy inventing and creating; those with an enterprising side will find satisfaction in demonstrating products for sale; social realistic people will do well in technical supervision.

To enter jobs in this area, take high school, community college, or adult education courses that are related to industry. And look into on-the-job training (OJT) in industry as well as apprenticeship programs through trades such as carpentry or cement working.

Education

Many careers are available in the field of education besides teaching in schools and colleges. Corporations hire specialists to develop basic learning programs, and business and industry carry on employee training programs. People who teach various skills or crafts at home or at community centers also participate in the field of education.

The enterprising and social personalities enjoy the task- or people-oriented interactions of teaching, leading, and motivating others. Those with a realistic bent enjoy teaching such subjects as physical education, military arts, and shop, whereas the artistic types drift toward humanities and fine arts, crafts, and design. Investigative interests are needed for scholarship and research and for teaching the liberal arts and sciences; conventional personalities do well in teaching the basics. In fact, all personality types can be found in education. It helps to be a jack of all trades in many areas of education.

Communication/Entertainment

The communication/entertainment arena attracts the artistic personality. Workplaces range from circus tents to TV studios. Opportunities tend to be more limited than those in any other area because these "glamour" fields are generally highly competitive. To succeed here, you need exceptional ability, great quantities of luck, lots of courage and perseverance, and either some enterprising qualities or a good agent! The electronic media continue to grow erratically, and sometimes positions for creative people with enterprising, conventional, realistic, or investigative sides can be found in the marketing, business administration, clerical, engineering, and research areas of media. Because creative people usually like to work alone or in unstructured settings, many find it difficult to do routine work even though the workplace may deal with a creative product.

Realistic types who are creative may enjoy careers such as industrial design, whereas conventional/artistic types may do well in such areas as computer-assisted drafting. Enterprising/artistic people may open their own galleries or become book publicists. With the incredible rise of the information society, opportunities will continue to open up for the creative person who is technically talented, word-wise, or number-nimble.

Health

Besides working in hospitals and medical offices, health care workers also find employment in business, industry, education, and military settings. Specialization and technological advances have expanded the health profession rapidly, but growth slows when recession and unemployment pinch health care budgets.

Alternative health care is a rapidly growing area as people choose such practitioners as chiropractors, acupuncturists, and homeopathists. Over half the nation's health care dollars go to these health providers.

The investigative person with a good social orientation will enjoy the challenge of helping people solve their health care problems, whereas conventional/social persons will like the established systems found in some health care facilities. The enterprising person will enjoy managing health care. There may be a great deal of physical work, which may be attractive to the realistic person who likes to work with people. Several hundred job titles are associated with health care delivery.

Government

People of all types find employment with government in every setting—from agricultural stations to hospitals, from prisons to the great outdoors. You must usually pass a "test" to become employed at the federal level (and often at state and county levels, too). The test may combine an oral interview and possibly a written examination. Job applicants frequently receive additional credit for years of education, military service, and past work experience that can give them preference in the hiring process. Any type of personality can find satisfiers as one of the great variety of government workers that includes narcotics agents, food program specialists, museum curators, and public health workers. Your state and other employment offices have information about these and other civil service jobs.

Traditionally, a government job has implied security but low pay. In past years, the pay increased along with the number of jobs, but growing taxpayers' concern about government spending has brought lower pay and insecurity for many government employees. You need persistence to obtain these jobs, but many are still there for the person who is willing to try for them.

Military

Realistic and conventional personalities are attracted most readily to military operations and procedures, but here people of all types can also find opportunities from cooking to hospital laboratory work to sophisticated industrial research and design, along with frontline fighting. During the 1990s, the military was downsized in certain areas for budgetary reasons, with many people in military jobs moving into other employment fields. Even so, new recruits may still apply and be accepted. More recently, the United States has experienced a surge in military recruitment and spending triggered by increasing concern about global terrorism. For those so inclined, the military provides a very structured working and living situation, training in a variety of skills, and good benefits, offset by the chances of being assigned to undesirable duties or locations, or having to participate in wars or other military actions.

You will find that workplaces have personalities just as people do. Some are austere, rigid, demanding, challenging, stressful; others are lavish, casual, supportive, easygoing. They reflect various combinations of the six personality types and tend to attract similar types who will be comfortable being together.

Choosing a category of workplace focuses your career exploration and can even get you started on a basic college curriculum or training program. Keep in mind the main functions your personality combination enjoys and imagine the sort of place where you would feel at home:

R: working with things   S: helping people

I: solving problems   E: initiating projects

A: creating new systems   C: following guidelines

CAREER LADDERS LARGE AND SMALL

You may find it helpful to match your satisfiers with one of the levels in the Career Ladder Chart on page 143 and to be aware of other closely related factors such as size, complexity, and setting, both indoor and outdoor. There are four major levels on any career ladder: entry, supervisory/technical, mid-management, and top management. Each level includes some support services such as human resources, purchasing, secretarial/clerical, and maintenance. Some companies are trying to group employees into a few broad job categories rather than naming them with the dozens of titles found in traditional systems. And others are flattening or shortening the ladder so that there are fewer managers. Moving up is still as difficult a climb with the short ladder. In some of these cases, moving over instead of up can be a good career strategy if the lateral move will help you gain new skills and confidence.[1]

Generally, the higher you climb on the career ladder, the higher your salary will be. One young woman started as a nurse's aide, moved up to registered nurse (RN) with a Bachelor of Science degree (BS) in nursing, and then went on to earn a Master of Science (MS) in nursing so she could teach. She could also have gotten a master's degree in hospital administration.

Your place on the career ladder may be in a large and complex structure, or it may be in one that is small and simple. It may have a rigid system like the military. It may have blurred lines of authority. No matter what size they are, all workplaces—lawyers' offices, large catering services, hospitals, or international manufacturing corporations—have similar structures and functions, sometimes repeated over and over in various divisions. A small staff might consist of the boss, who has many management functions, and one assistant, who does the rest.

In a larger workplace, entry-level workers can expect to do more limited and specialized jobs, such as putting lettuce leaves on a thousand sandwiches, soldering links in a thousand electronic circuits, or data processing a thousand letters. Possibilities for change, however, including moving both up and over, are greater in a larger than a smaller work environment. On the other hand, research shows that small and mid-sized companies create many more jobs than large companies; are usually more productive, flexible, and creative; and may grow dramatically to become huge corporations, which tend to lose productivity, flexibility, and creativity. Data gathered by the U.S. Census Bureau in 1999 on the size of all U.S. firms revealed that 98.3 percent have fewer than one hundred employees.[2]

Visualize the size of workplace you might enjoy within one of the seven categories. Is a multinational corporation for you, or a tiny business at home? A modest-sized company in a nearby city, or a cooperative venture in your neighborhood? Gather job titles that would work in these workplaces.

In the past decade or two, many corporations have grown dramatically, merged with or taken over others, and gone multinational. Smaller businesses have been able to fill much of the resulting employment gap in creative ways. They are able to respond more quickly, often at lower cost and with better customer services. Not necessarily high tech, small and family-owned companies may use technology to do tasks impossible without computers. Direct

THE CAREER LADDER

Position	Responsibility	Education	Support Staff
TOP LEVEL			
Top management and professionals, such as Presidents Board members Doctors Lawyers	The decision makers: responsible for nearly everything. There is more independence at this level.	PhD, DD, MD, MBA, etc. Technical and professional expertise	
MIDDLE LEVEL			
Middle management and professionals, such as Department heads Engineers Nurses Teachers Product managers	Share responsibility with the top level and enjoy some independence.	MA, MBA, MS, BS, BA, etc. Middle-level expertise	Operate at all levels to provide auxiliary services, such as Human Resources Finance Communications/ Graphics Legal counsel Research Purchasing Marketing Data processing Secretarial/ Clerical Maintenance
LOWER LEVEL			
Lower management and technicians, such as Supervisors Lead persons Legal assistants LVNs	Are responsible for a small part of decision making. May supervise others.	AA, AS, vocational, or on-the-job training	
THE WORKERS			
Basic production and service work, such as Trades, Crafts Assemblers Machinists Waiters/Waitresses	Are responsible for a particular function. Entry-level jobs; often repetitive work.	High school, apprenticeship. Usually *some* training or experience is needed.	

advertising, selling, and providing services on the Internet can take place even from home.

Erving Goffman wrote in *Asylums* that simply by reason of sheer numbers, institutions tend to become dehumanizing.[3] But large size doesn't always mean depersonalization. Within many large organizations, you can discover companies within companies and/or small, cohesive, caring groups of people looking out for each other's interests. This kind of support is sometimes missing in a small business with high demands.

Barbara Garson studied three workplaces in New York. She reported that two well-known companies had extremely restrictive policies for workers: no talking to other employees during work time, no personal phone calls about family emergencies, and other rigid rules. In contrast, the report described the accounting office of a community college where five older women worked very hard, often staying late to complete their tasks. They also managed to fit in noon parties, trips to the hospital to visit sick family members, and other personal ventures.[4] This is why it is important for you to do your homework when researching employers, so that you can understand their cultures, values, and norms and find companies whose values and style are consistent with yours.

Setting is another related factor. Some people like their career ladder outdoors where the structure is usually simpler; others like to be more on their own inside or on the road; others like a mix in which an office is their base but they move around inside the same plant, on the road, or outdoors; and still others like to be indoors in one spot. Such choices may move a person either farther away from or closer to the center of decision-making power in a company. This in turn may enhance or delay progress up the career ladder.

Remember that titles for the same job may differ from one company to another. You may find the most accurate information about a job title in the job description developed by companies when they advertise a position. Continue to develop a list of general functions you'd like to perform so that you'll recognize the ideal job when it comes your way.

Then, before you discard some job titles, be sure you aren't stereotyping them in a way that distorts their possibilities. Food services might seem to mean frying hamburgers, but if you stop there, you miss management at local, regional, and corporate levels, finance, accounting, marketing, planning, and all the functions of any corporation. The possible work settings include industry, schools, hospitals, airlines, and even executive dining rooms, where highly professional food service personnel work a five-day week serving upper management and their guests.[5]

And consider food engineering. Engineering students at the Massachusetts Institute of Technology (MIT) found a great project by working out a faster, more economical system to put the hard candy coating on M&Ms. The company sent them 1,500 pounds of M&Ms, not all of which went into the experiment! The students and professors grew in wisdom and weight and found that the food industry has "tremendous engineering prospects."[6]

Where do you want to fit in this scheme of things? How far up the ladder do you want to be? (It may be lonely at the top, but it's also exciting and challenging—but not everyone can get there. It may seem more comfortable

Reprinted with permission from Mal Hancock.

at the bottom, but often not so lucrative or so interesting!) You may want to move up the ladder within a career area but not to a level that requires more education and career commitment.

Determining the size and complexity as well as the type of workplace and the rung on the career ladder that feels right to you can be important factors in career choice. If you know where you want to be in a few years, you will make use of present opportunities and not choose dead-end jobs.

WANTED: REWARDS ON ALL LEVELS

Workplaces provide an income, which ideally satisfies basic physical/survival needs such as food, clothing, and shelter and some of the enriching wants on your agenda. In general, in the last three decades of the twentieth century, we have seen the buying power of low-skilled worker wages decline and their jobs disappear. New but lower-paying jobs have come on line, often without benefits. At this same time, a new, well-paid, upper middle class of "knowledge workers" has developed.

But also consider the areas of reward that go beyond a paycheck and that may bring more satisfaction to your work: opportunities for fringe benefits and advancement; a supportive atmosphere for you, your family, and your lifestyle; autonomy; and compatible values. After you start your new job and receive the first two or three paychecks, the money you are earning is usually taken for granted and, although a source of satisfaction, loses its initial powerful motivating influences.

Most people find that an important element for sustained satisfaction at work is to work for a company they admire and have a manager whom they trust and respect and who reciprocates the same. If you can't find employment at the very best company, looking for the very best manager in any company you select is important. Your manager can be your greatest advocate and mentor or a source of great dissatisfaction in your job. Choose wisely.

Although your career choice puts you on a path to certain rewards, the workplace you choose can enhance or subtract from them. Robert Levering and Milton Moskowitz say—and the cartoon "Dilbert" confirms—that "most companies offer dreadful work environments."[7]

On the other hand, companies are not as bleak as some people may think. Companies have to be competitive in salaries, benefits, and opportunities to attract and retain top talent. Companies are often creative in offering perks to keep their employees happy and, most important, productive.

Don't Overlook Benefits

Benefits are not just a minor attraction. These perquisites or "perks" represent a considerable, if hidden, part of your pay; if carefully considered, they can result in larger income and long-term savings as well as enriching activities off the job.

Health Care   Health care, for example, can include dental and vision care in addition to medical/hospital care. Many companies, especially smaller ones, find it a struggle to offer health benefits. As the cost of health care climbs, medical expenses can put someone without insurance deep into debt.

Stock Options   Stock options are the way companies may share control while sharing some profits—often a significant benefit. Though originally designed to reward worker productivity, some plans have lost sight of that. Nor are all such plans designed to give workers autonomy, though they may; rather, some may give the company advantages, such as reducing worker turnover. Before depending on these generous-looking benefits, research them carefully as to their short- and long-term effects. Given the corporate financial scandals of 2002, new corporate and accounting rules are being proposed and implemented concerning stock options, making them less attractive and generous to the employee and company.

Career Development   Consider too a company's record in career "pathing" or career development and the quality of their employee training programs, for these can lead to better-paying jobs. Some companies make a concerted effort to help their employees improve and grow on the job. They provide training on or off site, educational opportunities, and encouragement to employees to set goals and objectives—and help in meeting these goals. In the long run, this type of benefit may be vastly important.

Retirement   Although retirement can seem eons away, it's never too early to look at various options and plan for a financially worry-free retirement, one hopes with an ethical company where your retirement funds are secure. As women tend to live longer than men, they need to plan ahead carefully, since about 90 percent of them will be responsible for their own finances at some point.[8] With the prospect of increasing longevity, some people welcome the opportunity to work after age sixty-five. To others, retirement (as early as possible) means liberation. Some retirement plans can lead to considerable income. Several, like individual retirement accounts, both traditional or Roth IRAs, involve reduced or deferred income taxes. Some people manage to save and invest wisely enough to make their retirement free from financial worry. A T-shirt reads, "Retirement is a full-time job," as many who have retired will agree. With some creative planning, retirement can be on your career agenda sooner than you think.

Other Perks   Paid holidays and vacations; child/elder care subsidies; on-site recreation/health maintenance; personal, investment, and financial counseling; educational planning; courses for personal enrichment; use of a company car; expense accounts; dry-cleaning pick up; and even the use of vacation resorts are just a few of the benefits offered by some companies. Some give raises when workers acquire and broaden their skills; some provide sabbaticals that allow an employee, after some years on the job, to take several months off with pay for enrichment. Some offer "cafeteria style" benefits and allow employees to choose whichever combination suits them. Some may give you a vested interest in the company through a variety of employee–owner plans.

Companies are becoming more aware that when employees are frustrated and concerned about problems, their energy and productivity are drained. As a job hunter, you benefit by knowing which perquisites would help you solve important problems and which would simply enhance your work. Remember, when negotiating for your job, if you do not ask for the perks you want, they probably will not be offered. Be creative and reasonable when asking for the benefits you want.

Rewards of a Different Sort: The Emotional Contract

For some, work itself is rewarding. Some people say they would almost be glad to pay someone to let them do their jobs! However, salary and benefits are the usual prime motivators. Work also has intangible rewards on many levels that relate to the values of a company.

A company's "corporate culture" or "corporate climate" is a common and shared set of beliefs and values that shapes attitudes and behavior and makes for reduced conflict and greater efficiency. It includes the company's attitudes toward employees; its sense of respect, fairness, trust; its supportiveness toward people who work there, especially during tough times. It is something you depend on as if you had signed a contract with your employer.

For example, when you see others laid off abruptly and you live under the threat of your own "downsizing," you will find it hard to feel trusting of your workplace. The morale of everyone drops as salaries, benefits, and jobs are cut back. In 2000, Gladys West completed and defended her doctoral dissertation, which was a meta-analysis, a study of all available research, on the effects of downsizing in organizations. She confirmed that the remaining employees' morale, trust, productivity, and commitment to the company plummet in organizations that lay off workers.[9]

Many innovative companies recognize employee morale as an important concern. Southwest Airlines founder Herb Kelleher says, "Nothing kills your company's culture like a layoff." Southwest's mission statement talks about providing a stable work environment for its employees and treating them with the same concern and respect that its employees should have for Southwest's customers. So protecting its employees' jobs is paramount over trying to stabilize the company's fluctuating stock price or having to postpone scheduled deliveries of new airplanes.[10]

Most workers want to feel they are valued not only for the work they do but also for themselves. James Kouzes and Santa Clara University professor Barry Posner, made the following observation in the book *Credibility:* "Generally we will work harder and more effectively for people we like and we will like them in direct proportion to how they help make us feel." In their research they found that people felt *valued, motivated, enthusiastic, challenged, inspired, capable, supported, powerful, respected,* and *proud* when they had leaders they valued. Yet they also found that fewer than half the employees surveyed by the Opinion Research Corporation could say that their companies treated them with dignity and respect.[11]

Even so, a 1997 INC/Gallup survey showed that more than two-thirds of Americans said they were satisfied with their places of employment. The smaller the workplace, the more satisfied they were, with people owning their own business the most satisfied. Eighty-two percent said that they did every day what they do best. Less educated workers said they received less praise, less opportunity to grow, and were less satisfied with their jobs.[12]

As time goes by, the intangible characteristics of a job may change. One newly divorced woman enjoyed her work in a small savings and loan office where the boss and coworkers were supportive. But the boss, who had decided to work harder at moving up, began to be more restrictive. The work atmosphere became unpleasant—but changed again for the better when the boss left and the then-experienced woman became the manager!

No matter how carefully you plan your career, at some time you are likely to have a job that does not satisfy all your needs and wants. Some people have exaggerated expectations about the role the workplace and coworkers should play in their lives. For example, some people hope for more emotional support from coworkers and supervisors than these individuals are prepared to supply. Cultivating a reasonable amount of independence and a moderately strong skin can protect you against the ups and downs of the work world.

Some companies make a conscious effort to hire and keep only those employees who espouse their ideals, which can improve the emotional climate. Granite Rock, a rock-and-asphalt business in Watsonville, California, since the early 1900s and recipient of the 1992 Malcolm Baldrige National Quality Award, expects "their people" to value quality, service, and fairness.[13] Employees today, more than ten years later, consider it an exceptional place to work.

When you are hired, you agree to a company's beliefs and values, as though to an unwritten emotional contract. Your work life will be more satisfying if you choose an environment with just the right values and enough support for you. Other workplace motivators include enhanced self-esteem, prestige, rewarding relationships, and opportunities to actualize your unique potential. As you search out information about workplaces, try to find those ingredients—beyond money and benefits—that would inspire your loyalty to a job and the company.

WORKPLACE VALUES: ETHICS 101

What would you do if you found your employer involved in some illegal, unethical, or immoral actions? What if your workplace exploits workers: uses underage employees illegally at home or overseas; allows unsafe working conditions and the use of dangerous equipment by untrained personnel; pays below the legal wage requirement. In addition, what is legal is not always what is moral and ethical. Companies may fire someone legally, for example, who takes time off for a family emergency, or pressure workers to put in excessive overtime—but are such actions ethical?

The ethics of a company are a major part of the corporate culture. However, not everyone agrees on what ethical/moral behavior is. We can say, however, that people are ethical when they are honestly and consistently trying to behave according to their values without shirking their responsibilities. Today, responsible workplaces are paying serious attention to their values and ethics.

To avoid serious ethical dilemmas in the workplace, do a little research ahead of time about the principles of companies you are considering. More and more companies are being evaluated for their level of ethics and social responsibility, a concern not only to workers but also to investors. The magazine *Business Ethics* rates what its editors consider to be the 100 best corporate citizens.[14] A social screen was developed by U.S. Trust Company of Boston to advise concerned investors.[15] An expanded version of the social screen follows. You can use it to help you determine a given firm's level of social responsibility:

- Does it produce and sell safe, high-quality, and healthful products and services that affordably fulfill basic needs or enriching wants of its target markets?

- Is it honest, fair, and trustworthy, following ethical principles in its business dealings on both national and international levels, without exploiting others, especially children, or supporting repressive regimes?

- Does it provide a safe, healthy, humane work environment?

- Does it provide equal employment opportunities and implement fair labor practices for women, men, and minorities?

- Does it elicit worker loyalty through concern for employees' welfare, not just stockholders'?

- Does it provide workers with information, tools, and an environment that encourages high performance, supports workplace democracy, and respects and encourages worker participation?

- Does it respect and preserve the natural environment wherever it operates, practicing energy conservation, recycling, and use of renewable energy where possible?

- Does it contribute to and invest in the community where it operates without overwhelming its political, economic, and social life, while understanding its culture and the problems workers face in meeting their needs?

- Does it grow and compete in a balanced way?

- Is it willing to disclose information that gives answers to all these questions?

Companies who strive to be socially responsible win in many ways. They win the admiration and support of their stakeholders. For example, when Malden Mills—maker of Polartec fleece fabric—burned down, its president, Aaron Feurstein, continued to pay his employees while the plant was being rebuilt, a decision he said was a moral one. It definitely made good business sense for the company.[16] "Surveys show that up to 70 percent of American consumers say they won't buy products made under unsafe or unfair working conditions."[17]

Socially responsible investors have already diverted over $610 *billion* away from corporations whose policies they didn't support, and 80 percent of American consumers say that environmental concerns have led them to switch brands of the products they buy.[18] San Francisco-based Working Assets Funding Service, a $104-million company, has managed to combine twelve years of rapid growth with a socially responsible business mission.[19]

Some companies struggle valiantly to get high marks, but few are perfect. They do have to meet expenses; they do have mountains of governmental regulations to follow that sometimes hinder rather than help them; they may be in a period of difficult transition. Being socially responsible doesn't mean being impractical—for example, giving such lavish benefits that the company fails. But the bottom line is always a business's efforts to consider the needs of all its stakeholders, which include not only the stockholders but everyone with a stake in the company, such as clients, workers, the wider community, and the company's surrounding environment.

Corporate ethics, social responsibility, advancement, training, stability, and a host of other factors are considered by respondents in the survey conducted by *Fortune* magazine to compile its annual index of "The Best 100 Companies to Work For." Edward Jones, the investment and brokerage company, won first place in 2001 and 2002.[20]

Workers have ethical responsibilities to do their jobs well, to be honest, and to respect others. The personal responsibility skills you assessed in Chapter 2 will help you make yours a "high-performance" workplace where everyone profits. No amount of legislation or rules can take the place of the ethical behavior of individuals in a society. For both individuals and companies, "Free market competition works not because it is unfettered, but because of the moral dimension we each bring to it. Without these internalized social bonds, efficient competition becomes destructive chaos."[21]

Carefully research and ask questions about what a company really stands for. Sometimes advertising can be misleading. Do library research, including a review of the business section of newspapers and magazines. Ask around. You can be amazed at how much employees know about the ethics of their own company. The question, Can a company do well when doing good? (can it be both ethical *and* profitable) is being answered with a resounding Yes! It's important to find a company whose values match yours.

A group called Student Citizens for Social Responsibility at California's Humboldt State University initiated a pledge for graduates whereby they promised "to investigate thoroughly and take into account the social and environmental consequences of any job opportunity I consider." Now headquartered at Manchester College in Indiana, this pledge is spreading to other campuses.[22]

AUTONOMY DIMENSIONS: WHO'S BOSS?

Old industrial-style management techniques gave bosses complete authority over employees with whom they shared little about the business. In 1994, workers at a chicken plant in Mississippi complained that they needed a doctor's note to use the bathroom more than three times a week. Workers also needed to pay ten cents per cup for clean drinking water.[23] But authors Levering and Moskowitz assert, "The authoritarian work style . . . has failed."[24] Because the number of workers with college degrees is increasing, and because these workers are often underemployed, they are likely to challenge old-style management techniques with creative new ideas.

The information age is bringing marked changes. Many workers are taking responsibility for their own decisions based on access to computer data formerly reserved for management and now made available to people at all levels. The career ladder shortens as people become "more equal."

You see Brenda, I first ask folks what I can do to help them. You first demand their ticket number, receipt, ID, etc.; things that aren't really important to them.

Commenting on leadership, authors of *Credibility*, Kouzes and Posner, add: "Leaders we admire do not place themselves at the center; they place others there. They do not seek the attention of people; they give it to others."[25]

Some businesses are experimenting with "open book" management based on the principle that making money should be the work of all the workers in an organization. Financial as well as other information is shared openly with workers, giving them insider status. Ken Eberhard, owner of the Eberhard Equipment Company, has been training his workers with painstaking care toward a day when they can take over the company. Promoting from within gives people a feeling that their work is valued. Companies that clearly connect performance with earnings usually find that employees will work harder.

However, as the workplace automates routine jobs, "doing one's job" is not always enough. The jobs that are left require that workers act like owners and create the job as they go. As people begin to look around their workplaces, if they can stay flexible, they begin to see new possibilities to do what fits them best and to benefit the company in the long run. William Bridges writes of a nation of owners working for "You & Co."[26]

Autonomy options also include democratic decision making, skills sharing through job rotation, and education in job and cooperative skills, profit-and-loss sharing, and shared ownership by workers. Autonomy requires workers to assume greater individual responsibility.

Management is learning that the more workers take responsibility in their jobs to make suggestions, solve their own problems, and learn new skills, the more energy they will bring to their work, the more self-esteem and enjoyment they will derive from it, and the greater the profits will be for all. Yet even in companies that try to include everyone in decisions, there are struggles with communication, over equitable working conditions, and over salary and benefits for all levels of workers.

Not everyone likes to take more responsibility for their work, of course. Years ago autoworker Joe Rodriguez was sent to Sweden to learn teamwork techniques for his auto assembly line. He concluded, "If I've got to bust my ass to be meaningful, forget it. I'd rather be monotonous."[27]

Doing everything better as a continuous process may be exhausting—working for the latest, the best, *always* striving, trying to get ahead of the competition. For others, it is exhilarating. If autonomy is important for you, zero in on workplaces that encourage it.

WORKPLACE DIVERSITY

Up until the last quarter of the twentieth century, U.S. workers in all but the least skilled jobs were generally white males. The civil rights movement of the 1960s and the women's movement of the 1970s changed the complexion of the workplace dramatically. Not only did women and minorities enter workplaces in increasingly greater numbers, but the media and the global economy brought us into closer contact with diverse groups of people from all over the world. People in these groups, including you, are looking for satisfiers in the workplace.

Everyone is learning new ways of doing business with and working with people, both inside and outside their organizations. At one of the Fortune 500's fastest-growing companies, Harry Pforzheimer, director of corporate communications, says, "The population here reflects the world population. That makes for an exciting melting pot of ideas. And I think it adds dramatically to our success."[28]

The tendency for those in the mainstream, however, has been to stereotype and exclude others as a group before getting to know them as individuals. Those left out often feel like foreigners in their own land. Elie Wiesel, Nobel Peace Prize winner and Andrew Mellon Professor of Humanities at Boston University, said:

> It is enough for someone to treat me like a foreigner for me to be one. If I am excluded, it is because some one has pushed me out. Therefore, it is my fault, too, if the other person is excluded, that is to say, deprived of a feeling of security and of belonging, of a sense of identity. For it is up to me whether someone feels at home or not in our common world, and whether he feels tranquil or anxious when he looks around him.[29]

Gender in the Workplace

It's hard to believe that only thirty years ago it would have been considered extraordinary for a woman to become an astronaut or a zookeeper, to head a Fortune 500 company, to venture into the financial world, or as was true in some states, to write a check, buy stock or property, or open a business without her husband's permission.[30] And it would have seemed just as extraordinary for a man to do a significant share of housework and child care. Still, gender is possibly the most powerful and pervasive influence in our lives, and traditional stereotypes live on. Before a baby takes its first breath, people ask, "Is it a boy or a girl?"

Gender Bender: Women

Worldwide, women are scarcely counted in the statistics and barely have any rights at all. In the United States, women have come a long way since the early 1970s, when they could expect to earn just 57 percent of the salary paid a man for doing the same job. Now, women seem to be at parity with men or just a percentage point or two below. In addition, women received more than 50 percent of associate's, bachelors, and master's degrees granted in the 1990s.[31]

The number of women in roles and jobs traditionally reserved for men is increasing. Carleton "Carly" Fiorina, a superstar saleswoman and an outsider, was hired in 1999 as the new CEO at Hewlett-Packard Company, where, traditionally, long-term employees were groomed and promoted to the top positions. As HP's first woman CEO, she was the chief architect and proponent of HP's merger with Compaq Computers, a contentious project that was finally concluded in 2002.

Globally

- Of the estimated 1.3 billion people worldwide living in poverty, more than 70 percent are women and girls.[32]

- Women's work represents half the total global economic input, equaling about $11 trillion—but it is not included in the standard economic accounting systems.[33]

- Women receive only 26 percent of total earned income and constitute 70 percent of the poor.[34]

- Women are almost universally excluded from all but minimal education and from political and economic decision making.[35]

In the United States

- Two out of three poor adults are women.[36]

- Forty-five percent of female-headed households live on incomes below the poverty line.[37]

- The median income of female-maintained families in nonmetropolitan areas is $12,742, compared to $21,997 for male-maintained families and $37,080 for married-couple families.[38]

- Half of those living below the poverty line in the United States are children, representing 8 percent of all American children.[39]

- Women in unions earned over 40 percent more than nonunion women.[40]

- Sixty-two percent of mothers with children under six now work, up from 47 percent in 1980.[41]

- According to U.S. census data for and 2000 and 2001, on average, the median wages for white women were higher than those for African American women, whose wages were higher than those for Hispanic women.[42]

Although the world's women have experienced improved health and educational opportunities, they still have few options for using their abilities.[43] In some countries, women have virtually no rights at all.[44]

In the United States, a large proportion of women continue to cluster in traditional clerical and personal services jobs, which are often low-paying, part-time, and dead-end, instead of the more lucrative, nontraditional jobs (of which 75 percent or more are filled with men).[45] There is still considerable sexual harassment for many women in educational institutions, the military, and other civilian workplaces. However, new laws and policies are sending the message that *sexual harassment* is not to be tolerated.[46]

Women advanced significantly in the last half of the twentieth century. There are many more female CEOs, more women-owned businesses, more successful female politicians, doctors, and lawyers, often earning the same income as men at these higher levels. Still, they have a long way to go in some areas to achieve equality with men, not only in the workplace but also at home. Many women who earn more than their spouses (22 percent do) still find themselves doing more than two-thirds of the household chores.[47]

Balance in life is important

Gender Bender: Men

Over the past centuries, the male role has not evolved as much, though some men now help with housework and child care. Many men see their career as their main focus and a major element in their dreams and aspirations. They may experience crises as their careers and lives evolve, especially in their forties (mid-life) and sixties (retirement). However, marriage and family are also integral components of their self-image, as are friendships/peer relationships, ethnicity/religion, and leisure.

Career decisions men make are linked to their values. Workplace satisfaction, salary, prestige, commuting time, overtime, pressure, travel, and colleagues all have an impact on personal and family life for men as well as for women.

The results of the changes that many women have been making in their careers and personal lives have generally been positive for them. But these changes have forced men to change. For example, men now more frequently work with and are supervised by competent women. Trying to fit into new expectations about what they should do and how they should be is adding new layers of frustration and bewilderment to some men's lives. It is especially difficult when men are not sure what the new expectations really are or where these expectations will lead. Like many women, many men feel trapped in low-paying, monotonous, demanding, or demeaning jobs.

For Better or For Worse®   **by Lynn Johnston**

FOR BETTER OR FOR WORSE © Lynn Johnston Productions, Inc./Dist. by United Feature Syndicate, Inc.

Still, a study from the University of California, Los Angeles, noted that white males hold 95 percent of the positions of power in the United States, and minorities, including black, Asian, and Hispanic men and women, occupy only 1 percent of top corporate jobs.[48] Despite that, the successful man as well as the unsuccessful one may be leading a life of quiet desperation. Many have buried themselves in their work and cut themselves off from nurturing by family and friends and from taking the needed leisure time that can be critical, especially at times of crisis. As the late Paul Tsongas, former U.S. senator from Massachusetts, said, "No man ever said on his deathbed, 'I wish I had spent more time with my business.'"[49]

Workshops provided by such companies as Merrill Lynch, American Express, IBM, and Time-Warner help employees resolve issues dealing with conflicts over family and careers. Companies are finding that when both men and women are certain that family responsibilities are being covered, they work more efficiently, turnover is lower, and profits increase.[50]

Family, Career, or Both? Minding the Family

As it has become more common for both parents to work, career choices have had to be integrated more fully into family life. Even the definition of family, a highly important life component, has been changing. Today the adults who manage a household may both be working and married with fewer children than preceding generations, or without children, or remarried with part-time children, or not married; they may be two single mothers trying to make ends meet; they may be gay or lesbian partners.

Only about half of American children live in a family consisting of a mother, father, and full brothers and sisters.[51] Families headed by single men are the fastest-growing type of family in America, representing 15 percent of single-parent families.[52] Each year sees a drop in the number of traditional households. In the late 1990s, 24.9 percent of households consisted of one person, compared to 6.8 percent in 1970.[53]

At last count, women were entering the workplace in greater numbers than men. They will account for 63 percent of the growth in the labor force, according to the U.S. Department of Labor, and at least 55 percent of them will provide half the household income.

Most developed countries guarantee between 75 and 100 percent of a woman's pay for maternity leave that can range from eight to sixteen weeks, according to a study, "Maternity Protection at Work," by the International Labor Organization. The exceptions are the United States, Australia, and New Zealand.[54] At least 85 percent of new mothers return to work within six months after childbirth.

Fitting a career into the family equation presents singular problems, especially for women who still take major responsibility for home and children. Women who divorce find that raising children alone can be difficult, with finances often a serious problem.

Dazzled by two incomes, many trend-setting, successful working couples find themselves on the "trend-mill" toward a frenetic and hard-edged kind of success. Anne-Marie Foisy-Grusonik says, "Frequently, after telling others about my family and my career, they would respond, 'It sounds like you have the best of both worlds.' But in my heart I felt I had the worst of both worlds, and they were constantly at odds." Someone once gave her a coffee mug that said, "I am a working woman, I take care of a house. I hold down a job. I am nuts." And she responded, "I was!" She opted out of the work world after struggling with career and family concerns for some years.[55]

In her consulting work with women beginning businesses, Nancy K. Austin tells them, "The chances of 'having it all' are about as thin as a pinstripe." She adds, "I've learned that a love of work and a love of family, balanced so that one never injures the other, is only an illusion."[56]

As women move up in the workplace they are facing the dilemma that men have often faced—the prospect of being asked to relocate. If the decision involves a spouse and children, accommodations need to be made for the concerns of these significant others in the family: the spouse's career, the children's education, and perhaps care for elderly parents. Companies that wish to hold on to a valued employee will assist the family in the process, often helping the spouse with his or her job change, too.

Family fulfills some of our deepest needs and wants on many levels for physical, emotional, intellectual, and altruistic/spiritual support and growth. Families are those people who, theoretically, are enduringly present in a special way to see a person through the ups and downs of life and career. Trying to nurture both *is* a balancing act.

Child/Elder Care

For working parents, finding someone to care for their children—with care—while they work is a difficult, crucial, and often emotional task. The family-leave law provides up to twelve weeks of unpaid leave for specific family and medical needs.[57] If a person has elderly parents, perhaps living at a distance, elder care may also present challenges. Many men still are reluctant to stay home with children or elders, but that attitude is slowly changing.[58] In 1997, the U.S. Census Bureau estimated that 1.9 million fathers were their children's primary caregiver.[59]

An increasing number of companies provide child care, flexible or part-time work schedules, and some form of family leave that their employees can use to care for children and elders. Whatever arrangements are made, dropping children off in the morning and picking them up from the child care center or sitter adds yet another chore in the work race for working parents. The challenges and needs of diverse households are beginning to be acknowledged in the workplace.

Teenagers and Young Adults

Teenagers who have done well in high school are usually confident and college bound; numbers of their peers, however, have not yet learned necessary job skills or experienced many feelings of achievement. Approaching the first rung of the ladder is the most difficult step in the entire lifetime career process. Statistics show that the unemployment rate for young adults is much higher than the rate for the remainder of the population, with young African American teens having the most difficulty becoming employed.

Geographical locations add special constraints for young people. In rural areas, the upward-bound teen may have problems finding adequate higher education and good jobs. Inner cities may provide little support or career and educational opportunities for the ghetto teen.

Some people feel that for students to work while they are in school can be a valuable as well as a profitable experience, as long as their grades don't suffer. Such opportunities can help inexperienced workers gain badly needed work experience while they explore various facets of workplaces. Too much work, however, can add to the stress of adolescence and adversely affect grades, the low pay not worth the sacrifice of time or the encouragement it may give to overspending. Young people also need some time for social life and relaxation, time to become involved in a variety of activities, if their financial situation will allow it.

Schools can make the transition to work easier in other ways. Recognizing students' need to begin work, some high schools and colleges collaborate with businesses to offer them work experience, career and exploration programs, and internships. People in business are getting actively involved with young people, acting as mentors, and in some cases promising them college scholarships if they stay in school.

Supervised community service can help young adults get started. Such work often helps the environment and the community while the young person earns money. Entry into the job market for this age group should be easier in future years as many fewer young people will be in the job-market pipeline as we move into the twenty-first century.

The Aging Worker in the Workplace

People born today may well be alive in 2100,
since many more people will live to 100 and over.

As the U.S. family shrinks in size, the overall population is growing older and life expectancy is lengthening. The fastest growing segment of the population between now and 2050 will be those over 85. As the baby boom generation ages and fewer couples opt for children, the number of elderly people could outnumber the young.

Opportunities for rewarding work become fewer for both men and women as they grow older. Many workers stay at jobs they've outgrown rather than face possible rejection in applying for a more challenging position. It seems that our youth-oriented, throwaway culture sees little value in older people. In playwright Lillian Hellman's words, they have "the wisdom that comes with age that we can't make use of."[60]

Betty Friedan estimates that we are being given an extra thirty years of life compared to our grandparents. Zalman Schachter-Shalomi says in *From Age-ing to Sage-ing* that these years can be used profitably in "eldering" or guiding and mentoring young people using the accumulated wisdom gained over a lifetime.[61]

A national council reports that, although they remain unemployed longer when seeking work, older men and women hunt more diligently for jobs, hold a job longer with less absenteeism, perform as well as or better than younger people, and are more reliable and more willing to learn. One study showed that employee theft was much lower when companies hired retirees.[62]

Employers are hiring older people in entry-level service jobs as the teen population diminishes. With a declining employee pool, older people will continue to find opportunities for satisfying employment. Elders are returning to school not only for enrichment but to learn new skills. Many of them are using computers with great success.

For those who are younger, it is important to plan a career path and retirement so that those years will be financially secure and filled with satisfying involvements. Opportunities for moving in and up in a large company may shrink, but many "seasoned citizens" begin successful small businesses, volunteer in satisfying activities, and stay active beyond previous expectations.

Older people are providing positive role models as they plow new ground. Many are handling retirement, finances, leisure, health care, increased longevity, loneliness, loss of independence, inflation, and productive involvement quite well. Because of the increasing number of elderly, jobs providing for their needs such as those in leisure activities and health care should increase.

Minorities/Immigrants/Refugees: The "Other"

In today's world, we encounter people whose appearance, language, customs and culture, and social and economic background can seem worlds apart from our own. When Jesse Jackson was running for president in 1988 he told supporters, "Most people in the world are yellow, black, brown—they're poor, female, non-Christian, and young—and they don't speak English!"[63] We will see more and more diversity in the workplace. The numbers of Asians and Hispanics is expected to surge by 2050.[64] Hispanics were expected to become the largest ethnic group in the United States by the year 2005, a projection that was met two years early.[65] Overt prejudice involving African Americans, Hispanics, Native Americans, immigrants and refugees, and women, and the gap it creates in everything from job opportunities to education, is still a major and dismal hurdle.[66] Still, minority women and men are slowly increasing their numbers in better-paying jobs and positions of prestige. The number of interracial marriages and multiethnic children in the United States has also grown dramatically. Golf pro Tiger Woods includes his Caucasian, African American, Indian, and Thai ancestry when speaking of his heritage.[67]

Increasing numbers of Hispanics are entering the middle class. The number of Latino-owned businesses tripled and sales revenues surged in the 1980s and 1990s, growing nearly three times as fast as business overall.[68] According to the U.S. Census Bureau, Hispanics own more than 1.2 million businesses, representing 40 percent of all minority-owned businesses.[69] Hispanic buying power has become a factor in marketing with many companies.

The African American middle class, with its attendant affluence, is growing, and more African Americans than ever before are visible in positions of influence; however, there is still a great deal of improvement needed in the community of African Americans left behind. African Americans own nearly 20 percent of all minority-owned businesses and have the highest percentage of women-owned businesses relative to Hispanic, Asian, or Native American firms.[70] Racism is still a factor in American life, as evidenced by the push to dismantle some elements of civil rights legislation. Many in the Native American population have been left far behind also, and rarely are they even noted in the statistics.

MEDIAN ANNUAL EARNINGS OF YEAR-ROUND, FULL-TIME WORKERS, 2000[71]			
MEN	EARNINGS	WOMEN	EARNINGS
White	$38,869	White	$28,080
African American	$30,409	African American	$25,117
Asian & Pacific Islander	$40,946	Asian & Pacific Islander	$31,156
Hispanic	$24,638	Hispanic	$20,527

Immigrants and refugees face added burdens. Never before in history have so many people migrated in fear and suffering during such a short period of time as in these past decades. Not only do people migrate to other countries, but because of wars, environmental destruction, and economic inequities, increasingly millions of people are displaced within their own countries. These migrations have been due in part, according to former U.S. President Jimmy Carter, "to the failure on the part of the world to live by principles of peace and human rights." The struggle to compete in a strange land like the United States with its assertive brand of success can seem overwhelming to these newcomers.

The diversity Web site **www.imdiversity.com** is geared for career and job seekers and provides helpful articles and links to help members in minority communities and women network and find opportunities in companies that embrace and value diversity. A list of minority-friendly companies is provided. Résumés can be posted and listed jobs viewed.

The Web site **www.gaywork.com** is designed to help members of the gay and lesbian communities find jobs and careers; provides useful job information, articles, and links; has a message board to share job hunting ideas and suggestions; and offers résumé posting and job listings.

The Disabled and Their Abilities

A humorous article by Adair Lara says that, like the movie hero Forrest Gump, most people know how to do some things very well, and in the rest of life "kind of fake it."[72] Although everyone has some limitations, people whose disabilities are more visible have been assumed to be incapable of doing anything. That attitude seems to be changing, and society is finally recognizing that among people with unusual limitations there is a vast pool of valuable and important skills.

The Americans with Disabilities Act of 1992 made it illegal to discriminate in employment against anyone who has the skills, experience, education, and other requirements to do the essential functions of the job with or *without*

For Better or For Worse®   **by Lynn Johnston**

FOR BETTER OR FOR WORSE © Lynn Johnston Productions, Inc./Dist. by United Feature Syndicate, Inc.

reasonable accommodations by the employer.[73] High tech in the workplace is bringing greater support to people with obvious limitations: talking/Braille computers for the visually impaired, robots to assist with physical tasks.

Changing views has been the greatest help as people become comfortable with others who have differences. It has led us to the realization that everyone, regardless of role or job title, can make a positive contribution. Not only will you work with a greater variety of people, you will be supplying goods or services to an increasingly diverse population with new and different methods of supplying their needs and wants. It can lead to interesting new ways of working.

The Web site **www.disabilityinfo.gov** is a comprehensive online resource for job seekers with disabilities and provides a wealth of information and related links to help find employers throughout the United States and Canada. As a federal government Web site, relevant articles are presented and information is continually updated.

STRESSED FOR SUCCESS

Many of us work according to rigid schedules that don't match our natural rhythms or leave leeway for personal needs. We are continually caught in a time bind in an increasingly complex world of ever-longer commutes, more complicated personal business transactions, and more involved maintenance of homes and gadgets.

Work occupies prime time. For the past fifty years, the forty-hour week and the 2,000-hour, fifty-week year have been the standard. However, corporate cutbacks now often force remaining workers to work even more hours. The Families and Work Institute in New York tells us that 45 percent of Americans work more than forty hours a week and 10 percent work more than sixty hours.[74] Some are on call twenty-four hours a day by fax, e-mail, cell phones, beepers, and computer link-ups—even when they are driving down the freeway! Many people are working two or three jobs just to make ends meet. Work plus the demands of family and the business of living leave many people with little time for other enriched choices.

Workplace stress has become a concern as companies downsize, move away, and otherwise squeeze their employees to produce more, with the threat of unemployment often only a paycheck away. Stress in great enough quantities can cause exhaustion, illness, and even death.[75] Stress is magnified by the pace of innovation and the necessity to beat competitors to the market. A difficult boss can be a source of stress as well as a hindrance to productivity. Lack of time to relax with family and friends and simply have fun often causes a life to go out of balance. Stress results when the demands of life become too great.

Studies of some Silicon Valley, California, firms disclosed a higher divorce rate among their employees than for the United States as a whole; high rates of sexual and physical abuse of children; frequent drug use by children of families employed in high-tech firms; high numbers of strokes at work; and families living beyond their means.[76] Our biology has yet to catch up and blend with our technology without causing us to lose our identities or our health.

Many workers fear taking the time off that is due them for fear of falling behind or looking like they are not busy. (The boss may give them more work!) Shorter vacations have become the norm. U.S. workers average ten days of vacation a year, ranking them twentieth in a list of industrialized countries, with Austrian workers topping the list with thirty vacation days.[77] Oddly, people brag that they haven't had a vacation in years.

Not all studies agree, however, with some researchers showing that people work fewer hours than they did thirty years ago but have many more involvements that make them feel a time crunch. For example, people spend many hours watching TV, drive their children to many more activities, play sports, and socialize more than their parents did, and then feel the time crunch in other aspects of their lives.[78]

Hard work doesn't necessarily lead to excess stress if it is enjoyable. Zest and energy for life come with doing things that challenge us and make us feel valued. Some people, though they may be in a job that is not their preference, have the ability to put their energy into it and find enjoyment.

Here is a checklist to help you decide whether you are overstressed, with some tips for changes you can make to reduce your stress level:

- Are you very unhappy with your life or your work? It's time to reevaluate each life component to pinpoint and resolve the problem. Learning to accept yourself and appreciate your good points can be an important first step. Sometimes the changes needed may be very small.

- Are you feeling excessively fatigued? Do you feel overworked? Find some enjoyable activity outside of work that will give you new energy. Exercise, for example, can actually be energizing. Get someone to take over for you at home or at work for a couple of days while you spend time sorting out your priorities. What can you eliminate? How can you get the help you need? Plan regular meetings with a good friend or colleague to talk over your progress in keeping a balanced schedule.

- Do you feel regularly stressed? Take a minivacation—for example, a weekend at home doing nothing but soaking up leisure, letting other people deal with distractions. Alternate with a friend by providing respite time for each other. Watch funny movies, because humor is a great stress reliever and even tears can help. Meditate, do yoga, play soothing music, enjoy a romp with the dog, or brush your cat.

Stress-reduction and health maintenance workshops are available at many community centers, conferences, health care centers, and even many companies; these teach simple relaxation techniques that can become a habit. Some companies, like SC Johnson Wax, that provide exercise programs have found that their employees are more relaxed and productive and have fewer health problems.[79]

Leisure, for many, is hard won. John Kenneth Galbraith says, "Only if an individual has a choice as to the length of his working week or year, along with the option of taking unpaid leave for longer periods, does he or she have an effective choice between income and leisure."[80] Some workers are striking for more time at home—doing away with forced overtime and better pensions—rather than higher pay, a plus for family values.[81] Humans have always dreamed of a world without work or at least with less work. In BREAKTIME, *Living without Work in a Nine to Five World*, Bernard Lefkowitz discusses some alternatives to "work."[82]

Many more workers could be employed if some people worked fewer than forty hours a week, fifty weeks a year. The loss of income might be offset in many ways (even financially): saving energy and resources, enjoying a more enriched life, having more time for the business of living. Many people with special needs such as parents, the elderly, and the handicapped are able to work when they are provided with a shorter schedule.

In the next chapter we consider various workstyle options with a view to helping clarify your career decision.

SUMMARY

Workplaces can be divided into seven general categories, each with its own unique characteristics and requirements: business, industry, education, communication/entertainment, health, government, and military.

There are a variety of career ladders for you to climb based on position, responsibility, and education. Generally, workers with higher levels of education will rise to the top-level positions, have greater responsibilities, and earn more money. Job titles may differ among companies and industries for the same work, and the same kind of work may have different job titles in different businesses. Being able to define clearly what you want in a job helps make it easier to find the best one for you.

Jobs come with a variety of rewards. Salary is usually considered the most important one. Yet, the additional rewards of benefits, colleagues, managers, advancement opportunities, working conditions, retirement plans, stock options, and a variety of other perks should be carefully examined when considering a company for employment. Also, if your values match those of the company—for example, in ethics, social responsibility, or autonomy—then your satisfaction working there should be high. Having a good manager is also a key factor in job satisfaction.

Workplaces have become diverse, with jobs becoming more gender-neutral, opening up more opportunities to women. Companies actively employ more minorities, women, gays and lesbians, and people with disabilities and continually encourage these qualified candidates to apply. Further, the number of minority-owned businesses has increased, providing additional opportunities for entrepreneurs. This increase in employment opportunities has caused men and women to reconsider how having families will affect their careers and how important it is to have balance in their lives.

 SELF-ASSESSMENT EXERCISES

The following exercises will help you decide on a category of workplace and understand its important rewards and characteristics.

1. Where Do You Fit In?

a. Number the categories of workplace in order of importance to you:

   _3_ Business   _2_ Education   _6_ Government

   _5_ Industry   _4_ Health   _7_ Military

   _1_ Entertainment/Communication

b. Check the workplace/location that most appeals to you:

  ✔ Very small   ____ Moderate   ____ Very large   ____ Multinational

____ Local   ____ Regional   ____ Global

Tell why it is important: _____

_____

c. Check all the settings and styles you prefer:

____ Indoors   ✔ Outdoors

✔ Traveling/Fieldwork   ✔ Varied work setting

____ Alone   ____ With a team

____ Close supervision   ✔ Independent

Tell why:

_____

_____

d. How far up the career ladder do you think you want to go? Explain.

_____

_____

2. Workplace Rewards

Rate these workplace rewards H, M, or L (meaning high, medium, or low) in importance to you as a potential employee. Put an E on any that are essential for you.

H Salary

H Paid holidays/vacation

H Medical care benefits

H Dental care benefits

M Employer stock option plan

___L___ Career support and development

___H___ Compatible values

___H___ Supportive emotional climate

___L___ Help with child/elder care

___M___ Such personal care rewards as on-site recreation, financial counseling

___H___ Retirement benefits

___M___ Autonomy

3. Workplace Values

a. Rate this summary of corporate values H, M, or L (meaning high, medium, or low) in importance to you as a potential employee. Put an E on any that are essential for you in a company you might consider working for.

___M___ Makes safe, quality, attractive, affordable products that fulfill legitimate needs and wants

___L___ Is environmentally conscious

___H___ Is an equal opportunity employer; follows fair and safe labor practices

___M___ Supports workplace democracy and worker participation

___H___ Is honest and fair in business dealings

___H___ Respects people of all backgrounds

___L___ Does not depend on repressive governments or military weapons contracts

___M___ Is a good member of the community

4. Identifying Major Components of Your Life

a. Rank these components of your life in order of importance to you.

_5_ Career   _7_ Ethnic/National ties

_2_ Marriage   _1_ Religion/Spiritual development

_3_ Family   _6_ Leisure

_4_ Education   ___ What else? _____

b. What problems do you see in fitting each of these components into your life? Into the lives of those around you?

_____ Money in education and _____

_____

_____

5. Stress

a. Which elements of your life components cause you the most stress?

_____ School, finances _____

b. How do you take care of stress in your life?

_____ music + friends _____

6. Thinking about Your Roles

On a separate sheet of paper, briefly describe yourself by means of ten roles, such as your gender, race, ethnic background, nationality, religion, student status, major, job/career, and other features that define (or that you feel do not define) you. Describe strong feelings associated with any of these roles.

 GROUP DISCUSSION QUESTIONS

1. Write about or describe your ideal workplace and schedule to your group. Include your ideal community/geographical location. relationship

2. Do you believe most companies could live up to socially responsible guidelines? Name some that do. Could they improve? How?

3. What factors prevent workplace environments from improving? In what areas have they improved?

4. Name two successful people that you admire. Tell why. Did the various roles they play influence your choices? How?

5. Do you feel that affirmative action programs have been successful enough so that we no longer need them? Why? How might we bring gender and race equity into the workplace? Give reasons you think it is important (or not) to do so.

6

Timestyles/
Workstyles

Alternatives
That Work

 GOALS

- Explore and evaluate various workstyles and schedules.

- Consider a business of your own.

- Learn how to research workplaces behind the scene and on site.

- Use information interviewing to gain practical knowledge about interesting careers.

Years ago, many people went to work in companies that paid a salary, required forty hours per week of work for fifty weeks per year, and provided some benefits and a job that often lasted for life. These days, there are many other ways you might connect to the workplace—from very close and traditional to distant and innovative. You may work different schedules with varying styles. You may work "long distance," combine work in a company with a business of your own, or simply start your own business. About 15 percent of the U.S. work force are using alternative work schedules.[1] Two-thirds of Americans say they would be willing to sacrifice pay just to have one or two more days off each week. Between 1991 and 1996, 28 percent of Americans voluntarily made changes that led to less income but a more balanced life, opting for time over money.[2] Here we will explore some workstyle options that might shed more light on your career decision.

FULL-TIME ALTERNATIVES

Flextime / Choice Time Flextime allows employees to work any eight hours between specified times, such as 7 A.M. to 6 P.M. Compressed work schedules, such as four ten-hour days per week, are a variation on flextime. Three twelve-hour shifts, another variation, enable college students to work three weekend nights and still attend classes, or let working parents share child care.

Some employers allow employees to choose which holidays they will take off; some allow them to accumulate and use sick leave as paid time off. Some allow full-time employees to reduce work hours for a period of time in exchange for reduced compensation. Some allow "comp" (compensatory) time which gives an employee the option of time off instead of pay for overtime, work. Instead of laying off large numbers of people, companies sometimes ask all employees to work fewer hours at a reduced salary.

The Bechtel Group, a worldwide engineering company based in San Francisco, felt that it would have an edge in recruiting valuable workers if it offered employees a nine-hour day, four days a week, with every other Friday off and the alternate Friday an eight-hour day. The employees now look forward to twenty-six three-day weekends a year.[3]

Thirty for Forty Some innovative employers advertise a thirty-hour week for forty hours' pay. Sam Morris, plant manager at Metro Plastics Technologies, Inc., in Columbus, Indiana, decided to try that system to lure workers during a time of low unemployment. It was so successful in increasing productivity and keeping workers happy that other companies are trying it.[4]

Job Sharing   Sharing one job allows two qualified people to work at one full-time position, in any combination of time schedules they can work out with their employer. One person might work mornings, the other, afternoons. They work out a system for sharing needed information.

Part-Time Work   More than 32 million Americans, or 25 percent as of 2001, are part-time employees—that is, they work from one to thirty-four hours a week. Thirty-eight percent are men; 62 percent are women; and 46 percent are between the ages of sixteen and twenty-four. A large majority of part-time workers prefer having a part-time job.[5] Often, people work several part-time jobs just to make enough to live on since part-time work pays less well than a similar full-time job.

Temporary Work   A growing number of people opt for full-time but time-limited jobs. Such work is available in many areas, such as office, technical, professional, industrial, and medical. All these fields require a wide range of skills for trained or trainable workers. People in these jobs may learn new skills and find access to jobs that are often available to those inside a company. In a survey of temporary workers, 38 percent said they were offered full-time employment by a company they entered on a temporary assignment.[6]

Manpower, Inc., the largest temporary agency in the United States, is also the U.S.'s largest nongovernment staffing services company, employing more than 1.6 million people worldwide. In 1997, more than one-third of its temporary workers found full-time jobs as a result of temporary placement. Manpower offers an array of free training modules, skills testing, and a welfare-to-work program.[7] Some temporary agencies are moving toward being a person's main employer and may even provide a variety of benefits. Called contingent work, the trend toward part-time and temporary work seems to be emerging as a major feature in employment.

Although some people find that working part time or full time at intervals is quite to their liking, others find there are disadvantages. Full-time work is more likely to include benefits including health care, retirement benefits, better wages, and a chance for promotion, although more temporary agencies are now offering benefits.

Part-time and temporary workers are often considered expendable as companies strive to make business more profitable. The continual uprooting of workers due to the greater ease with which employers can hire and fire affects both the workplace and the community. The U.S. Office of Personnel Management has issued regulations to limit the amount of time federal agencies can keep employees in temporary jobs.[8]

Overall, time flexibility may add to the work and cost of management, and part-time and temporary workers may demonstrate less commitment to the job, but research shows that absenteeism drops and productivity rises when companies adopt less rigid work hours. Businesses find that they benefit from the flexibility and the ability to change workers' hours and utilize work stations more efficiently.

THE COMPUTER COMMUTE

Only in the last half of the twentieth century did people begin to commute to work on a large scale. Before that, most of the United States was rural, and a great percentage of people either had their own farms or home businesses or they worked very close to home. In time, the easy commute became overtime spent in giant traffic jams.

Today there is a trend back to the old workstead, as technology can bring people within sight and sound of each other even though they are hundreds of miles apart. One production plant was kept running weekends, even though the person in charge was three miles away. Equipment that is thousands of miles in outer space can be operated and repaired from the Earth by remote control.

A judge in Alaska hears cases at a distance by closed circuit TV, and sometimes she hears defendants who are at home by using a speaker phone in court. Telecommuting—using computers to communicate with others—has enormous potential for unclogging roads and saving energy, too. Productivity often increases for those who work at home.

Single parents, the elderly, and the disabled can find new opportunities worksteading. Lack of safety guides, however, and possible exploitation by an employing firm—meaning low wages, no vacations or benefits, and long hours—are causes for some concern. Isolation is another issue to consider. Career development may be put on hold when a person works at home.

Cost can be an issue. In some cases, workers may have to buy or lease equipment or office furniture. People may find their utility bills (for example, telephone link-up) and energy costs rising. A good computer system is very affordable. A person who wants to telecommute needs to work out the parameters with his or her boss, including costs of computer, printer, Internet connection, fax machine, telephone, and copier along with time restrictions and how to keep in touch with the main workplace.

Not all telecommuters chose this method just because they wanted to be home with children. Most of these workers do not feel isolated from peers; they took only moderate time off for breaks; and they smoked, drank, and took drugs less than regular nine-to-five, office-bound workers. Combining child raising with work at home, however, can prove to be a stressful alternative. This and other family issues must be resolved: who can interrupt when; how late to work; whether to read a fax coming in at midnight; whether to do the laundry in the middle of the day.

According to one study, in 1999, more than 21 million people telecommuted to work, and it was estimated that 51 million workers would do so by 2030. Given the advances and quick adoption of new technology (computers, laptops, cell phones, personal digital assistants, instant messaging, and so on), the dependence on computers to perform many work tasks, the rise of cable and high-speed modems for fast data access, the increasing dependence on the Internet for commerce, and society's desire to eliminate time wasted in driving to the office or polluting the environment make telecommuting an attractive alternative to the traditional work model. However, not everyone agrees that telecommuting is a good idea. There are bosses who like to see their workers work in person, and there are people who enjoy going out to work rather than working at home. Some telecommute part time; some only temporarily. Many people find it highly satisfying and successful; companies find in many cases that productivity and morale improve among telecommuters.[9]

A down side to the ability to work long distance is that some companies have moved their data processing as well as manufacturing work to developing countries where worker wages as well as worker protection are minimal. This action subtracts from the available pool of jobs in the United States,[10] sometimes decimates the economy of a town or region, and often results in the exploitation of workers abroad.

WORK IN THE IN-BETWEEN

Some people would like more work independence but aren't ready to go out completely on their own. For them, here are some possibilities.

The *intrapreneur* holds an intermediate position between the corporation and being on one's own. It is a term coined by Gifford Pinchot III, a consultant to such companies as Exxon, to describe the *intracorporate entrepreneur.*[11] Intrapreneurs remain company employees while contracting their services to their employer. Using company resources and support, they act as self-employed persons, often developing services or products that the company wants but to which it is unwilling to commit with large-scale expenditures.

For example, one artistically talented employee negotiated a contract with her electronics company to make a number of working engineering models at home. As another example, an engineer could gather a team to do creative research. A teacher could be given a special assignment to develop a curriculum for his or her school district. A company benefits because it does not lose either a valued employee who might move to a competitor or that person's good idea. Intrapreneurship may require some capital, but it involves less risk than entrepreneurship. Look around your workplace for a possible intrapreneurial opportunity.

Franchises are for people who would like to be independent business owners but would prefer less risk and more support than they would have if they were totally on their own. Franchises have moved beyond fast food into such growing areas as hairstyling, quick-stop shopping, weight-loss systems, home/garden maintenance and remodeling, computer sales, and a whole host of other types of business ventures. A new franchise opens every eight minutes of each business day; one out of twelve business establishments is a franchise. Although Fortune 500 companies downsized by more than a million jobs during the past ten years, franchises were adding nearly 2 million jobs to the economy. In 2000, franchises had over 320,000 locations throughout the United States spanning 75 industries, employing over 8 million people, accounting for over 40 percent of all retail sales, and generating $1 trillion in sales,[12] with home health care one of the leaders.[13] Franchises fail far less often than other small businesses and generally need less start-up financing. Many franchise companies are targeting young, energetic, and organized new college graduates as potential owners. The advantage of franchising to the parent firm is the opportunity to expand more rapidly than would be possible if it had to raise all the money necessary for moving into new markets.

Cooperatives, group-owned and democratically run enterprises, are an option for people to improve their work environments without having to strike out on their own. When a group begins a cooperative business, the venture often creates a kind of community and autonomy. Cooperative enterprises often display social responsibility along with profit making and community involvement. They range from grocery markets to print shops, from forestry trusts to sewing cooperatives.[14] For example, food co-ops sometimes sell memberships to individuals who agree to work a certain number of hours a week in exchange for lower-cost food. These joint undertakings often result in increased motivation, sense of control, and productivity.

In the 1960s, women in Japan began a milk-buying cooperative that gave them more say about price, quality, and environmental issues in food production. Now working directly with farmers, the cooperative has a membership of more than 218,000 households in over 100 branches, each member contributing about $9 a month. With its own line of sixty products, the co-op employs a full-time staff of over 700. As the fourth-largest co-op in Japan, it has $120 million in investments and in 1993 did $650 million in business.[15]

A *buyout*—buying the company you work for—is one way to achieve greater autonomy, ensure that the company's value system matches yours, and become an owner. We don't envision an untested recruit buying out a company single-handedly, but some individuals and groups of seasoned workers have done so successfully when their plants have closed or one of their divisions have been "spun off." United Zipper Company in Woodland, North Carolina, became an employee-owned reality after months of hard,

Reprinted with permission from Harley Schwadron.

persistent work following near-panic when the factory closed. And in 1994, 54,000 United Airlines employees sported buttons that declared, "You are talking to the owner!"[16]

WORK OF ONE'S OWN: THE ENTREPRENEUR

In time, the work you look for may be your own. Although a life without work may be beyond the dreams or desires of most people, many often wish they could be their own bosses. In the early twenty-first century, self-employment is growing at a faster rate than wage- and salary-paying jobs. "Most new jobs in the United States are being created by small, service-oriented firms or suppliers of parts—many of them women-owned—and this trend is predicted to grow at the start of the twenty-first century."[17]

In the 1980s and 1990s, while large corporations were cutting back, small businesses were providing 80 percent of the net new jobs in the economy and almost all the innovation; many were based on socially and environmentally responsible practices. A survey found a surprising 37 percent, or more than one in three, American households involved in entrepreneurship.[18]

Women are starting businesses at nearly twice the national average. The largest share is in the service sector, but there is huge growth in such nontraditional areas as wholesale trade, transportation/communications, agriculture, and manufacturing.[19] And although small businesses seem to fail, a survey by Bruce Phillips (of the Small Business Administration) and Bruce Kirchoff (of the New Jersey Institute of Technology) found that in reality only about 18 percent of all new businesses end in real failure. Some owners sell out, close a company, and begin another—perhaps in a different industry or location. Nearly 70 percent of companies formed in 1985 were still viable nine years later, with smaller ones having a higher survival rate than the larger ones. Kirchoff found that only about 20 percent to 25 percent of failed businesses he studied ended up owing money.[20] The bursting of the "economic bubble" in 2001, triggered by the many dot-com businesses that disappeared because of unsustainable business models, will increase the statistics of true failures, with the bulk of companies affected being in computer- and Internet-related endeavors. Small firms—those with fewer than twenty employees, and especially those with less than four employees—will continue to play a dominant role in job creation. Women and minorities will continue to gain prominence in small business ownership.[21] Although half of the private sector U.S. work force work in small businesses, new jobs are created in them at a greater proportion. This trend is expected to continue.

It may seem beyond possible that a small, local company can enter the global market. But tiny Trek Bicycle in Wisconsin, which made its first bike in a rented barn, is now the world's biggest specialty bicycle maker. Its move into international marketing began with a small sale to Canada. The governor noted that "every time you sell one billion dollars of goods and services, you create 22,000 good jobs here in the state of Wisconsin."[22]

With increasing globalization of economies and affordable technology, many people find that they can begin a worldwide business on a desk at home. Called the "new entrepreneurs," the people who begin businesses are knowledgeable, experienced, technology literate, and willing to work with others; they set reasonable goals and work hard to achieve them. They are open to both creative and tried-and-true ideas about how to acquire a company, how to organize it, and how to keep it running well. Many of them are young people.

Small grassroots financial institutions are springing up around the world. They are dedicated to developing their communities and to helping all the community members, including the poor, to participate in the local economy. Some development programs begun by these institutions work with "incubators" that provide support, information, office space, and equipment for fledgling businesses. The Pajaro Valley Community Development Corporation in

Watsonville, California, has supported a restaurant, produce market, soccer shop, bookstore, children's clothing store, hair stylist, and gift shop.

Some advisers encourage the budding entrepreneur to start with a flourish; others counsel going slowly and in small steps. It's hard to disagree that having a creative edge and perseverance with a new idea are pluses. At 3M, an engineer tried inventing a super glue that did not stick things together very successfully. Someone else tried the product and found a way to keep bookmark slips removable yet secure on the page. After he spent years trying to convince management the product had promise, the "Post-it" was born.[23] Each case is unique, but the facts show that planning and experimenting as well as having capital are essential. Most successful entrepreneurs have degrees, experience, and money, but we still hear and read about people with little background who begin small businesses with few resources and in no time are making a profit. "Find a need and fill it" says an old adage that still works.

Some people decide to quit their jobs and create a home-based business. Pessimists say the day of the "Mom and Pop" venture is long gone, but this may not be so. Even though the competition from large chains is fierce, if Mom and Pop go high tech in a specialized market niche, they may well be developing highly efficient and successful companies.[24] Luke Elliott says that "even today, in the era of corporate cannibalism, it's possible to start a business on a shoestring." He and his wife Cindy started Photo Vision, a retail outlet for solar electric systems and other energy-related products, with "$1,500 and a kitchen table."[25]

Here's what George Hellyer, a worksteading attorney, advises for someone who intends to replace a job by worksteading[26]:

> If a person is going to leave a job to work at home, [he or she] needs a very clear attitude about how [he or she] is going to live. I set up a rather modest goal of the kind of security I wanted to have before I left the law firm. I don't buy expensive clothes, for instance. I enjoy cooking so I don't go to restaurants much. If you have a place to live, where you can also work, you can get along on very little. The rest of life doesn't really take too much money if you have a place to be.

Who knows what goods and services will be produced from the electronic cottage of the future?

Many famous companies, including Apple Computer and Microsoft, began on a shoestring and became very successful. Millard Fuller, founder of Habitat for Humanity, started on his path to millionaire status while he was in college. He provided a service delivering birthday cakes from bakeries to students, paid for by their parents with a cut for him. Karen Scott tested the possibility of a mail-order baby-products business in a unique way. She contacted

250 new mothers listed over time in her local newspaper, asking them by phone what products they sought. She began to focus on travel items, and now Chelsea & Scott's travel items are top sellers in the $28 million business.[27]

You can avoid investing a fortune; start small by having a simple, inexpensive business card made. You can design it by computer and have it copied quickly on card stock at your local copy store. Your first card does not have to be fancy. Then begin handing your cards out to friends and relatives, perhaps offering to do your first work free or for a small fee.

Using appropriate technology can be a plus for any business. Through the Internet you can network with people all over the world to gather information, share and test ideas, make contacts, and develop markets. Small businesses find that they can have as much exposure as large ones on the Web.

Media messages to the contrary, the best advertisement is word-of-mouth by satisfied customers. You can use evenings and weekends to test the waters while keeping your paying job as a backup. Because of the expenses of setting up an office if you are a beginner, therapist Richard Patocchi advises you to rent office space part time; only after you have enough clients to justify expansion should you agree to rent the space for more time per week. If you need to hire some employees, providing the equipment for computer-at-home work can be a highly cost-effective way to expand your own business.

Contracting is a way many people begin a business. Companies both large and small may find that contracting with another entity can provide them with resources and skilled people they lack or can relieve them of burdens at a small cost. Contracting also enables businesses to focus their resources more closely on fewer tasks at the home company and to do what they do best. Also called *outsourcing,* this way of doing business lets companies hire out such jobs as specialized parts manufacture, data processing, warehouse storage, accounting, human relations/development, and health care provision. Such contracting entities may form a group with other companies and procure cheaper health insurance. Owners of small businesses as well as contingent workers often do not have access to health care or legal services as well as volume purchasing of such items as office supplies.

Community enhancement offers another entrepreneurial opportunity. Some businesses are set up to help solve community social problems such as homelessness or drug addiction. The social sector is the fastest growing of the country's sectors and the largest employer. There are nearly 1 million nonprofit organizations in the United States. Well over 90 million people are involved in nonprofit activities, including both volunteers and employed staff.[28] They often work with their municipalities and other government and nonprofit entities to obtain funding.

Some entrepreneurs are beginning nonprofit organizations that are supported by for-profit components, making fundraising less of a chore. Delancey Street in San Francisco, a self-help, no-nonsense program, with *no*

MOST POPULAR START-UP BUSINESSES[29]

Arts and crafts	Investment broker
Audiovisual production services	Landscape / Lawn maintenance
Automotive services/repair	Marketing programs/services
Beauty shop	Painting
Building contractor (remodel/paint)	Real estate
Communications consulting	Residential/Commercial cleaning
Computer services/repair	Restaurant
Construction	Retail store
Consulting / Business management	Trucking
Designing	Wholesale trade: nonperishable goods
Internet/Technology	

---

government funding, is located in a beautiful home and business complex built by its residents with donations of money and material from the business community. Its elegant restaurant with a view of San Francisco Bay nets $1 million each year; its moving company earns $3 million. Other businesses it has developed and run, such as printing and catering, add more. The five hundred well-dressed and well-mannered men and women who live and work there were all headed for prison terms, some having committed violent crimes. With lots of hard work, they are able to turn their lives around, help those coming after them, and move on to respectable lives.[30] The Roberts Foundation book, *The New Social Entrepreneurs,* contains numerous case studies of recent such nonprofits that have an income-generating entity and are set up to help the disadvantaged.[31]

The person with a product or service to offer, the energy to do it all, and the personality to make customers feel valued by giving them excellent service can find great satisfaction in being an entrepreneur. There is no question that beginning a business may be hazardous to your health on many levels, but you get to be your own boss—twenty-four hours a day! From the five-year-old selling lemonade to the weekend do-it-yourselfer remodeling the kitchen, self-interest is a powerful motivator for getting work done. Generally, business owners are happier with their independent work than are people who are employees.

Ventures with a better than average success rate include services to private education, health services, legal services, insurance agents and brokers, and personal services. Amusement and recreation services had a very high failure rate, as did oil and gas extraction and lumber and wood manufacturing; general building contractors and furniture and home-furnishings stores also ranked high in rate of failure.[32]

Creative careers are simply unusual ways to work that can be successful in a company or on your own. As you interview people and observe them on their jobs, look for those who have taken an ordinary job and brought it to life in a creative way, sometimes within a very structured bureaucracy. The position of "store manager" with its attendant duties may sound formidable or dull. But Monique Benoit of San Francisco gave it new life. Well known for her community involvement, she loved to shop in expensive antique stores and boutiques. She also cherished her independence and loved to travel, so she created her own job to satisfy these qualities. She sent a carefully composed letter to managers of her favorite stores, offering to "shop sit" if they had to be away from the store for business or personal reasons. She received a good response and subsequent offers of part-time, temporary, and permanent full-time employment.

In Santa Monica, California, two women began a vehicle-repair referral service to put people in touch with affordable, honest, and reliable mechanics. They generated $750,000 in sales in 1992.[33] "Susie Skates" indulges in her favorite sport while delivering messages. "Flying Fur" delivers pampered pets around the country, and "Sherlock Bones" searches for missing pets. After being laid off, Geoffrey Macon decided to begin a business that designs and produces upscale ethnic dinnerware with African American motifs.[34] From Clutter Cutter, Rent-a-Yenta or Rent-a-Goat, Eco-Tourism or Eco-Weddings, to Mama's Llamas and Rent-a-Thief, people create careers with imagination instead of capital.

Here are a few ideas for small-scale, more traditional although not always lucrative careers: house sitting, pet sitting, matching housemates or travel companions; child care that includes instruction in a craft or hobby; shopping, transportation, or exercise classes for the elderly and disabled; photography at special events; house calls for sick plants; servant-in-costume at parties—for example, at parties for children's birthdays; teaching do-it-yourself house or auto repair. Add producing and marketing very special gourmet homegrown/homemade food and herbs, sometimes by prearranged purchase, and pick-your-own flowers; combining photography with a host of activities both recreational and professional; combining art with science; designing/evaluating children's toys for companies; designing play space, books, or furniture; making treasures from trash—for example, rag rugs and quilts; conducting estate sales. The homeless in one community market their own home-grown vegetables raised on a city lot; they also sell used clothing and other treasures gleaned from donations. The possibilities are endless. One major mark of a fulfilling job is the invigorating and energy-giving feelings it provides.

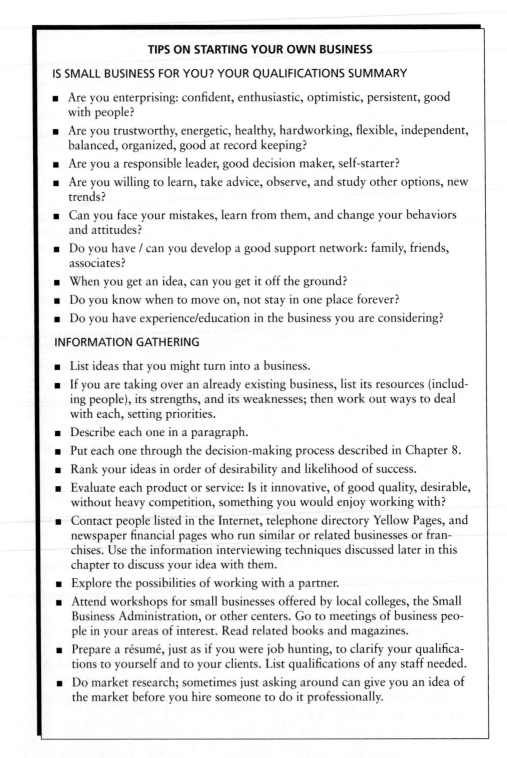

TIPS ON STARTING YOUR OWN BUSINESS

IS SMALL BUSINESS FOR YOU? YOUR QUALIFICATIONS SUMMARY

- Are you enterprising: confident, enthusiastic, optimistic, persistent, good with people?
- Are you trustworthy, energetic, healthy, hardworking, flexible, independent, balanced, organized, good at record keeping?
- Are you a responsible leader, good decision maker, self-starter?
- Are you willing to learn, take advice, observe, and study other options, new trends?
- Can you face your mistakes, learn from them, and change your behaviors and attitudes?
- Do you have / can you develop a good support network: family, friends, associates?
- When you get an idea, can you get it off the ground?
- Do you know when to move on, not stay in one place forever?
- Do you have experience/education in the business you are considering?

INFORMATION GATHERING

- List ideas that you might turn into a business.
- If you are taking over an already existing business, list its resources (including people), its strengths, and its weaknesses; then work out ways to deal with each, setting priorities.
- Describe each one in a paragraph.
- Put each one through the decision-making process described in Chapter 8.
- Rank your ideas in order of desirability and likelihood of success.
- Evaluate each product or service: Is it innovative, of good quality, desirable, without heavy competition, something you would enjoy working with?
- Contact people listed in the Internet, telephone directory Yellow Pages, and newspaper financial pages who run similar or related businesses or franchises. Use the information interviewing techniques discussed later in this chapter to discuss your idea with them.
- Explore the possibilities of working with a partner.
- Attend workshops for small businesses offered by local colleges, the Small Business Administration, or other centers. Go to meetings of business people in your areas of interest. Read related books and magazines.
- Prepare a résumé, just as if you were job hunting, to clarify your qualifications to yourself and to your clients. List qualifications of any staff needed.
- Do market research; sometimes just asking around can give you an idea of the market before you hire someone to do it professionally.

TIPS ON STARTING YOUR OWN BUSINESS *(continued)*

- Explore locations/types of spaces available and their cost. Consider sharing space, providing a service to a company in exchange for space; remodel a home space and telecommunicate with employees.
- Consider asking for help from people who later could become your advisory board.

FINANCIAL/LEGAL PLANNING

- Begin with a clear statement of purpose.
- Develop a sample product or prototype and find out whether people will buy it. Have people test it.
- Cost out possible expenditures: goods, services, equipment, insurance, real estate, advertising; develop a good accounting system.
- Find out about permits, licenses, and other documents you may need to get started. Taxes vary widely from state to state.
- Work out a financial plan as carefully as you would a résumé or term paper. Do a complete description of the business, estimate of cash flow, one-, two-, and five-year projections, your own financial assets and liabilities, the amount of money you need to "tide you over" until the business gets going.
- Talk to a knowledgeable financial planner about various funding options.
- Get to know your banker. Getting credit is one of the largest hurdles, especially for women!
- Develop a credit rating by repaying a small personal loan promptly.
- Look into loans from banks and private foundations; taxes, partnerships, stocks.
- Negotiate the terms of loans and other contracts and expenses; don't just accept the first suggestion.
- See a knowledgeable lawyer about various legal aspects of the business.
- Software is available that will "walk you through" the process of developing a business plan including those financial projections so loved by lenders.

Note that, like the founder of Togo's restaurant chain, some entrepreneurs break all the rules and end up as resounding successes!

The U.S. Small Business Administration Web site (**www.sba.gov**) lists information and local groups that provide assistance to budding entrepreneurs. Local chambers of commerce can be quite helpful. The Department of Transportation, Office of Small and Disadvantaged Business Utilization (**http://osdbuweb.dot.gov**) will also send information. The Additional

ADDITIONAL RESOURCES

The following are resources you may want to use for follow-up. This listing does not imply an endorsement. It is up to you to evaluate the data you find. For further information you might check this text and endnotes.

Business Ethics
http://www.business-ethics.com

Business Plan: Sample business plans
http://www.bplans.com

Co-op America: Information about cooperative organizations
http://www.coopamerica.com

Council of Better Business Bureaus, Inc.
http://www.bbb.org

Entrepreneurial Parent: Information about balancing work and life
http://www.en-parent.com

Find Law: Source of legal information
http://www.findlaw.com

Good Money: Information about 176 socially responsible companies
http://www.goodmoney.com

Green Pages Online: Directory of "green" businesses
http://www.greenpages.org

Home-Based Working Moms: Helps moms stay closer to their kids
http://www.hbwm.com

Hoover's Online: Business information
http://hbn.hoovers.com

Journal of Small Business Management
http://www.be.wvu.edu/serve/bureau/jsbm

Manual of Corporate Investigation: Document file for corporate analysis
http://134.68.115.97/organizeindiana/Documents/
Manual%20of%20Corporate%20Investigation.pdf

Nolo: Legal information, books, forms, and software
http://www.nolo.com

OMB Watch: Watching for government fiscal responsibility
http://www.ombwatch.org

Small Business Development Centers Information (SBA)
http://www.sba.gov/sbdc
(800)8ASK-SBA
8275-722

Union Label & Services Trades Department of the AFL-CIO: For union-friendly companies
http://www.unionlabel.org

U.S. Government Securities and Exchange Corporate Data Base (EDGAR)
http://www.sec.gov/edgar.shtml

Women's Bureau—Bureau of Labor Statistics
http://www.dol.gov/wb

World Franchising: Information about franchises
http://www.worldfranchising.com

Work-at-Home Moms: Site for jobs
http://www.wahm.com

Resources chart lists Web site addresses for follow-up information. Your library can refer you to organizations and publications that can guide you. Community colleges, chambers of commerce, and other local groups often run workshops for prospective and current small business owners. These free resources have been enough to get many businesses off the ground.

As a business starts growing, an owner has to decide whether to brave the world of venture capital. Experience, competence at what you have already accomplished, and a good adviser are usually essential before you go into the deep water of big business. A good beginning might include a microloan from a microlending organization, as described in Chapter 4. We can count on small businesses to continue creating more jobs than large corporations well into the twenty-first century, and much of that work is happening at home.

THIRD-WAVE PROSUMERS

When a truck driver with a college degree was asked what he intended to do with his education, he replied, "I will practice living, I will develop my intellect, which may incidentally contribute to the elevation of the esthetic and cultural levels of society. I will try to develop the noble and creative elements within me. I will contribute very little to the *grossness* of the national product."[35]

Some idealistic people prefer not to contribute to an economy they feel encourages the mindless consumption of goods, wastes energy and resources, and contributes to a poor quality of life. These nonconformists are carving out unique lifestyles. Do-it-yourself and self-help tasks, bartering, and sharing are all parts of their diverse lifestyle. The psychologist who helps people grow at the office may come home to a small farm and grow vegetables for self and sale. Veterinarian Richard Pitcairn's varied schedule at one time included part-time spaying of dogs and cats at an animal shelter, along with research, writing, and private consulting. He and his artist wife grew many of their own vegetables and repaired their own car. Their book, *Dr. Pitcairn's Complete Guide to Natural Health for Dogs and Cats,* reflects their caring lifestyle.[36] Families garden and raise chickens for eggs, bees for honey, and fruit for jam for barter and table. One artist bartered a stained glass window for dental work.

Bill Cane lives a frugal, solar-powered lifestyle, gardening and bartering many of his goods and services for others. He gives workshops and publishes a quarterly journal called *Integrities* four times a year. His small nonprofit supports projects in Latin American countries for women and men in need of support and development help. Cane wrote in his book, *Through Crisis to Freedom,* "In crisis, you are somehow enabled to get in touch with sources of life deep inside yourself—sources you never knew were there. And then mysteriously, like the blades of grass, you begin to know how to grow."[37]

These new "old" lifestyles aren't for everyone, but they are options in a nine-to-five world for those willing to take the risk. Many people lived these simpler lifestyles years ago. In the technological future, we may be able to do less work and enjoy more of life's good things.

NEW VIEWS

Most people, especially males, begin work after graduating from high school or college and keep at it until retirement. But even the most exciting of career fields can pall after many years, and workers must take steps to keep up their motivation. Going back to school, seeking a promotion, changing positions or companies, looking for a unique approach to your job, finding enriching hobbies, fostering personal growth on all levels are ways to keep up your work energy. Some industries such as Intel, Rolm, and Seagate have experimented with giving their employees leaves of absence for social action, educational projects, or pure recreation.

An engineer working in Silicon Valley found that his boss expected him to live a very upscale personal life. He was urged to trade in his ten-year-old Honda for a new BMW, and in general he was criticized for many of his lifestyle choices. He decided to let his wife carry them financially for a few years while he went back to school to earn a degree in spiritual theology. He is back with a new electronics company and a whole new perspective on life. By riding the train to work, he has time to read in his new field, and he does church work on weekends, to his great satisfaction.

As people explore alternatives, they create a variety of new workstyles. Many find they can make a living by working part time at several jobs. People who teach a course or two at community colleges may run their own businesses on the side, publish articles, or do graphics and some computer consulting. They may fish in the summer, teach skiing in the winter, and do a little farming and construction work in between. Some live very frugally, trading income for flexibility.

LEISURE STYLES

The suggestions offered earlier are aimed at helping you not only to find satisfying work but also to find time for satisfying leisure. Many people are opting for a less pressured, more serene life with less frantic activity. They start small home businesses that require only two or three days of work a week, retire early, take time off to be with children instead of trying to juggle work and child care. Busy people are asserting their need for daily meditation, exercise, or other forms of relaxation to help them get in touch with deeper values.

But most of us need *some* structure in our lives, even though we might like to think of ourselves as free spirits. Work is the basic organizing principle for most people; therefore planning and learning how to balance work and leisure so that both are enriching is a never-ending process. Too much work can consume us; too much free time can bore us. Too much materialism suffocates us; too little frightens us. Many people are continually trying to find the balance, but they are further ahead than those who don't even *know* their lives are out of balance.

When we look at basic needs and wants and compare them with the work that is being done, we may be tempted to say that *much of the work we do is not the work that needs to be done.* Aware people are evaluating their own work to see whether it not only meets their own needs, wants, and values but is socially responsible as well. After a certain point, they may wonder if the *money* is worth the *time.* They are often people with ideals, education, and skills who have some money behind them to aid in a unique transition. They find themselves working hard, often at jobs they themselves have designed, and doing work they feel benefits society. Leisure can enrich not only individuals but the planet as well.

COMMUNITY

A workplace is not an isolated entity. No matter how aloof it tries to stand, it is enmeshed in its community in innumerable ways. From farm to city, from ocean to mountains, from prairies to wetlands, the geography of a locale affects a major part of a worker's life and workstyle. The predominant products and services provided by the area—logs or jam, silicon chips or potato chips—certainly influence a place.

A workplace, whether it be a huge corporation in a small town or a small business in a big city, affects and in turn is affected by its location. The style of dress, housing, and transportation, the kinds of leisure activities, schools, social life, and economic achievement will vary slightly or greatly from one place to another.

We expect a good community to include elements that are equally to everyone's advantage such as affordable health care, effective public safety, peace among various groups, a just legal system, and an unpolluted environment.[38] In a speech, Senator Bill Bradley said,

> Civil society . . . is the sphere of our most basic humanity—the personal, everyday realm that is governed by values such as responsibility, trust, fraternity, solidarity, and love. . . . What both Democrats and Republicans fail to see is that government and the market are not enough to make a civilization.

There must also be a healthy, robust civic sector—a space in which the bonds of community can flourish.[39]

All over the country, communities are asserting their importance as unique places. Watsonville, California, salutes its large Hispanic population with festivals of dance and music and celebrates both its agricultural heritage and its scenic beauty.

In North Carolina, Mayland Community College teams up with Penland School of Crafts (one of the most prestigious in the country) to highlight and develop job training in local crafts. A collaboration of nonprofits works with government and business to create the Cultural Diversity project in Fargo, North Dakota, and neighboring Moorhead, Minnesota.[40] Logging companies and environmentalists get together to create agreements beneficial to the local community.

Many job seekers will choose a place that encourages the type of lifestyle they would like to lead. A person seeking a more sophisticated style may choose a Manhattan apartment and wear the latest fashions, whereas the Big Sur Coast of California is dotted with the tiny and isolated cabins of artists and writers in sweatshirts and jeans.

But beyond the physical level, people seek "community" that nourishes their emotional, intellectual, and spiritual needs. Just as in a company, a community has an unwritten psychological contract about how it treats its members and what it values. Many people will seek out a community for these qualities: It is a hospitable and human-scale place that does not force people to join in but provides opportunities for them to share experiences with like-minded people and to feel that each of them is valued and supported; it enables individuals to have a sense of belonging to a place and a say in what goes on there. It is, in short, a place where people can feel at home. Sometimes just the design of a place can make it easy for people to meet. The local post office or friendly coffee shop may draw people together, or an activity centered around religion, community service, sports, recreation, politics, theater, or music may provide opportunities to gather.

But some people value isolation whether they live in the forest or the busy streets of a large city. There is always a trade-off between privacy and community. Many new living styles are developing to give people the best of both worlds, shared housing and co-housing among them, where people have private spaces but may share some meals, child care, and recreational space with a community.

Former English professor and farmer-poet Wendell Barry sees the United States as Thomas Jefferson did—a collection of communities where people share more values than just economic ones. These include hard work, devotion, memory, and association. He questions what we mean by "progress" if it satisfies the loss of land and community.[41] Generally, the more a location is taken over by gigantic businesses and mammoth traffic systems, and the more people absorb themselves in technologies such as television and computers, the more difficult it is to find human-scale community.

Workplaces, too, are valued not only for the way they treat workers but also how they treat their local communities. Giving away tax breaks and other advantages to lure large companies may be a poor trade-off. These businesses usually require increases of infrastructure and services; they may leave when conditions look better elsewhere. Municipalities are finding that encouraging a vigorous turnover of small businesses "as needed" creates a lively, lucrative, though tumultuous economy. Workplaces are good neighbors when they use local people and resources as much as possible; spend profits locally; and enhance community life by positive participation, not depleting it by adding to its problems. When businesses serve the community by satisfying the basic needs of its members and fulfilling wants that really enrich them, including employment, the lives of all the residents improve.

THE INS AND OUTS OF WORKPLACES: DOING THE RESEARCH

You have been surveying various and important aspects of both traditional and nontraditional workplaces and workstyles of interest to you. *Now* it is time to collect specific information about workplaces you might consider. First, get a view from the outside in by reading about workplaces and eliminating those that don't match your needs and wants. The next step is the information interview: getting the inside story about careers and companies by talking to people on site.

How can you find out what services your community needs that you might provide? Imagine how much archaeologists of the year A.D. 10,000 will learn about us if they get a look at some of our old telephone Yellow Pages. Scanning the Yellow Pages is one of the best ways to survey not only the businesses in an area but also the lifestyles. These listings reveal surprising ideas for both employment and beginning businesses. Looking at the Yellow Pages from other geographic areas can also tell you about businesses that may work in your community. You can determine whether a town is somewhat affluent by the number of upscale restaurant ads you find and the types of car dealers who advertise. Rural places will advertise a great deal of farm equipment; Silicon Valley will have pages of electronics firms. Comparing old phone books with new ones will tell you what businesses have failed; for example, solar energy companies took a beating when government subsidies were withdrawn in the 1980s and the message went out that energy conservation was not a priority.

Talking to people who have similar businesses or who might order from you and showing your product to people who might buy it are some ways to test your idea. Look for "niche" markets, those small areas where there is a possibility for a product or service. Think of new businesses in your area that attract people, such as coffee or frozen yogurt shops with a flair.

Information about companies is available from many sources, which may also help you learn whether the claims a business makes are true. Most libraries have a business reference section; most librarians love to help people and take pride in knowing where to find data. Company unions, labor groups, environmental organizations, and consumer groups are other sources of information. Ask for an annual report and other literature from a company; notice who is on the board of directors and what their affiliations are; ask what legislation the company supports or has helped to get passed; attend a meeting of the company if these are open to the public. Business and professional journals in your field will provide a wealth of information. For further information, check the Additional Resources chart presented earlier in this chapter.

Professional organizations, a source of job leads, also hire personnel—for example, in public relations and finance. Look at chambers of commerce, Better Business Bureaus, real estate boards, and trade associations at the national, state, and local levels, not only for information but also for possible jobs.[42]

The U.S. Department of Labor (**www.dol.gov**) has general and statistical information on all aspects of the labor market in the United States for those doing research for themselves or their businesses. This agency also has regional offices. The U.S. Bureau of Industrial Economics has information on trends in various fields. Your local chamber of commerce can inform you about the businesses in your town. College career center libraries, placement offices, and state employment offices are often stocked with material about companies. Some companies have public relations departments that send information if you write or call.

Don't forget to use the Yellow Pages of your phone book, a gold mine of ideas because just about every business in your area is listed there according to what it does. If you read the business section of your local newspaper regularly, you will know who is doing what and where in the work world in your community.

You can access the Internet from the convenience of your home or from a computer in your local college or library to surf your way into a wealth of free information. Free business directories are available on some networks. The Department of Labor's Office of Safety and Health Administration (OSHA) (**www.osha.gov**) has computerized records of workplaces that have been cited for worker safety violations, listed by industry. Environmental impact statements and records of environmental violations are available from the federal Environmental Protection Agency (**www.epa.gov**). The financial reports (quarterly, annual, and others) that publicly traded companies are required to submit to the U.S. Securities and Exchange Commission (SEC) can be viewed online in the SEC's database called EDGAR (**www.sec.gov/edgar.shtml**). Information on local companies such as deeds and licenses are kept by city or county governments.

Reading about jobs can leave some pieces of the puzzle missing. Those descriptions are only the bare bones of the job. You can put flesh on those skeletons by visiting workplaces and interviewing people about what they do. From here on, it's important to be *out*—talking to everyone about his or her job, observing work environments, talking to people with inside information to share about places of interest to you.

Unless you are an experienced and sophisticated job seeker with a broad knowledge of jobs, you need to gather as much firsthand information as you can *before* you choose a career, and perhaps plan courses and get a degree. Some guides list "hot careers" with high salaries. On talking with people in the field, you may find there is more education and experience required than you care to take on or that openings are very scarce. Why not learn all you can before you commit to a career that could turn out to be different from your expectations? You can also eliminate misconceptions about the preparation you need to be hired.

INFORMATION INTERVIEWING

You probably have already done a great deal of information interviewing and didn't even realize it. How often have working friends given you a blow-by-blow description of life at Picky Products, Inc.? (Or how often have you gotten good information from friends about a class, or an instructor, for that matter.) If *you've* worked for a company (or taken a course), you have information about it that's not easily available to an outsider. You know the people who are likely to help beginners; you know how tough or easy the supervisors/teachers are, how interesting or boring the work is—what it's *really* like. Obtaining this inside information about a workplace answers two questions: Is this a job you would really like? Is this a place you would really like to work?

Don't be afraid to contact people who sound interesting. Ask them to tell you more about what they do or congratulate them on some accomplishment or promotion. People appreciate positive feedback. Let them know that you are sincerely interested in some aspect of their work or workplace.

If you feel timid about approaching a stranger, practice by interviewing people in your family, then a friend or neighbor about his or her job. Talk to all the people you meet about what they do and how they like it, and whom

PEANUTS reprinted by permission of United Features Syndicate, Inc.

they can introduce you to in your career field. Ask people you know for names of willing interviewees. It's amazing how you can usually find someone who knows someone who knows someone. Your school alumni office is often in touch with graduates in different fields. An instructor in a field of interest may know a person who will talk to you. Use professional society meetings, trade shows, business conferences, job fairs, and your local chamber of commerce as other venues in which to meet people in your areas of interest. Have them refer you on to the specific people whom you wish to meet. Seek someone close to the level at which you are applying. Don't ask to see the president of a company if you are searching out information about safety engineering. Rather, find a person who *is* a safety engineer or industrial technologist or technical supervisor.

Make an appointment ahead of time. Avoid calling during lunch hour, early mornings—especially Mondays, when everyone is getting organized— and late afternoons, especially Fridays, when people are getting ready to wrap up the day's or week's work. If you feel uncertain about going to an interview alone, ask a friend to introduce you, or ask someone with a mutual interest to go along. If it seems appropriate and you are comfortable with the idea, invite the person you will interview out for coffee or lunch after you visit the workplace.

Remember that any meeting, whether in person or over the telephone, is an interview situation and should be treated seriously for you to maximize its benefit. Making a positive impression is as important as getting the information you want. Each informational interview adds a potential new person to your network contacts list; gives another person, potentially someone who could hire you, a chance to evaluate you for employment; results in a source who can refer you to other individuals and companies; and offers an opportunity to refine your interviewing skills. Chapter 7 describes tips and techniques for effective interviewing and networking; brush up on them before you go on your first information interview.

Use the information interview sparingly, not casually. Wait until you have some idea of your direction. Then have carefully prepared questions you haven't been able to find answers to through your research. You want to encourage people to talk easily about their work. Most people are sincerely interested in helping information seekers, but sometimes they cannot spare the time. Don't feel discouraged if you are refused an interview.

Find out whether the company you are interested in (or one like it) gives tours. In some cases, you can spend a whole day observing someone doing a job you might like. Remember, when you talk with people in your career field of interest, you are gathering all their biases. Each person likes and dislikes certain things about the job. Each one will give you a different view. Keep your antennae out to receive the emotional content of the messages. Then weigh all these messages against your good feelings and reasoned judgment.

There are other ways to meet people in your field of interest besides visiting their workplaces. Many professional groups welcome students to their meetings and have special rates for student/lay participation; the Society of Women Engineers, for example, is one of these. The *Occupational Outlook Handbook* you used for your research in Chapter 4 lists names and addresses of such organizations. Throughout the United States, the American Society for Training and Development (**www.astd.com**) has chapters that hold monthly meetings and annual conventions. At such times you can meet people who have access to local business information and contacts. Chambers of commerce and other community organizations hold regular luncheons with speakers. In social settings like these, it's possible to make contacts easily and explore possibilities for on-site visits. Many of these organizations are also putting up Web sites faster than the click of a mouse. At workshops or classes in your career area of interest, speakers and participants can share information with you both formally and informally. Trade or business fairs can be a great way to see products and visit with people from a variety of companies in the same or related markets.

Much of your success will come from keeping your eyes and ears open. Begin to wonder what just about everyone you meet is doing. Almost every media news item is about what people are doing. Which activities attract you? How can you learn more about these activities? Keep on looking, listening, asking questions—it's your best source of information. Eventually you will be talking to people who are doing work you would like to do. Something will click as you begin to share experiences and enthusiasms. You will make a network of friends who may later wish to hire you.

One caution. Most people are happy to answer most questions about their jobs until you come to salary, but there are ways to get an idea of what you may expect. Here are some possible approaches: "What is the approximate salary *range* for a position like yours?" "How much might an entry-level person expect to earn in this area?" A call to a local or state employment office can also provide approximate salary levels.

At first, many people hesitate to call a stranger in a large company—or even an acquaintance in a small one. One student, whose talents were apparent to everyone but herself, was terrified at the prospect. She grimly made the first phone call. To her amazement, the interview was delightful—that is, until she was advised to explore a graduate program at a nearby university. She forced herself to see the department head that same day. Another warm reception. Elated, she rushed out to call her career counselor from the nearest phone booth. She was chuckling, "Here I am, thirty-five years old, and as excited as any kid over talking to two human beings!"

Another student given the same class assignment simply didn't do it. She had been a psychology major with a love for art; she changed to business because it seemed more "practical," although it didn't seem to fit her creative "people" needs. Then she discovered organizational development and talked about her interests to someone who knew a management consultant who used graphic arts in his work. Her reluctance to interview vanished as possibilities began to open up.

If you plan your information interviewing carefully, you may find a well-respected, experienced person who can listen to you, keep what you say confidential, and be a guide in finding other people to interview. This person may even become a mentor, someone who will give you tips not only on finding a job but also on advancing your career. Over time, your relationship may become so trustworthy that your mentor may give you constructive, perhaps painful, but helpful, critiques. You may have more than one such person; you may have someone in your company whom you feel comfortable with and can trust, a person who can help you develop a special skill; someone who can support you through tough times, even stand up for you if you are in the same company. With restructuring, companies have fewer managers, and employees have fewer opportunities to get help with their career development. A mentor can fill in, and a fulfilling relationship may result. Some companies are even setting up mentor programs. Mentors find, too, that they learn from those coming up behind them: new ways of doing things, new problems that arise that they never had to face. It is not just a one-way street.[43]

Perhaps not everyone you meet will be helpful. You may meet a "Queen Bee" or a "King Pin"—someone who has made it and is unwilling to help others. Sometimes people are absorbed in a complex problem, are truly too busy, or have yet to learn what all self-actualizing people know: the more you help others, the more successful you'll be. Many successful people enjoy sharing their expertise. So if you don't give up, you will find warmhearted people who understand your needs, your confusion, and you! Keep on searching for those who are sensitive to your concerns.

When people have spent time with you, follow up with thank-you notes. This courtesy will be appreciated and help employers to remember you when you begin the job hunt. Your informational interview is an opportunity for you to gain information and insight about a specific job, company, or industry. It is also an opportunity to gain a better understanding of the interviewer, who is making time in a busy schedule to accommodate you. Reciprocating the favor by asking during the interview what you can do to help the interviewer will add to the positive impression you make and may give you a chance to build a stronger relationship with that person. The information interview process puts you in the hiring network. It can be an adventure—and it can be very profitable.

The applicants best prepared for a job interview are those who not only know the company they want to work for but also have a broad knowledge of the work world, its people and challenges, and the ways they can help with options. Knowing some of the basics about a company, an industry, and its competition gives you confidence during the job hunt.

WORK EXPERIENCE

Work experience—even if you have to volunteer—is one of the best ways to get information. Try your school or state employment placement office for positions at different workplaces. Or sign up at a temporary employment agency with a good reputation so you can survey businesses, make contacts, and earn money on your own schedule. Once inside a company, you can get acquainted with people—the cafeteria can be a great meeting place—and watch the bulletin boards for job announcements.

Internships are sometimes available for students to do course research and cooperative work experience, sometimes with pay. These positions can last a day or two, a whole semester, or even a year. Although these sorts of activities give you the opportunity to survey companies, they also give employers a chance to get to know you. Such contacts may be valuable resources for you in the future.

With some actual work experience, a young person who loves animals may find working at the veterinarian's office exciting or, with sick animals and worried owners, traumatic. On the other hand, every job will gradually (or quickly) demonstrate some unpleasant aspects. Work is often hard work! You must function within the economic and time parameters of an organization or, if you are self-employed, meet clients' and society's demands. When both time and money are in short supply, deadlines and shortages create pressure.

As you become familiar with workplaces and as you make friends there, your confidence will grow. By the time you are ready for an interview, you will understand the job and some of its problems. You will know some of the

WORKPLACE TAKE-CHARGE GROUPS

These groups—each with a different focus—provide job leads and ideas and support for workplace owners and workers to cooperate to effect positive change. They encourage businesses to show greater fairness toward employees and customers. They show companies ways to improve their relationships with their physical environment and with their host communities. Contact those that interest you.

Center for Economic Conversion: Information about sustainable economics
  http://www.conversion.org

Environmental Research Foundation: Resources for environmental justice
  http://www.rachel.org

Good Money: Site for socially concerned investors
  http://www.goodmoney.com

Good Works: National directory of social change organizations
  http://goodworksfirst.org

Job Seeker: National environmental job site
  http://www.thejobseeker.net

Micro Credit Summit: Loans for poor entrepreneurs
  http://www.microcreditsummit.org

National Center for Employee Ownership: Provides information on employee stock ownership plans (ESOPs)
  http://www.nceo.org

New Road Map Foundation: Tools to master basic life challenges
  http://www.newroadmap.org

New Ways to Work: Prepares young people for the world of work
  http://www.nww.org

North American Students of Cooperation: Co-op education resources
  http://www.umich.edu/~nasco

---

latest techniques in your trade or profession. You will know people in the field who may recommend or even hire you. Many people find out about job openings not yet listed simply by asking everyone they know for information about future possibilities. And with your newfound self-confidence, that first job interview will be duck soup—not sitting duck! You will be ready to hire an employer.

SUMMARY

The working world offers many opportunities, from full-time or part-time employment working for a company or business; being self-employed working as an independent contractor; or being an entrepreneur starting a new business, buying an existing business, franchise, or a co-op. Determining the characteristics you want in an ideal workplace (location, office, manager, coworkers, and so on) is important to help focus your search toward the best career, industry, company, and job.

Starting a business, although often difficult, can be very rewarding. Conducting extensive research to determine if your temperament is suited for the demands of a start-up and completing the necessary business analyses and plans to ensure the operation's viability are vital factors for success. There are federal, state, and local resources to help you research or start your business and a variety of information sources available at libraries, in career centers, and on the Internet.

Talking with people already in the business or industry you like, through informational interviews, is one of the best ways to gather firsthand information about what can be expected if you should pursue similar employment. Not only do you get a chance to build a network of people in the industry whom you can contact when actually looking for employment, you can polish your interviewing skills. You can seek opportunities to try out potential jobs or careers by volunteering or through an internship.

◎ SELF-ASSESSMENT EXERCISES

The following exercises will help you decide what kinds of workstyles you prefer and will then help you locate those that match your preferences.

1. Identifying Alternative Workstyles

Choose one (or several that go together) of these alternative workstyles that interest you most and tell how you would (or would not) like to live it out: entrepreneur, intrapreneur, contract work, telecommuter/worksteader, career creator, third-wave prosumer.

_____

_____

2. Finding Interesting Careers

Name three people you know who are in interesting careers, in order of importance to you. Include the job title of each person.

_____   _____

_____   _____

_____   _____

Describe the characteristics you like of the most interesting of these careers.

_____

Describe the characteristics you dislike.

_____

3. Locating Contacts

List three businesses in your field of interest from the phone book Yellow Pages.

_____

_____

_____

4. Researching Workplaces

Using library/computer resources as much as possible, research one workplace in your career area. Use the information interview to ask for answers this research does not provide.

Name of workplace _____ Phone number _____

Address _____ City/State/Zip _____

Organization

Divisions and locations _____

_____

_____

Products/services _____

Number of employees _____ Job titles of interest to you _____

_____

Performance

Past and present market _____

_____

Company earnings as of past year _____

Future projections for growth and profit _____

Stability _____

Competitors _____

Other factors

Reputation/integrity _____

Environmental record _____

Social concern _____

5. Information Interview

Interview workers in a career field that interests you. Write the results of one such interview either here or on a separate sheet of paper.

_____

Name of person   Company name

_____

Job title   Address

_____

Phone number   City/State/Zip

Here are some questions you might ask.

a. Why did you choose this field?

_____

_____

b. How did you get your job?

_____

_____

c. What do you really do all day?

_____

_____

d. If you could redesign your job, which parts would you keep? Which would you get rid of?

_____

_____

e. What were your most positive career decisions?

_____

_____

f. If you had it to do all over again, what would you do differently in your career? Are there any decisions you regret?

_____

_____

_____

g. What are the major issues in your career field? The important books, journals, organizations?

_____

_____

_____

h. What is the entry-level job title and its salary range?

_____

i. What steps would a typical career ladder have? About how long would it take to move through each step, and what would each one involve—for example, job duties, salary?

_____

_____

_____

j. How available are jobs in this field expected to be in the future?

_____

k. What are the requirements for the job: training, certificates, licenses, degrees, tools, union membership?

_____

l. Will your company have openings in this field soon? _____ Yes _____ No

m. Could you recommend someone else I might interview?

Name of person	Company name
Job title	Address
Phone number	City/State/Zip

5. Workplace Checklist

Using both the library/Internet and the information interview for information, rate one workplace of interest to you on the following checklist.

Put a "+" in front of the ten qualities that are of most interest to you.

Company name _____   Phone number _____

Address _____   City/State/Zip _____

Management Characteristics

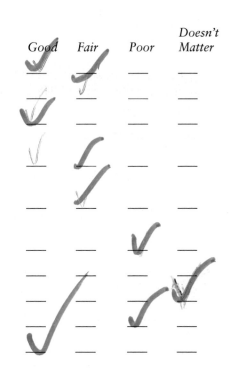

	Good	Fair	Poor	Doesn't Matter
_____ Honest/fair/ethical				
_____ Respectful of you as a person				
_____ Gives helpful performance feedback				
_____ Shows appreciation for good work				
_____ Open about the status of the company				
_____ Willing to answer questions				
_____ Cooperative				
_____ Sets clear goals				
_____ Stable management style				
_____ Makes positive contribution to locale				

	Good	Fair	Poor	Doesn't Matter
Makes workers feel proud of its goals	✓			
Is open to innovation		✓		
Flexible		✓		
Promotes job security		✓		
Adequate preparation for layoffs			✓	
Encourages teamwork			✓	
Mentors or coaches		✓		
Actively listens	✓			

Use of Skills/Interests

	Good	Fair	Poor	Doesn't Matter
Respects/encourages autonomy/ideas	✓			
Provides varied experience		✓		
Acknowledges achievements	✓		✓	
Is open to transfers/promotions		✓	✓	
Offers education/growth opportunities		✓		
Provides training/development		✓		

Work Environment

	Good	Fair	Poor	Doesn't Matter
Location/setting		✓		
Appearance of buildings	✓			
Work stations	✓			
Cafeteria			✓	
Restrooms		✓		
Colors	✓	✓		
Light		✓		

	Good	Fair	Poor	Doesn't Matter
_____ Furnishings/equipment	✔	___	___	___
_____ Safe/environmentally conscious	___	✔	___	___
_____ Compatible coworkers	___	✔	___	___
_____ Friendliness	✔	___	___	___
_____ Orderliness	___	___	✔	___

Salary/Benefits

	Good	Fair	Poor	Doesn't Matter
_____ Salary	✔	___	___	___
_____ Medical/dental/vision care	✔	___	___	✔
_____ Life/disability insurance	___	___	___	✔
_____ Profit sharing	✔	✔	___	___
_____ Retirement benefits	___	✔	___	___
_____ Vacations/holidays	___	✔	___	___
_____ Maternity/paternity leaves	✔	___	___	___
_____ Child care	___	✔	___	___
_____ "Business of living" personal time	___	___	✔	___
_____ Travel benefits	___	___	✔	___
_____ Compensation in case of layoff	✔	___	✔	___
_____ Fitness facilities	___	___	✔	___
_____ Flexible schedules	✔	✔	___	___
_____ Moving/travel expenses	___	✔	___	___

Financial Stability

	Good	Fair	Poor	Doesn't Matter
_____ Sales prospering	✔	___	___	✔
_____ No likely takeovers	___	✔	___	✔
_____ Manageable debt	___	✔	✔	___
_____ Positive cash flow	___	___	✔	___

	Good	Fair	Poor	Doesn't Matter
_____ Special product or service	✓	__	__	__
_____ Little serious competition	__	✓	✓	__
_____ Shows foresight and plans ahead	__	✓	__	__

The Community

	Good	Fair	Poor	Doesn't Matter
_____ Recreational/cultural facilities	__	✓	__	__
_____ Medical/dental facilities	✓	__	__	__
_____ Acceptable schools	✓	__	__	__
_____ Good transportation	✓	__	✓	__
_____ Reasonable cost of living	✓	__	✓	__
_____ Other amenities	__	__	✓	__
_____ Benefits to the community	__	__	__	✓

c. Complete this statement: I would (or would not) like to work there because _of benefits and enjoying a work environment that is in my element_

d. What other questions might you like to ask a person you interview? _What hobbies they have._

 GROUP DISCUSSION QUESTIONS

1. Describe in detail an alternative workstyle you might enjoy and why.
2. Describe a business you might like to own and why.
3. Share any insights you gained from the information interviewing process.
4. Ask for career information from members of your study group. Trade resources and contacts for information interviewing.
5. Explain the following quote and give examples: "Much of the work we do is not the work that needs to be done."

7

The Job Hunt

Tools for Breaking and Entering

 **GOALS**

- Develop job search objectives, strategies, and tactics.

- Find hiring managers and discover what makes them tick.

- Create and use a job search network effectively.

- Manage job recruiters and agencies.

- Respond to job ads carefully.

- Design and craft an effective résumé and cover letter.

- Generate job and personal references.

- Complete a job application.

- Master the interview.

- Close the deal.

- Navigate electronic communications and the Internet.

You have assessed your needs, wants, values, and interests. You have envisioned your ideal lifestyle. You have researched your skills thoroughly. You have collected many words to describe yourself. You have looked over the job market and found jobs that will suit you well. You have reflected on many societal issues that will affect your life and your work. You have interviewed people, researched companies, and explored workplaces. You have considered the job versus career issue, the career ladder, possibilities for future goals, creative careers, and owning your own business. You have zeroed in on a job title or two and some companies where you have contacts. In short, if you need no further training or education, you may be ready at last for the job hunt!

You will find that your best strategy is actively to drive the job hunting process, to seek out and make opportunities within organizations. In doing so, you probably will approach companies and talk with prospective employers who may not have an open requisition for the job you want, who may have an opening for something completely different, or who may have no job openings at all. It will be incumbent on you to convince these potential employers that you are a valuable asset. This style of job hunting mandates an aggressive and proactive approach.

It is also possible that you have not completed some of these initial steps. If your job hunt is several years down the road, you may be tempted to wait to learn the process. However, putting it off might leave you unprepared if a great job opportunity should arise or if your current position should disappear. Being prepared puts you steps ahead. And learning the process can sometimes facilitate decision making because it helps you focus on what a job will require of you. However you use this chapter, reviewing it just before you go out to job hunt can enhance your chances for success.

> I am rather
> like a mosquito in a nudist camp;
> I know what I ought to do,
> but I don't know where to begin.
> —*Stephen Bayne*

DEVELOP JOB SEARCH OBJECTIVES, STRATEGIES, AND TACTICS

Job hunting is full-time work. It can be hard work, whether you are hunting for full-time, part-time, or temporary employment. What will be your overall strategy, and what tactics will you employ to get your job? How are you going to manage the job-hunt process and not let it manage you? Effective planning and organization are necessary tactics that will help you navigate the many activities you will be doing concurrently to reach your new job.

A job search can take a day, six months, or a year, and it can certainly take longer during depressed economic times or if there is a glut of people with your skill set. A key determinant in how long your job search will take is how quickly you can get interviews. The sooner you can meet with a hiring manager, the closer you will be to having a job. The time it takes to get a job will depend entirely on you and your motivation, planning, persistence, and stamina.

Identifying and meeting the people who can actually hire you should be your paramount objective. First, identify one or more hiring managers in your target companies. Next, contact the hiring managers and secure an interview, preferably one in person. Today, multiple pre-hire interviews with different people, including your potential coworkers, are common. After you participate in one or more interviews, if everyone concurs that you are a "good fit" to the group and have the appropriate talents and skills for the position, you may be offered a job. Last, work with the hiring manager to secure the job offer, finalize its details to your mutual satisfaction, and accept the job. You can breath a sigh of relief, for this job search is over, but the process will undoubtedly be repeated as your career needs and wants change, with you regularly moving to enhance your career development and satisfaction.

For you to develop the strategies and tactics that are right for you, it is important that you know something about different sources for jobs. Most people typically think of pursuing the want ads in the newspaper, sifting through ads placed on a company's Web site, or just sending a résumé to an online job listing as the best way to find the job of their dreams. Sometimes they get lucky, most often not. Another source is recruiters, commonly referred to as "headhunters," or employment agencies that find a job for you, with them acting like your personal talent agent. Sometimes people elect to go into government service positions, like the military or civil service, where the career paths are clear. Some opt to become self-employed and make their own destinies. Another, and by far the most effective way to find your ideal job, is through what is called the "hidden job market." This is an ever-expanding network of people you interact with to discover job opportunities, hiring managers, and new directions to take in your search, all moving you closer to your dream job. Using this source for employment puts the responsibility and onus on you to research companies and people, network effectively with others, diligently follow up leads, and seek out employment opportunities that may not openly exist.

Government and university studies have shown the following distribution for all jobs found: about 75 percent through the hidden job market, about 10 percent through newspaper ads, about 10 percent through recruiters and agencies, and the remaining 5 percent through civil service, self-employment, and the like. Further, about 40 percent of the jobs found in the hidden job market are created for the individual[1,2]! What this means is that your best efforts and time should be devoted to exploring and using the hidden job market. Your competition will be minimal or nonexistent relative to the large number of job seekers who respond to newspaper or Web site ads and who use recruiters and agencies, and your likelihood of getting the ideal job rather than settling for something less will be improved. The only catch to navigating successfully through the hidden job market is that you must be diligent, proactive, and persistent.

The best strategy and tactics to use will be tailored to your specific situation. The most important goal in your strategy, which should temper your activities, is always to remember that effective job hunting is about building good relationships through telephone calls, face-to-face meetings, interviews, networking, correspondence, and the Internet. You can never have enough friends or know enough people to contact. Even the most remote contact could leverage you into meeting the right person who could offer you your dream job. The cliché is often true: "It is not what you know, it is who you know." It may seem unfair, but ultimately, a clear and purposeful approach will win out over an unfocused and lackadaisical one. It is up to you to take every advantage that you can to win the job. Keeping your wits about you and keeping up your courage are essential skills to use in your tactical plans for managing your job-hunt relationships.

A vital component of being able to create, maintain, and grow good networks or to be successful in human interactions is to have good manners and be able to project and manage the image you wish others to have of you. Written to help people dress effectively, which is certainly applicable for job seekers, John Molloy's classic book, *New Dress for Success,*[3] reinforces the adage that you never get a second chance to make a good first impression. You have the power to develop and project the image you wish to convey to others. Because you will be meeting many people, asking for their time, and depending upon their assistance, you should constantly strive to have people perceive you as being positive, pleasant, and nice. *Please, Thank you,* and *You're welcome* are good words to have in your vocabulary, whether you say them or write them. A businesslike, polite phone style is a plus, and be sure the message that greets callers on your answering machine reflects this same politeness. Shaking hands firmly, making friendly eye contact, climbing in and out of a car smoothly—all the things you've been doing forever—can quickly come undone in a stressful situation, so practice these behaviors consciously to be sure you perform them automatically, even at difficult times. Good table manners will make the right impression if you find yourself invited to coffee or a meal. Waiting until others are seated before you sit down, seeing that they are served before you begin gobbling the first course, and handling your knife and fork with confidence will put you on the right track. Some colleges now offer courses on manners. If you feel shaky and need some review, look around your area for workshops teaching good manners or check your library for a basic book on etiquette.

If you are already employed, you may want to consider your strategy for bridging the gap between your old job and your new one. Will your present employer be unhappy if he or she finds out you are job hunting? Will that make your current situation uncomfortable? If you have a good relationship with your employer, would it be better for you to share the news that you *are* looking for a new position and ask for a good recommendation, for support, and leads? If you wish to keep your job hunting to yourself, you must be sure that prospective employers do not leave messages for you at work. If you quit without having a new job lined up, will you have enough money to live on for the weeks or months it may take to land another position?

Your plan of activity is important, because you must wisely allocate your time to those things that move you closer to landing the job. You must overcome and manage continually the following tasks: identify people who can hire you, secure an interview with them, convince them that you are the best person for the job, get a job offer, finalize the offer, and accept the job. A piece of cake, right?

Following are some Web sites that are great stepping-off points for you in your job hunt and provide information and links to other sites.

The Riley Guide (**www.rileyguide.com**) is dynamic and regularly up-dated as its manager identifies and incorporates new, relevant information. With its multitude of links, it is a gateway to job and career data that will keep your interest for a long time.

Quintessential Careers (**www.quintcareers.com**) is a commercial site that can give the Riley Guide a good run for its money, with plenty of links and information.

Job-hunt.org (**www.job-hunt.org**) is another comprehensive site offering career and job-related advice, articles, and links to more than 8,000 other relevant sites. You will find its Getting Started section invaluable, especially the job search information and advice tips.

America's CAREERInfoNet (**www.acinet.org/acinet/default.asp**) is a commercial site that provides a comprehensive list of 5,000 links to relevant job and career-related sites, more than 300 video clips describing a wide range of jobs, numerous articles on career and job hunting topics, and job posting and listing services.

The University of Waterloo in Ontario, Canada, presents a very helpful and enlightening electronic manual on career development (**www.cdm .uwaterloo.ca**).

A great general site that is targeted for college graduates and new entrants to the work force is sponsored by the National Association of Colleges and Employers (**www.jobweb.com/catapult**).

Hiring Managers

You must understand how hiring managers think and behave so that your approach and interactions ensure the best possible outcomes for you. Hiring managers are typically juggling a myriad of tasks, like solving problems, wrestling with interpersonal issues among employees, responding to deadlines and demands from upper management, and hammering out agreements with other departments. As a hiring manager, given all of these demands, what would you want in a new employee? What would you be thinking about when interviewing a potential new team member? As you identify with, communicate with, and meet with hiring managers, remember that they are looking, either consciously or unconsciously, at each potential candidate while seeking answers to four key questions, whether candidates are being evaluated by résumé, e-mail, correspondence, telephone call, interview, or reference check.

1. *What can you do to make me rich?* Hiring managers are looking for new employees who can either bring new revenues into the company or find ways to save the company money. Being a salesperson is an obvious example of the former, but developing a new time-saving form for use in the office or finding a way to help people learn something faster and easier exemplify the latter. Hiring managers in for-profit corporations, nonprofit companies, or educational institutions will prefer candidates whose talents can benefit the organization by making money, saving money, decreasing costs, improving efficiencies, or saving time.
2. *What can you do to make me a hero?* Managers want to advance, make more money, and "look good" to higher-level managers in the company. Anything you as a new employee in the department can do to make your manager look good will make you an attractive candidate.
3. *What can you do to make my problems go away?* There are always problems to solve in any organization. Identifying and successfully resolving problems, especially under your own initiative, is an asset you should bring to the organization.
4. *Do I like you?* Would you want to work eight to twelve hours a day with a brilliantly competent person whose personality grated on you like fingernails scratching across a blackboard, or would you prefer someone who may be only competent but is likable and easy to get along with? The answer may seem unfair, yet it is part of human nature. We want to be around and work with people we like. Managers are no different.

Projecting positive answers to any or all of these questions will get you interviews, advance your standing against any competition you may have, and ultimately help you win the job.

Hey, Eric. I think I've found our new VP of Marketing.

NETWORKING

Networking means using all of your contacts to get hired. People are net-working when they shake hands and exchange business cards. People talk business everywhere, including the business of sharing job opportunities—in hallways, over coffee, on the golf course. These casual conversations may sound trivial, but they strengthen the links in the network.

Networking is *not* the same as information interviewing, although the two use similar techniques. When you do information interviewing, you are simply asking for information about careers and companies. But networking implies that you are using various contacts, including those acquired while information hunting, to find out about job openings. Networking requires patience. Job openings are often only in the minds of the people who may be thinking of retiring or moving out or over. Delays are commonplace. The company could be reorganizing. Managers could be feuding or be new on the job or both. Consultant Martha Stoodley, author of *Interviewing: What It Is and How to Use It*, reminds us that "companies are run by human beings who are trying to juggle their professional challenges and personal lives."[4]

Where do you stand in the networking game? How often have you or people you know heard about a job opening from a friend? Suppose you want to hire someone to take care of a child or ailing parent, fix your car, clean your house. No doubt you would feel safer asking for a referral from a friend. Employers feel better, too, when they hire someone they know or someone recommended by a trusted friend or colleague.

If you have already done information interviewing, you have a good start on networking. Use the same process and the same contacts to find out about job openings and how to approach a given workplace. These insiders can offer you the inside story as well as moral support. And one contact can lead to another. Successful job hunter Mel Fuller says, "Believe the statistic that 70 percent of people are hired by word-of-mouth." He urged people to talk to their relatives, neighbors, friends, clergy, business contacts such as bankers, stockbrokers, insurance agents, doctors, and dentists—in short, anyone who knows you. Go to association meetings, job fairs, and trade shows. But then target a few people who can and will help you specifically. Prepare for meeting them by knowing key points about them, even their leisure activities, as an icebreaker. And schedule follow-up meetings.

Even if you haven't developed a network of personal contacts, call on as many companies (or clients) as you can and apply for possible openings. Plan a schedule: exercise, eat well, get plenty of rest, and talk to as many positive people as you can. In a tight job market it's important to keep up your courage. Remember that rejections are part of the game; they do not mean you are unacceptable. Chances are you are just one of many good candidates. Later, the company you are interested in may offer you a different job from the one you had in mind. If the business is a good one, you may be smart to take the alternate job; this will get you inside the company, where changes in position are more easily arranged.

There are some important things to remember when developing a successful network:

1. Always be prepared. You never know where you may be and under what circumstances you will encounter someone who can provide wonderful news, ideas, suggestions, or references to help you meet a hiring manager. You should have clear in your mind what you want to say and do when you meet networking contacts. So, in a chance encounter when someone asks you what kind of job you are looking for, you need to be able to describe what you want. If you cannot clearly articulate what it is that you want, then it will be hard for people to help you.
2. Try to make it as easy as possible for your contact to help you. You will be amazed how helpful people, even strangers, will be to you if you can tell them what you need. Ask for their advice, and do it in a friendly, non-threatening manner. You may find that engaging in small talk before prob-

ing for job-related information is a better strategy for interacting with one person, whereas being direct and to the point may work best for someone else. People love to be asked for their opinions, advice, and/or recommendations. Using these words in a question—"What advice can you give me about finding a job doing . . ."—will help elicit responses from almost anyone.

3. The more descriptive and explicit you can be about what you want or what help you need, the easier it will be for people to help you. Providing some background information can help your contacts direct you appropriately. A job title may help crystallize what you are trying to convey rather than a list of job functions.

4. Have your "elevator speech," your 30-second-or-less practiced response to questions like, "What do you do?" or "What kind of job are you looking for?" ready to go, and tailor it to the situation you are in when delivering it. When you meet and are talking with one or more people and the conversation gets around to you, telling them succinctly what you want can move the subsequent conversations to topics that benefit you. Be prepared to meet and talk with people via the Internet. Written messages do not typically have the same impact nor the ease and quickness of communication of a personal meeting, but they do provide a valid way to network.

5. Always keep control of the networking process. If someone says that he or she will contact the boss on your behalf and will get back to you in the future, politely confirm when you can expect a call back or when it would be convenient for you to follow up. Your contacts will have good intentions of helping you, but they may fall prey to their own work and family responsibilities.

6. Be prepared to help others. It is always good to ask what you can do to help the people in your network and follow up diligently when told to ensure fair exchange. Your gesture of help can score you additional points and motivate the people in your network to want to help you further. Giving people in your network feedback on your progress can stimulate them to provide additional information or give them an opportunity to help you overcome a roadblock to your progress on a path they suggested. Often, just thanking them is sufficient.

Seeing everyone you meet or know as a possible source of help can make your networking efforts more fruitful. Three questions need to be answered by everyone you meet.

1. *Could you be my boss?* Find out if the acquaintance or stranger with whom you are speaking could be the person in a position to hire you. If the answer appears to be Yes, then you are in a job interview, even if you happen to bump into this person in an elevator, a restaurant, or on a sidewalk at a traffic light.

2. *Do you know my boss?* Now you are relying on your contact to provide potential hiring manager contacts based on his or her knowledge of what you want and have explained. Your networking contact may refer you to other managers within his or her organization or to other managers in different companies. It may be that the next-door neighbor of your contact is a manager in an organization you would love to work in. If this avenue of questioning is unproductive, then it is time for the last question.

3 *Do you know where my boss may be?* This invites your contact to provide leads, whether specific people, companies, magazine articles, or industries that may benefit you. Getting an answer to this and the other two questions can provide you with valuable data that will replenish your "To Do" list and keep you progressing forward.

There are so many venues in which to network that it seems like you are limited only by your imagination. It is best to start with people you know and expand from there. Colleges and universities have career centers to provide students and alumni with a wealth of career-related assistance and information; some even offer courses on career management. Networking through your alumni association can provide great contacts and help renew college friendships. Cities hold job fairs where many employers are accessible in one location to answer your questions and review your résumé. Sometimes companies host their own job fairs, so check local media services routinely for a calendar of upcoming events. Trade shows and industry conferences can yield a plethora of wonderful contacts from the companies present and the attendees. You may even land an interview on the spot, so be prepared. Casual small talk with conference attendees can give you new leads to follow. Professional organizations have formal and informal networking activities for members. If you are a member of an organization and have not attended a meeting in a long time, go. Find relevant organizations to join or attend the sessions they have open to the public.

States have employment departments or divisions to provide a variety of job- and career-related programs and information from fundamentals of job hunting to support groups for networking. California, for example, has the state Employment Development Department (EDD), which hosts a wealth of local service groups: PROMatch, PRONet, and One-Stop-Career Center, chartered with training job seekers in workshops on résumé writing, networking, and interviewing, or hosting job support groups where members meet weekly. A local organization, the NOrth VAlley Job Training Consortium (NOVA, **www.novaworks.org**) provides career-related services for people in Silicon Valley. Some people find these work groups invaluable for emotional support, inspiration, and coaching throughout the job search. Researching federal, state, and local government career support services via the Internet is a fast and efficient way to link up with people motivated to help you succeed in your area. Regardless of which venues you choose to explore, be sure to take sufficient copies of your résumé with you to hand out when needed.

Networking can be a little scary and intimidating, especially for those people who are shy about meeting new people. It takes active, continued persistence on your part to make your networking efforts successful. And always, friends and family can be sources of ideas and emotional support if and when the going gets tough, to bolster your confidence so you can jump into the networking arena again reinvigorated.

MIT's Web site (**web.mit.edu/career/www/workshops/networking /whatis_networking.htm**) provides articles and tips on how to start, run, and profit from your network.

The web site **www.tradeshowweek.com** is a source for trade show and expos around the country.

The Web site **www.brassring.com/EN/ASP/CIM/br_home.asp** is a typical commercial site that offers job postings and listings, and it also provides an index for upcoming career fairs and shows.

The Web site **www.utahbizlist.com/bizlist.html** contains hundreds of links to major businesses and companies throughout the United States.

Links to each state's employment and labor statistics can be found at **www.acinet.org/acinet/library.asp?category=1.6**.

Job Recruiters and Agencies

Recruiters provide a valuable service to job seekers. *Retained recruiters* are paid a fixed fee by a company to find qualified candidates; *contingency-based recruiters* are paid a percentage of the first year's compensation of people hired by the company. Retained recruiters are usually hired to fill upper-level managerial or senior technical positions within a company. Contingency-based recruiters usually fill lower-level positions. Either kind of recruiter will specialize in certain kinds of searches; for example, management-level employees for the pharmaceutical industry or computer programmers across many industries. John Lucht's book, *Rites of Passage at $100,000+*,[5] provides a good reference on how to understand and use recruiters successfully. Don't let the title of the book intimidate you; the information presented is relevant for everyone hunting for a job.

Since recruiters are paid by the company looking to fill a position, they will be more motivated to satisfy the desires of the company than to satisfy you. Hence, you should be cautious when using a recruiter, since their goals may be different from yours.

1. If you are right out of college, a recruiter may take you as a client, especially if you have a degree in a "hot" discipline like computer programming or chip design. Otherwise, the recruiter may have no interest in you. Obviously, people with a work history, especially ones who have gained

progressive experience toward a successful career, are more attractive as candidates for recruiters.

2. The recruiter will interview you, usually over the telephone, review your résumé, and if acceptable, will present you to the company. The recruiter will not divulge the company to you for fear that you may go directly to the company, bypassing the recruiter and eliminating the fee that would be paid, which ranges between 15 and 40 percent of your salary for the first year. Thus, you come to the company at a premium if you are hired using a contingency recruiter. Will you be worth the extra percentage cost the company will have to pay to hire you versus its finding a candidate who applies without a recruiter? This is why finding the company on your own rather than using a recruiter is an advantage for you.

3. Recruiters are typically looking for specific kinds of candidates. If you do not fit the profile for their search, they will quickly tell you to look else-where and may not even bother taking your résumé. Contingency-based recruiters will take your résumé and file it in their database if they have no clients looking for someone like you. You may or may not hear back from them, or you may hear from one of their colleagues if he or she has a client looking for someone like you.

4. Most recruiters are honest and ethical. However, when you give a recruiter your résumé, you will have no guarantee that he or she will not distribute it to every potential employer. You should care about this, because if you later go to a company where the recruiter sent your résumé and you get hired, the recruiter may claim a finder's fee for you, thus putting you and the company in an awkward position. You are wise to make an arrange-ment with the recruiter to secure your permission for each company to which he or she wants to send your résumé. This will keep you in control of your job search.

5. The recruiter is motivated to "sell" you on the job and the company, even if one or both are not exactly to your liking. Thus, you may be enticed to settle for something that you do not really want.

6. If you reject more than a couple of job offerings the recruiter finds for you, you will be dropped as a client. Recruiters want to "sell" you as quickly as possible.

7. The recruiter may tell you to sit back and wait while he or she finds you a job. Don't do it; always keep looking and following your plans.

The commercial Web site **www.recruitersonline.com** contains a search engine to find recruiters specializing in your field and corresponding links, along with job listing and job posting services.

There are many local and international employment agencies that match skilled people with employers, from entry-level jobs up to CEO positions. These agencies are contracted to supply workers to client companies. The workers are employees of the agency and not of the client company. Job assignments are temporary, depending on the nature of the work and the duration of contract. Agencies will interview you to determine if your skills and background match the client companies' needs. If there is a match, you are sent to the client company to work or to be interviewed before starting to work. If your performance is acceptable, you stay until your assignment is complete. The client company pays the agency for your work, and you are paid by the agency.

Adecco (**www.adecco.com/Channels/adecco/home/home1.asp**) is one of the world's largest employment agencies.

Robert Half (**www.roberthalf.com**) specializes in accounting and finance-related placements.

Kelly Services (**www.kellyservices.com/kcn/jobsearch/jobsearch.asp**) caters to a broad spectrum of clients needing workers from many different career areas.

Certain kinds of firms will charge you a fee, sometimes thousands of dollars, to introduce you to prospective companies that may hire you. They may help write or revise your résumé, print it, send it out, coach you on interviewing techniques, and provide other job search services. It is usually people who become desperate in their job search that buy the services from these organizations. You should try to avoid these companies and, instead, invest the money in your own networking and job search efforts.

Job Ads

When you respond to a newspaper ad or an ad on a company's Web site, your response will most likely go to someone in the human resources department who is charged with screening potential applicants, selecting the best of the résumés submitted, and forwarding them to the hiring manager for further consideration. Companies receive hundreds or thousands of unsolicited résumés monthly (especially popular companies or during difficult economic times) in addition to those sent in for the specific jobs advertised. The chance of your résumé being selected is inversely related to the number of résumés received. You may be screened out of the job you want, depending on the competition you face, how rushed the people in human resources are, or because you don't have enough key words in your résumé to match on a computer search. Your challenge is to avoid the traps within the company that screen your résumé out and send your résumé directly to the hiring manager.

Responding to solicitations for jobs when the name of the company is not listed should be avoided, because you do not know who will receive your résumé or what are the intentions of that company or its hiring manager. If the company is named in the ad and the department the job is in is obvious, you can call the company and ask the operator for the name of the department's manager, or call randomly within the company to reach someone who can help you. You will be pleasantly surprised how much information and help people within the company can provide. Not everyone will be cooperative; just keep calling until someone is. This same tactic is useful researching companies where the department for the job is not apparent. For newspaper ads that list only a post office box, you can call the post office and ask for the name of the company that rents that box. If you cannot determine the company from an online job posting—usually on recruiter or some large posting Web sites—you may want to avoid posting your résumé there and explore other avenues, less dependent on luck, to keep you in control of the job hunt process and your private information.

The Web site **www.usnpl.com** links you with most major newspapers in the United States where you can investigate the want ads for jobs of interest from the comfort of your computer.

Networking is not meant to give less-qualified people an unfair advantage over others, although it sometimes does. It can help you access the job market, but be aware that employers are required to follow legal hiring practices. They must advertise widely and screen an adequate number of applicants. This procedure gives as many people as possible a fair chance at the job and helps employers hire the best-qualified person. Some companies and government agencies have helpful material available about their hiring processes. Some will try to ensure that the help they give is available to all prospective employees. And some employers will simply be equally "unavailable" to all!

THE RÉSUMÉ

A résumé is a summary of personal information about you that is relevant to the job you seek. A good one marks you as a serious job seeker. Much has been written about the résumé. Some regard it as a sacred cow, *the* most important item to use in presenting yourself; others believe preparing a résumé is a worthless exercise. Still, many employers require them, so job hunters, an obliging lot, will continue to oblige, even though they realize that often they are one among hundreds of applicants.

Your résumé is crafted to present you in the best possible light to prospective hiring managers. It has three important functions. First, and foremost, your résumé needs to excite and compel hiring managers to call you for an interview. Second, creating your résumé helps you understand the important things you have done in your academic and professional careers. Last, your résumé is the source for questions generated during the interview.

Sometimes people tend to get so involved with developing the perfect résumé that they lose sight of what is important. Having a fantastic résumé will not necessarily get you a job; being a fantastic person will. Creating a good résumé will take time and considerable effort on your part. The ideal résumé creates a positive image about you and communicates that you can successfully address the four key questions managers think about with potential new hires. After viewing your résumé, hiring managers will be compelled to speak with you, and your telephone will ring with requests for interviews.

There are two basic types of résumés: chronological and functional. A hybrid résumé, integrating elements of both the chronological and functional résumés, is a third alternative. Chronological résumés present your employment history and accomplishments sequentially, starting with your most current job and working backward in time. The companies, job titles, employment dates, and accomplishments are clearly listed, making it easy for a hiring manager to see what you did, when, and where. A functional résumé is used when making a major transition to a new career without having specific job experience, coming back to the workforce after an extended time away, or dealing with gaps in your employment history. In its most elemental form, your functional résumé lists several key skill categories relevant to the new job, with each skill having accomplishments affirming your abilities, irrespective of when the accomplishments were made. You hope the hiring manager will see your accomplishments as reasonable and valuable, thereby enabling you to "bridge over" any unemployed times and seemingly unrelated jobs or careers to win a telephone interview. Listing the companies in which you worked, especially in chronological order, is a further embellishment to your functional résumé, converting it into a hybrid résumé.

However, hiring managers often do not like ambiguities in how much relevant experience a candidate has, how current his or her skills and accomplishments are, or how stable the candidate's employment history is when reading a functional or hybrid résumé. So, stick with a chronological résumé if possible; it is the easiest one for the hiring manager to understand. Regardless of résumé style, if a hiring manager cannot find something intriguing about your résumé in the first 5 to 15 seconds of being read, your résumé will get eliminated. This is why it is so important to craft your résumé to capture and hold the hiring manager's attention. Moreover, since your résumé is a reflection of you, it should be perfect: a great format, easy-to-read font, excellent use of space, powerful and compelling accomplishments, printed on quality paper, and of course, addressing the managers' four questions.

Plan to invest plenty of time writing a good résumé; then set it aside and come back to it later for a fresh look. Be sure to have someone else read your résumé and give you feedback. Following these guidelines will help ensure your résumé is easy to read and best represents you to hiring managers.

- *Tools:* Using a word processor to write your résumé will give you the greatest flexibility and ease in producing and subsequently tailoring your documents. If you do not have a personal computer, public libraries, friends, copy centers, or schools can provide you access to one.

- *Content:* Every entry you make in your résumé should bolster your position as the most viable candidate. Do not include anything that could screen you out from further consideration. Remember, the mindset of a hiring manager reviewing a résumé is to look for reasons to eliminate the candidate. Give the hiring manager every reason to want to call you; review your résumé critically, from his or her perspective, to make certain everything on it validates your candidacy.

- *Paper:* Use a premium grade 8.5-×-11-inch, 20-pound (or preferably 24-pound) paper in white, off-white, or a pastel shade. Use plain paper without background designs, marble column decorations, or other such artwork. People pursuing jobs in artistic fields—like graphic artists or designers, where something untraditional may get them favorably noticed—may make an exception to this.

- *Length:* The length of a résumé is one to two pages, and on the second page finish about three-quarters or four-fifths from the bottom. New entrants to the job market will probably fit everything on one page; those with an extensive work history will use two pages.

- *Font:* Choose a "normal" serif (with the little extra lines at the tops and bottoms of some characters—Times New Roman, for example) or sans serif (without the extra lines—Arial or Universal, for example) that is easy to read. The font size can range from 10 to 14 points.

- *Spacing:* Adequate use of "white space" is essential for making your résumé easy to read. Margins should be about one inch on either side and about one-half to three-quarter inch on the top and bottom. Adding an extra one to three points of space between accomplishment statements to make them more discrete invites the reader to dwell longer to read each one.

- *Format:* Using **bold print**, *italics,* or <u>underlining</u> will make your entries stand out. Using bullets to clearly identify accomplishments catches the reader's eye by denoting separate, discrete "eye bites" of information. Like sound bites (those short statements made by people speaking on the radio or television in news interviews), eye bites are short statements that are easily discernable as discrete, complete thoughts. Be consistent throughout your résumé when bolding, italicizing, or otherwise differentiating its parts. Using left-justified margins is typical; although trying both left and right justification can add a little extra flair, too. Do not be afraid to experiment to see what looks best.

- *Grammar:* Résumés have their own grammar and syntax rules. Typically, you will start your accomplishment statements with action verbs using the present tense for your current job and the past tense for previous jobs. Use appropriate punctuation marks to denote separation of multiple items in your statements, and end accomplishments with periods.

Yes, Paul, I got your resume. ALL 327 PAGES!!! Send me the Cliff Notes version and MAYBE we'll talk.

- *Action words:* Use words that clearly and specifically express what you can bring to the job, not words that only impress. A woman who worked for a sanitation district said she "gave messages to the guys in their trucks." On her résumé, this phrase was translated to "communicated by radio with personnel in the field." Be sure that all words are spelled correctly.

- *Personal information:* Do not put information about your health, age, marital status, children, race, religious preferences, hobbies, or other personal items. There is no need to provide anything that doesn't directly relate to the job you are seeking.

- *Truthfulness:* Sometimes people get too creative and embellish their accomplishments, education, or other experience to impress prospective employers. Sometimes, people outright lie. It is the "kiss of death" for you if a prospective boss finds that you have falsified information; you won't be hired. And, if you managed to get hired under fraudulent circumstances, you can and probably will be fired. Companies now more than ever conduct background checks, scrutinizing an applicant's criminal, employment, credit, driving, and educational records.[6] Commercially done résumés may cast some suspicion or give rise to concerns about you if they are constructed from standard templates or use boilerplate text.

- *Scanability:* Designing résumés to be sent electronically or scanned into a company's database is discussed at the end of this chapter.

The Chronological Résumé

The sections in a chronological résumé are presented following. Examples of chronological résumés appear on pages 228–229 and page 230.

- *Header:* This section contains your name, address, telephone number, cell phone number, e-mail address, and, if applicable, fax number. Typically these elements are centered at the top of the page and presented as shown in the résumé examples. Your name stands out more prominently if you boldface it and make it two or three type points larger. Try to avoid using nicknames. Academic degrees, like B.A., Ph.D., or degrees conferred by professional organizations, like C.M.C. (certified management consultant) should be omitted. Sometimes people get creative and place their names on the right or left side of the page and contact information on the right side. Do not include your work telephone number or e-mail address. If your résumé is two pages long, put your name on the upper left corner of the second page to ensure that interviewers know which pages go together, should they become separated.

- *Objective:* This is a short description of the position you are seeking. If you are applying for a specific job, especially one that has been advertised, including an objective may be reasonable. However, writing an objective may be unnecessary if you send your résumé with a cover letter, the latter indicating what kind of position you want.

- *Summary:* This provides a brief listing of accomplishments throughout your career, whether you have been in the workforce for years or are just out of school. These descriptors illustrate who you are and what you can do. Including things like "Excellent communication and written skills," "Manages multiple tasks easily," or "Self-starter who sees tasks to successful conclusion" will start painting a positive picture of you in the reader's mind.

- *Professional experience:* This involves two sets of information. The first set includes your title, company, its address, dates of employment, and possibly a very brief paragraph of what the company does (if you believe the reader will not know). The other and most important set of information is your accomplishments. Those descriptive statements are the heart of your résumé and are the things a hiring manager will read to see if you can meet his or her needs. Spend time analyzing what you do at work, how good you are at doing it, and the effect you have in your department or company. Clearly articulate the results of what you have done or contributed to demonstrate how you have made a positive difference in your company.

If you find yourself at a loss to generate accomplishment statements, use the problem-solution-result method to stimulate your recollection about the significant and unique contributions you made at work. Ask yourself the following questions:

> "What was beneficial to the company, my coworkers, or my customers about me being in my job?"
>
> "What did I do that differentiated me from my colleagues?"
>
> "How do I know that I did a good job?"

Your answers to these questions will help you determine what problems, issues, activities, or circumstances arose that you had to address in some way. Pick a problem or issue and thoroughly describe what it was, what you did to address it, and what result you obtained. If at all possible, quantify the result or use qualifying adjectives to describe the outcome of your actions. Using the problem-solution-result method is very helpful for dredging up those significant contributions you made at work that validate your manager's wise decision to hire you. With a little careful thought, you will be able to remember your major accomplishments and describe them in powerfully written statements.

The best way to start an accomplishment statement is by using an action verb—present tense for your current job and past tense for previous jobs—for example: *advise/advised, create/created, direct/directed, design/designed, increase/increased, manage/managed, negotiate/negotiated, plan/planned, research/researched, schedule/scheduled, teach/taught*. A test for having written a powerful accomplishment statement is to read the statement and then ask yourself, "So what?" If the answer to that question is not apparent, you need to revise the accomplishment statement. Following are examples of accomplishment statements with increasing clarity and impact:

- Designed a marketing management program. (So what? Poor—reads like a job description, indicating nothing about how well it was done or its results.)

- Designed an effective marketing program. (So what? Better—has a qualitative descriptor providing some representation of the result.)

- Designed an effective marketing management program that resulted in a 60 percent sales increase. (So what? Best—answers the question with a clear, quantitative result.)

- Increased sales 60 percent by designing an effective marketing management program. (So what? Best—another way, illustrating the result first followed by the action taken.)

Present quantitative information using numbers wherever possible to illustrate your accomplishments, whether using dollars (saved $50,000 per year, manage $2,000,000 budget), percentages (improved efficiency 12 percent, decreased cost 22 percent), or numbers (direct a staff of 32 professionals, wrote eight 400-page customer proposals in six months). Numbers in your accomplishments break up the monotony of having all words and attract the eye of the reader, which is what you want to do when crafting a good résumé.

Use bullets and appropriate spacing to separate your accomplishment statements into discrete eye bites of information to avoid your accomplishments merging together and looking like a giant paragraph. Why use this method? Hiring managers generally hate reading what they perceive to be paragraphs and want to glean the pertinent information about you from your résumé quickly and easily, which using eye bites affords.

Balance your accomplishments with the time you have spent in the various jobs you have held. Having eight accomplishments in your most recent job, where you have been working for one year, and only three accomplishments for your previous job of four years is unbalanced.

Put your most important and powerful accomplishments in rank order at the top of each job section. Managers will look at the first couple of accomplishments, and if not impressed, will toss your résumé aside. You can change the sequence of your accomplishment statements based on their relevance to the company and people you are targeting to optimize your résumé for maximum effectiveness.

- *Education:* This section of the résumé contains a list of your academic or professional training, starting with the most recent degree first. List the degree and discipline (A.A. History, B.S. Chemistry, M.B.A. Economics, or Ph.D. Astronomy), followed by the degree-granting institution and its location. If you are in the process of completing your degree, or if you left school years ago without finishing, you can account for your progress by adding a simple statement saying, "Expected graduation 2004" for the former and "Three years completed" for the latter.

- *Professional skills:* This section lists any specialized training or skills you have with specific equipment, computers, software, and so on. Sometimes, people title this section "Computer Skills," "Computer Expertise," or "Technical Skills" to show all of the computer systems, software applications, and programming languages they know or have used. Sometimes technical people will put this section at the beginning of their résumés so interviewers can quickly ascertain relevant technical skills and background. Expertise in any specialized equipment, like heavy construction machinery or complex laboratory instruments, should also be mentioned in this section.

- *Professional training:* Any training you completed related to your work requirements are listed here; for example, Dale Carnegie public speaking, TQM practices, and such. Also, certificates, credentials, licenses, or degrees from professional training institutes are listed here; for example:

FOR BETTER OR FOR WORSE © Lynn Johnston Productions, Inc./Dist. by United Feature Syndicate, Inc.

teaching certificates, real estate credentials, Series 6 (insurance sales), and C.M.C. (certified management consultant).

- *Additional skills/information:* Any other skills you have that relate to the job for which you are seeking are listed here. Typically, people include foreign language skills or emergency first-aid training here. Special school or civic awards are also placed in this section. *Whatever you list here should be relevant to the job.*

- *Professional associations:* List those organizations in which you are an active member in some type of management position or have been responsible for completing a major task.

Functional and Hybrid Résumés

The other two kinds of résumés people use are functional and hybrid résumés. Functional résumés emphasize several skill categories, complete with appropriate accomplishments, based on the skills the hiring manager values most, and omit mention of your employment history. Hybrid résumés integrate the skill categories and accomplishments with employment history. If you can speak with the hiring manager and make a personal connection before sending your résumé, you dramatically increase the chances of a functional or hybrid résumé being read carefully. Here are the two sections that are unique to a functional résumé. Examples of functional résumés appear on pages 231 and 232; a hybrid résumé appears on page 233.

- *Accomplishments:* These will be the same entries you would make for a chronological résumé. In a functional or hybrid résumé, however, you will identify several key skill categories, like leadership, communication, customer service, or problem solving, that are relevant to the company or hiring manager reading the résumé. Place the most impressive accomplishments

John A. Wilson
123 Smith Street
Santa Cruz, CA 95060
home (831) 555-4590   cell (831) 555-8734
jawil@anyisp.com

OBJECTIVE: Production Director

SUMMARY:

A forward-thinking design specialist, producer, project manager, and developer for over 450 voiceovers, 40 videodiscs, over 30 stock footage CDs, 12 electronic books, 350 animations, 200 video clips, 30 Web-based courses, and approximately 40,000 still images. Excellent managerial, leadership, and team-building skills to meet tight deadlines and budget targets.

EXPERIENCE:

Senior Project Manager   2000–Present
GENUINE FILM COMPANY, Cupertino, CA
A $50,000,000 company, with offices in the U.S. and Europe, producing over 100 distance learning products delivered on video, film, CD-ROM, and the Web annually. http://www.gfc.com/

- Supervise construction and design of audio/video recording facilities and develop engineering staff, saving the company approximately $600,000 in recording fees.
- Determine critical path for developing and delivering 30 to 40 accredited courses on the Web by June 2003, at 50% under budget and 20% ahead of schedule.
- Systematize scheduling and budgeting for four $1,000,000 projects and supervise department budget of $3,500,000 and staff of 12 professionals.
- Develop and manage four teams of sound engineers, AFTRA professionals, and media coordinators producing over 450, 20-minute voiceovers and 200 video clips for delivery on CD-ROM.
- Direct A/V staff in research of technology, compression, and editing technique for streaming high-bandwidth media to develop new product technology currently submitted for patent approval.

Education Manager   1997–1999
WE TRAIN EVERYONE, INC., San Francisco, CA
A $10,000,000 venture-funded start-up that designs, develops, and produces training products and tools for the Fortune 100 companies worldwide on video and audio media, with offices in San Francisco and New York.
http://www.wtei.org/

- Successfully organized and marketed high-tech seminars in video, animation, and special effects, selling over $2,000,000 annually. Clients include: Lucas Arts, Colossal Pictures, and MGM.
- Set compression specifications for audio and video files for four $1,000,000 products.

Figure 7-1   Chronological Résumé of a Technical Professional

John A. Wilson   **Page 2**

- Developed routes for distributing calendar, which increased enrollment and brought the education program into black for two consecutive years, generating over 32% per year growth.
- Designed and implemented a new training program for advanced digital A/V graphic techniques to train in-house staff, subsequently spun off as separate company product offering, generating $50,000 revenue the first year.
- Established the company as a Northern California A/V Training Center to gain worldwide recognition as a leader in the training industry.

Design Specialist
GRAPHIC ARTS DEVELOPMENT, INC., San Jose, CA   1995–1997

A $5,000,000 graphic arts development and production company supplying television and movie studios with unique digital animations.

- Designed 23 digital animations for MGM incorporated into three feature films grossing $1,000,000,000 worldwide.
- Evaluated industry and technology trends for use in strategic management planning resulting in the growth of the graphics R&D staff by 40%.

EDUCATION:

M.S. (Digital Broadcasting) University of San Francisco, San Francisco, CA (1/6 completed)
B.A. (Radio and Television) Sacramento State University, Sacramento, CA

TECHNICAL SKILLS:

Audio/Video: Avid, Premiere, AfterEffects, Media Cleaner Pro, QuickTime, Pro Tools, Real Media, QuickTime, Emblaze, Sorensen, Qualcomm, QDesign, IMA.

Management: Microsoft Project, FileMaker Pro, Microsoft Word, Netscape HTML, Fetch

Desktop: QuarkXpress, Photoshop, Illustrator, Debabelizer, Quick Keys, Toast

Platforms: PC, MacIntosh, SUN Sparc
Hardware: Abekus 3000 digital mixer

ADDITIONAL SKILLS/TRAINING:

Toastmasters

PROFESSIONAL ASSOCIATIONS:

Vice President, International Training Industry Council, San Francisco, CA (2001–Present)

Kevin Donovan
643 Eagle Drive
Dubuque, Iowa 52001
Kevdonovan222@aol.com
home (319) 555-1234   cell (319) 555-4567

OBJECTIVE: Customer Service Management Trainee

SUMMARY:

A quick learner not afraid of hard work. Excellent public relations and customer service skills. Can work independently or as an active member of a team. Good driving record.

PROFESSIONAL EXPERIENCE:

Customer Service/Bagger   2002–Present
K-Mart, Dubuque, IA
- Help customers with merchandise, stock shelves, maintain appearance of the store, bring carts from parking lot into building, and bag merchandise from check stands always ensuring customer satisfaction.
- Train new employees in merchandise stocking and rotations and monitor their progress; 22 employees trained to date.

Gym Instructor   2000–2002
Dubuque Gymnastic Association, Dubuque, IA
- Sold over 183 memberships and $800,000 of exercise equipment and vitamin supplements.
- Served as personal trainer for 38 clients, averaging four to seven clients per day.
- Conducted sales presentations and tours with highest close rate of any employee.
- Balanced daily customer receipts and opened and closed facility when manager was away on vacation.
- Ensured the smooth operation of the facility and received lots of very positive customer feedback on facilities operation, equipment maintenance, and satisfaction.

Iron Handler   1999–2000
S & S Wrought Iron, East Dubuque, IA
- Loaded and unloaded trucks with iron products and merchandise, always keeping on schedule.

Warehouse Worker   1998–1999
Van's Furniture and Mattress Co., Dubuque, IA
- Moved furniture and equipment for receipts and shipments and delivered to customers, always keeping them pleased with the service.
- Conducted inventory audits quickly with 100% accuracy.

EDUCATION:

B.A. (Business) Loras College, Dubuque, IA (expected graduation summer 2004)

COMPUTER EXPERTISE:

IBM PC: WIndows, Microsoft Office

ADDITIONAL INFORMATION:

Currenty working 30 hours per week, attending college full time, GPA: 3.74

Figure 7-2   Chronological Résumé of a College Student

Betty A. Bug
5403 West Monrovia St.
Chicago, IL 60644
(312) 555-9829

OBJECTIVE: Industrial Employee Trainer

SUMMARY:

Over 15 years of demonstrated success in instruction, supervision, communications, and human relations. Expert at making complex subjects and topics simple to learn.

EXPERIENCE:

INSTRUCTION:

- Planned, organized, presented language and mathematical instructional material to elementary school students, whose test scores were second highest in the county.
- Developed over 50 teaching modules to solve specific learning problems.
- Designed and coded 20 computer programs for instruction and compatible resource materials enabling students to master material 15% faster than with traditional instructional methods.
- Directed the curriculum development committee to create seven new instructional programs for mathematics.
- Introduced latest motivational techniques to improve attention span and minimize in-class student disruptions by 42%. Instructed other teachers in this same process.
- Conducted 23 staff in-service workshops on new training methodologies and teaching technology, which improved teaching instruction throughout the entire school.

SUPERVISION:

- Supervised over 100 student groups, 34 teacher interns, and 52 classroom aides.
- Conducted performance reviews for teacher interns and classroom aides, providing feedback resulting in significant improvement in the quality of classroom instruction.
- Interviewed and recommended for employment teacher interns and classroom aides.

HUMAN RELATIONS:

- Conducted problem solving and conflict resolution interventions between students, student groups, instructors, and other staff members.
- Initiated a successful program of student self-governance, which served as a model for schools throughout the county.
- Served as liaison between families of diverse cultural, ethnic, and economic backgrounds and school personnel services, successfully overcoming difficulties to secure services.

EDUCATION:

B.S. (Mathematics) University of Chicago, Chicago, IL

TECHNICAL EXPERTISE:

PC and MacIntosh: WIndows, OS8, BASIC, WORD

ADDITIONAL SKILLS:

Spanish—fluent speaking, reading, and writing

Figure 7-3   Functional Résumé of a Teacher in Transition to Industry

William Reaume
361 Calle de Florencia
Santa Fe, New Mexico 87501
(505) 555-9743

OBJECTIVE: Public Relations Specialist

SUMMARY:

Self-starter who is an excellent organizer and a resourceful team player. Excellent communication and persuasion skills. Works well in fast-paced, time-critical situations.

EXPERIENCE:

WRITING/PUBLICITY

- Compiled and published public service directory ahead of schedule and under budget.
- Coordinated and edited corporate newsletter monthly for circulation throughout a 300-person company.
- Designed publicity brochure, which increased public awareness of the community service programs company was doing and increased community goodwill.
- Developed and implemented the style and formatting for the company employee handbook. Feedback from employees indicated it was much easier to read and understand over previous versions.
- Gave over 50 presentations to local government, civic groups, schools, and employees on company's innovative policies.
- Contacted media regarding personnel changes and events of interest to the community to garner publicity and goodwill for the company, which was instrumental in helping secure favorable tax treatment by the city government for a new building addition.

ADMINISTRATION AND ORGANIZATION

- Hired, supervised, and trained 21 contract employees; served as mentor and coach, helping them become productive quickly.
- Established and maintained resource/reference library, which was a benefit to marketing and sales by having timely competitive information and industry trends data readily available.
- Planned, organized, and promoted company picnic, congratulated by management for 78% increase in employee participation over next best previous year.
- Developed and conducted new hire orientation program, which was adopted for use throughout the company and helped employees.
- Coordinated and presented 27 work-effectiveness seminars for all departments resulting in a company-wide average cost savings of $300,000 annually.

EDUCATION:

M.B.A. (Advertising) Golden Gate University, San Francisco, CA (1/3 completed)
B.A. (English) [cum laude] University of Wisconsin, Whitewater, WI

TECHNICAL EXPERTISE:

PC and MacIntosh: WORD, Excel, PowerPoint

Figure 7-4   Functional Résumé of a Man Moving into Pubic Relations from Secretarial Work

Helen B. Bell
432 Spruce St.
Junction City, Kansas 66441
(913) 555-7035

OBJECTIVE: Office Manager with Accounting Responsibilities

SUMMARY:

Over 19 years of successful accounting experience. Thrive on ensuring smooth flow, efficiency, and accuracy for company accounting function. Highly organized with an excellent memory and have exceptional numerical and computational skills. Resolve complex accounting problems quickly and deftly.

EXPERIENCE:

Successful Accounting Activities:
- Managed payroll, payroll taxes, accounts receivable, accounts payable, bank reconciliation, and executive credit card expense accounts for a variety of medium-sized manufacturing and service companies of up to 160 people and $30,000,000 in sales.
- Served as full-charge bookkeeper through monthly and annual profit and loss statements, completing all tasks ahead of schedule.
- Developed and implemented spreadsheet application for accounts receivable and accounts payable, which cut end-of-quarter books close-times significantly.

Supervision and Management:
- Directed office functions such as secretarial, accounting, customer relations, sales, employee performance, and schedules, managing up to 12 people.
- Acknowledged by company management for outstanding leadership for three consecutive years.

EMPLOYMENT:

Kindergarten Supplier, USA, Inc., Wichita, KS Accountant	10 years
Electra Corporation, Wichita, KA Receptionist	1 year
Ridgeway Company, Topeka, KS Accountant/Secretary	1 year
Rod's Van and Storage Company, Topeka, KS Accountant/Secretary	2 years
Humphrey Motor Company, Junction City, KS Accountant/Secretary	9 years

EDUCATION:
B.A. (Accounting) Kansas State University, Manhattan, KS

COMPUTER EXPERTISE:
PC: Windows, Excel, Lotus 123

Figure 7-5   Hybrid Résumé of a Senior Citizen/Housewife Returning to the Job Market

first. The idea is to convince the hiring manager by painting the picture, with your résumé, that your skills and accomplishments will be of benefit.

- *Employment:* This section usually contains a list of all of the companies in which you worked and the job titles you had. The list is usually written in reverse chronological order, with employment dates, the total years of employment, or no date information at all, depending on the purpose of the résumé. Adding company information makes your résumé a hybrid. The hybrid résumé gives you many options for combining accomplishments and employment history. The more cryptic your employment history appears, however, the quicker your résumé will be rejected.

Here are some final points to consider about résumés. You may send your résumé with an individual letter addressed to a specific person in a company. If you plan to mail it, prepare a carefully typed, matching envelope addressed to the correct person. The idea is to give the employer a preview of you before an interview takes place. Always have your résumé handy and bring several copies to the interview, because more than one person may want to talk with you. You want your résumé to get a second look rather than the usual 10-second glance. And yes, you do need a separate résumé for each job title and sometimes even for each company. As your career advances, you will not simply add new jobs to the list on your résumé; you will probably change the entire format. You may summarize early jobs, stress your newer high-level qualifications, and recast earlier entries to point toward your new job goal. The résumé is a living document that will change to emphasize your achievements, and each job entry will show increasingly greater connections to the next job goal.

The commercial Web site **www.free-resume-tips.com** shows elements from a variety of different résumés and cover letters, plus offers tips to make your résumés more powerful.

The University of Minnesota (**www1.umn.edu/ohr/ecep/resum**) provides an online résumé tutor to help craft the perfect résumé.

Résumé writing and cover letter links can be found at the Canadian site: **www.accesswave.ca/~hgunn/virtual/resumes.html.**

The University of California–Davis Career Center (**ucdavis .placementmanual.com/resume/index.html**) shows examples of different kinds of résumés.

COVER LETTERS

Employment counselors and personnel managers say that a well-written cover letter is an excellent door opener for an interview; it links you to the employer and acts as a lead for your résumé. After you have made personal

October 21, 2002

Ms. Jill Jones
Director of Marketing
PTT Corporation
Dogwood, AL 36309

Dear Ms. Jones:

As a word processor at Datatime Company last summer, I had occasion to meet with people from PTT. Your sales representative, Joan Carl, referred me to you. I was impressed with both your product and your personnel. I am a senior at Peachtree University. I would like to be considered for an internship position in marketing for the Spring Semester of 2003.

I am an energetic, enthusiastic person with a commitment to whatever I take on. My involvement in student affairs led me to plan and execute a successful campaign for student body vice president. As vice president, I met and negotiated with faculty representatives and members of the board of trustees and hosted visiting guests of the college. My junior project in marketing won departmental recognition, and my 3.2 GPA put me on the dean's honor list.

With these qualifications, I feel that I can make a positive contribution to PTT. I look forward to meeting your campus recruiter, A. J. Lupin, next month to explore a marketing internship position.

Sincerely yours,

Chris Cross
5401 Monroe St.
Mobile, AL 36608

Figure 7-6   Cover Letter of a College Student Applying for an Internship

Chris Cross
5401 Monroe St.
Mobile, AL 36608
(205) 555-0983

OBJECTIVE: Internship in Marketing

SUMMARY:

B.A. candidate in Marketing and Sales. Won departmental honors in Marketing. Word processor for two summers on PTT Systems. Good human relations skills, energetic, and goal oriented. Excellent communication skills.

PROFESSIONAL EXPERIENCE:

Data Entry

Datatime Company, Mobile, AL   (Summers) 2001–2002

- Entered data for marketing and sales departments for subsequent generation of eight different monthly or quarterly management reports.
- Logged product sales, sales personnel progress, and regional growth daily with all entries completed daily before day's end.
- Provided customer, sales, and technical information to service representatives quickly, which helped close over $100,000 of business in one quarter alone.

Wait Staff

McDougal's Hamburger Shop, Mobile, AL   1999–2000

- Waited on customers, conducted cash register transactions, and was only person assigned to train new employees.
- Created a successful coupon marketing strategy that raised sales 11% in three months.
- Served as store manager during her absence, received positive customer feedback.
- Entered data for marketing and sales departments for subsequent generation of eight different monthly or quarterly management reports.

EDUCATION:

B.A. (Marketing and Sales) Peachtree University, Peachtree, GA (graduation June, 2004)

RELATED EXPERIENCE:

Vice President

Peachtree University Student Body, Peachtree, GA   2001–2002

- Planned and executed my election campaign, received 73% of votes.
- Championed new student services center in extensive meetings with faculty, administration, and board of trustees, gaining approval for a new $3,000,000 facility whose construction starts in 2003.
- Spearheaded senior projects like the Homecoming Dance and Career Day.

Senior Class Secretary
Junior Class Vice President

Blossom High School, Mobile, AL   1998–1999

- Active participant throughout high school in student body activities, science club, and intramural basketball and soccer.

Figure 7-7   Chronological Résumé of a Marketing Student to Accompany Cover Letter Requesting an Internship

January 24, 2003

Dierk Van Symms
Manager of Technical Services
Effective Micro Systems, Inc.
130 Meridian Dr., Suite 411
Aurora, IL 60505

Dear Mr. Van Symms:

EMS Marketing Representative Kevin Skahan acquainted me with your company, felt that I could be a significant asset for you, and recommended I contact you. He was impressed with my hands-on experience, both manual and computerized, in a manufacturing environment and believed that I could offer a special attention to detail that a manufacturing company like EMS deserves.

My effective problem solving, communication, and planning skills in my current position resolving office and factory applications issues have resulted in higher customer satisfaction and fewer complaints about scheduling and delivery. The enclosed résumé will acquaint you with my background and skills in providing quality technical services and includes these notable accomplishments:

- Developed a cross-checking system that improved on-time deliveries for 12 major customers a minimum of 18%.
- Designed and implemented a computerized raw materials purchasing system, installed ahead of schedule and under budget, that saved $320,000 annually in excess raw materials inventory.

I am now seeking a technical business position with your team to tackle the greater challenges that are faced by a company like EMS. I will call you next Thursday to set up a time when we can meet and discuss how I can become a valuable member of your team, contributing to its success.

Sincerely yours,

Joanne M. Malatia
5405 Monroe St.
Aurora, IL 60504

Enclosure: Resume

Figure 7-8   Cover Letter to Accompany a System Analyst's Résumé

Joanne M. Malatia
5405 Monroe St.
Aurora, IL 60504
jmmalatia@yahoo.com
home: (708) 555.1478
cell: (708) 555.4321

SUMMARY:

An efficient systems expert with over seven years of experience achieving system and operations improvements, increasing productivity, and decreasing costs. A team player with excellent analytical, written, and communication skills, who leads and drives projects through to completion on time and within budget.

PROFESSIONAL EXPERIENCE:

Watlow Electric Manufacturing Company, Batavia, IL   1999–Present
Systems Analyst (2001–Present)
- Develop a cross-checking system that improved on-time deliveries for 12 major customers a minimum of 18%.
- Design and implement a computerized raw materials purchasing system, installed ahead of schedule and under budget, that saved $320,000 annually in excess raw materials inventory.
- Coordinate implementation of corporate-side order processing and sales analysis system, ensuring effective transition with no disruption to order processing or sales teams.
- Conduct semi-annual system audits (mainframe, mid-sized, and PC-based system) to determine future needs, configure necessary hardware and software requirements, develop system strategy, and present findings to management, maintaining company's premier position in the industry in all productivity per employee measures.

Computer Programmer (1999–2000)
- Defined data sets, processing problems, and objectives using MAPPER database language to improve production run changeovers by 16%.
- Performed general maintenance on all computer hardware systems at Batavia plant, minimizing downtime and disruptions to plant operations.
- Instructed team members and plant users (over 60 people) on a variety of business and manufacturing computer applications.

Figure 7-9   Chronological Résumé of a Systems Analyst to Accompany Cover Letter Seeking New Employment

Joanne M. Malatia   Page 2

Lovejoy Rehabilitation Center, West Chicago, IL   1997–1999
Data Collector for Research/Education Department
- Directed a system investigation of the Materials Management Department to determine system requirements for upgrade and efficiency improvements. Results led to $832,000 investment in new equipment, standardization of software applications, and productivity improvements up to 37% in departments transitioning from manual to computerized systems.
- Coordinated acquisition and installations of new system upgrades to ensure smooth transition.
- Designed and implemented software application training programs for staff to master new applications and procedures quickly.
- Conducted 130 patient telephone interviews to determine specific system needs and prepared management report with findings.
- Implemented a successful follow-up tracking system to gather patient feedback to measure service performance goals and fine where new modifications could yield improved patient satisfaction.

McDonald's of Stratford, Bloomingdale, IL   1995–1997
Administrative Assistant to General Manager
- Managed and balanced daily books and cash sheets while maintaining cash flow to ensure efficient operations.
- Scheduled and planned employee activities and supply deliveries according to management goals.
- Oriented and trained all new employees.

EDUCATION:
B.S. (Computer Information Systems) DeVry Institute of Technology, Lombard, IL

COMPUTER EXPERIENCE:
Hardware: IBM3033, AS400, PCs
Operating Systems: OS/MVS, OS/400, Windows XP, Windows 2000,
                              Windows NT
Languages: COBOL, BASIC, RPGII, Pascal, JCL. Assembler
Applications: MS Office, Access, Oracle SQL, SAS, SPPS, MAPPER

contact with someone in the company who seems interested in hiring you, targeting your résumé to that company and addressing a cover letter to that person, both geared to a specific job, is usually an excellent strategy. In other cases, a cover letter may be superfluous and even undesirable. Some employers, such as school districts and government agencies, have step-by-step procedures that make cover letters unnecessary. These employers may want only an application with your résumé attached. It's wise to learn and follow the expected procedures when these are clearly stated. In companies with less formal application procedures, employers often appreciate a short and clear cover letter stating in a sentence or two what you are interested in. You can use it to amplify an important aspect of your résumé and to form a chain linking you directly to the employer (see pages 235–237).

- *Connect:* State your reason for writing and your employment objective. Mention the person who referred you to this employer or the source of the reference, such as a classified ad.

- *Add more links:* Describe your experience in brief—one or two sentences should be ample.

- *Solder the links:* State what you can do to help the company in a sentence or two, or simply include two or three of your most impressive, relevant accomplishments, presented in bullet form, just like on your résumé.

- *Hold onto the chain:* Prepare the way for the next step by asking for an interview and indicating when you will call to set it up.

Stating a specific day that you will call for an interview demonstrates your initiative, keeps you active in your job hunt with follow-up tasks, and can provide an effective ploy for overcoming challenges from the hiring manager's administrative assistant intended to shield him or her from your call. Be ready to win over the boss when you've connected.

Sometimes you will get a negative response when you call for an interview. Rather than answering with a stunned silence, be ready with a positive answer to reinforce your possible contribution to the company. For example, to "We don't hire people without experience," your reply might be, "I do learn very quickly," or "I have had a great deal of experience as a student doing similar tasks such as . . ."

LETTERS OF REFERENCE

Be prepared to supply the names of people who have written or will write letters of reference for you or who will answer questions about you when called. *Do not* name someone until you have asked that person's permission to be listed as a reference and he or she has agreed. The people you ask should generally be professionals who know you, teachers, school advisers, clergy, or doctors. The most valuable references come from individuals who can speak from personal experience about your work abilities. These may include supervisors, coworkers, and people who work for you. If possible, ask a person with the same background as your prospective employer to write a reference for you. Keep in mind that a potential employer may call anyone from any place you have worked, so keep your human relations with your coworkers as smooth as possible.

Ask the person writing the letter to mention your specific job and personal responsibility skills that relate to the position you are seeking. Some people who write many letters of reference may ask you to write the letter for them to revise and sign. And some may decline your request entirely.

Given the propensity for lawsuits in our society today, some companies prohibit current employees from disclosing any information about those seeking jobs elsewhere to callers doing reference checks. Such calls are directed to people in the human resources office, who will provide only basic information about employment dates and job titles for the former employee in question. Thus, employers are unwilling to give out information about former employees that may be damaging to the job seeker, even though they know that person might cause severe problems for a future employer.

When you apply for a job, the usual procedure is to provide names of references if they are requested, or to bring copies of letters to the interview. A reference list (page 242) should contain the name, title, contact information, and a sentence or two describing the areas upon which the reference will comment. Hiring managers prefer to speak directly with your references, as this can provide an interactive dialogue rich with examples about your accomplishments, attitudes, and working habits. Reference letters, unless written and made current for the specific job you are considering, look dated, nonspecific, and impersonal for the reader, typically being addressed, "To Whom It May Concern."

Some college placement offices keep a file for each of their graduates with copies of letters of reference, a current résumé, and transcripts; the placement office will send these out to prospective employers for a nominal fee. If you have letters of reference on file at your college, have them sent to the prospective employer either right before or soon after your interview. If the competition is fierce and you are almost certain this is a job you want, it may be appropriate to ask a couple of key people to write or even make phone calls to the person who may hire you. Ask a teacher or counselor who knows your skills, an acquaintance in the company to which you are applying, or some other professional acquaintance known to the interviewer or to the person you will be working for to speak on your behalf. Understand, however, that this is not the usual procedure and should be used with discrimination.

Chris Cross
5401 Monroe St.
Mobile, AL 36608
(205) 555-0983

REFERENCE LIST

Mr. William Ralphson, Computer Operations Manager
Datatime Company
1819 Lee Ave.
Mobile, AL 36609
(205) 354-8891

Mr. Ralphson can describe how I developed a question and answer data pool from which to quickly provide correct responses to our sales representatives for their customer inquiries. Further, he can detail the steps I took with the sales representatives to determine what kinds of questions their customers typically asked, how I researched the answers, and how I integrated the information to be retrieved quickly.

Ms Wendy Cotton, Owner
McDougal's Hamburger Shop
45678 Barrett Rd.
Mobile, AL 36610
(205) 523-1515

Ms. Cotton can discuss the coupon marketing project I designed and implemented to improve sales. She can address the steps I completed to research competitor coupon strategies, design our program, work with the printer to generate the coupons, train the staff to collect the coupons, and assess the program's results.

Dr. Anna Pekovia, Professor
Peachtree University
1298 1st Ave.
Peachtree, GA 30302
(404) 631-9734

Dr. Pekovia advised and mentored me on the student council. She can provide information about my activities spearheading and channeling student input to the faculty team on the new student services building project. She can talk about the PowerPoint presentations I created and delivered to the faculty panel highlighting student concerns and desires for the new building.

Mr. Paul Franks, Coach
Blossom High School
4500 Addison Rd.
Mobile, AL 36610
(205) 881-9000 x231

Mr. Franks can talk about how I helped encourage the members of the basketball and soccer teams to work more effectively as a cohesive group to make our practice sessions more effective and increase our victories.

Figure 7-10   The Reference List for a Job Seeker

THE APPLICATION FORM

Applications request much more information than what your résumé would divulge, which provides an advantage to the company. If at all possible, you should try to get the job without completing an application beforehand. If an application is required as a prerequisite to an interview, make sure to recheck the information in your résumé and in the application for continuity and consistency. It is becoming more common for companies to use online e-forms to gather applicant data in lieu of traditional paper applications. Application information can be entered directly through automated, online forms that prompt for each entry, which you can manually type in or cut-and-paste from your electronic résumé. Care should be exercised when using this method of submitting personal information to ensure the security and privacy of your data.

Applications vary from one company to another, but they usually require an accurate record of your past work experience and education. To help you in preparing every application you will make, create your own file containing all the information you may need to include, using the format in the Data File exercise in Chapter 1. A sample application is on page 276. Check the records carefully for accuracy. You will need names, addresses, and dates for both education and work experience. Obtain this information now if you do not have it. Employers often verify these facts, and the information on your application must match what they learn from your former employers or educational institutions. The more careful you are, the better you look. Be clear if you are asked what you did. Know exact job titles, the types of equipment you've used, and your desired salary range. Some firms may accept—and even require—e-mail, fax, or Internet applications. Here are some helpful hints to remember.

- Read the *whole* application form *before* you begin to fill it in. Follow all directions, and note the fine print.
- Print with a blue or black pen, or better still, type answers carefully and completely, but succinctly.
- Fill in all blanks. Write in N/A (not applicable) if a question does not apply to you.
- Have your Social Security number available. Some companies ask to see a driver's license. (Revocation or denial of a driver's license can indicate a problem.)
- Your reason for interest in the position should state an advantage to the employer. Research the company and know what you can do for it.
- An arrest is not a conviction. Arrests need not be mentioned.
- Provide accurate names and addresses of those who have given you permission to use their names as references. Have original reference letters

available, plus copies to leave if requested or agree to have them sent if they are on file or if the individual providing the reference wishes to send the letter personally.

- Reread the application carefully. Typos or other errors give a bad impression.
- Sign the application.

THE INTERVIEW

An interview is a purposeful conversation between an employer or delegated interviewer and a prospective employee. Its purpose is to exchange information. The interviewer needs to learn whether the interviewee has the qualifications necessary to do the job. The applicant needs to make sure that he or she understands the job, the company, and what is expected. In the following section we cover the key points in the interview and review a set of practice questions and answers.

An employer interviews individuals whose applications, letters, or résumés have proven interesting, those who have made a personal contact, or those who have been referred. Many managers feel uncomfortable with the interview and are not skilled at it, so be prepared to participate actively while letting the manager guide it. Have some key points you would like to tell the interviewer. Some school districts and government agencies have a very formal interview procedure, asking the same questions in the same sequence to each candidate. Try to learn whether the employer uses a structured or an informal interview so as to be better prepared.

Interviews may be conducted by a department head or project director, or a series of people familiar with various aspects of the job may act together as an interviewing committee. In a small business, you may be interviewed by the owner. Large corporations often employ professional interviewers.

If the hiring manager to whom you sent your résumé is interested in you, you will receive a telephone call from that person, from someone from the human resources department, or possibly from a professional interviewer to conduct a screening interview. If possible, set up a quiet place in your home to lay out your job hunting materials, so that whenever the interviewer's call comes in, you can refresh yourself with the correspondence and company. You need to concentrate on making a positive impression in the first few seconds of your conversation to quickly strengthen your rapport with the interviewer, while actively listening to the interviewer's vocal cues and trying to determine his or her communication style preference (short, direct responses; broad generalizations; concrete examples) to help you best respond. Building rapport and mutual trust with the caller during your conversation will improve your chances of being invited for a personal interview, especially

It's nice, Mr. Houdini, that you can appear in a puff of smoke, turn lead into gold, and pull a rabbit out of your hat. But can you program a computer?

when you clearly articulate your skills, accomplishments, and value you bring to the company.

Like a good composition, the interview usually has a beginning, a middle, and an ending. Introductions and casual conversation are designed to help you feel at ease. After a few minutes, most interviewers will guide you to the purpose of the meeting, which is to find out what you can *do* for the company and what your qualifications are for the job. A good interviewer will also give you information along the way to help you make your decision. You and the interviewer are looking to determine the next step: continuing on to the next round of interviews or deciding that the match is not right. Your participation in the process needs to be as intense, or even more so, than the interviewer's, continually evaluating what you can do to make the interview go better and whether what you hear about the job, company, and people are to your liking. The interviewer may discuss job duties, hours and overtime, salary and benefits, vacation and sick leave, opportunities for advancement, and company policies and procedures.

Interviews catch people when they are on their best behavior. Companies wish they could try an applicant. AlphaGraphics in San Francisco does. They hire likely applicants for one day for $100. Both employer and employee have been successful in making good matches.[7] Some companies even try tests of various sorts. Some may give an interviewee problems or situations to solve.

Some interviewers will give you a tour of the workplace. Depending on the level for which you are being considered, an interview may be over in fifteen minutes, last several hours, or even extend over some days, with many different people. When your prospective boss queries the other interviewers about you, responses may relate to your personality and their like or dislike for you rather than expound on your skills and abilities. Being liked is important, and being liked the best can mean the difference between getting a job offer or a rejection letter. Interviewers bring these meetings to an end and usually tell you when you will be notified about their selection of an applicant. They are generally seeing other people interested in the job, sometimes many others.

A successful interview may be one in which you *don't* get the job. In some cases, the interview reveals that hiring you would not be good for either you or the company, which only means that the interview has accomplished its purpose. *In any event, you want to appear at your best.*

Getting Prepared

When you are meeting someone you wish to impress, common sense and courtesy are your most reliable guides. Your goal here is to make a better impression than your competition and make it to the next round of interviews. If you are in doubt about dress and manner, it's best to lean slightly toward the conservative. Prepare what you will wear ahead of time. Be sure that your outfit is clean, pressed, polished, and *comfortable.* When purchasing your "dress for success" outfit, try sitting in it, moving in it. Then wear it a time or two, perhaps to an information interview. *And of course, be on time.* If you are a smoker, refrain from smoking during the interview even if others are smoking. Make sure your clothing and breath do not give your habit away. What you may not notice, others will. Many employers tend to look with disfavor on someone who does smoke. Seattle University professor of business William L. Weiss says that "in a race for a job between two equally qualified people, a nonsmoker will win 94 percent of the time."[8]

The very best preparation for an interview is practice—practice talking to people about their jobs; practice calling for appointments to see people in order to ask for career information. If you have done information interviewing and networking, you will be accustomed to sharing enthusiasm about the career of your choice, and this enthusiasm will come across naturally at the interview. Videotaping yourself in a mock interview provides invaluable feedback that can help you polish your responses to questions, improve your interpersonal communication style, and learn to focus your attention on what the interviewer is doing and saying, both verbally and nonverbally. It may

INTERVIEW OVERVIEW

GET READY

Check: The company (from reference section of library, public relations department of firm, contacts, friends)

  Location
  Products/services
  Potential market
  Earnings
  Policies

Check: Important items you wish to cover:

  How you fit in
  Your strengths
  Your experiences
  Your interests

GET SET

Check: Items for your application:

  Social Security number
  References
  Person to notify in case of accident
  Details of past experience:
    Name of company
    Full address and phone number of company
    Dates worked
    Salary
    Job titles
    Supervisors
    Duties, projects, skills
  Education (dates, majors, degrees)
  Copies of résumé
  Examples of work, if relevant

Check: Exact time, date, location (building and room)
  Availability of parking
  Name of interviewer (and pronunciation)

GO

Check: Your appearance:

  Neat, clean, conservative outfit
  No gum, no smoking, no fidgeting
  No sunglasses or outdoor clothing
  Comfortable sitting posture, straight but at ease

Check: Your attitude:

  A serious job seeker
  Definite goals
  Willing to work and work up
  Reasonable approach to salary, hours, benefits, or other aspects of the job
  Uncritical of past employers, teachers, coworkers
  Evidence of good human relations
  Sense of humor
  High personal values
  Wide interests, openness, flexibility

Check: Your manner:

  Confident, not overbearing
  Firm handshake
  Enthusiastic but not desperate or gushy
  Courteous, attentive
  Good voice, expression
  On target answering questions
  Prompt departure after the interview

Go alone

seem uncomfortable at first being videotaped, but after a few minutes, you will shift into the role of job candidate and be serious about answering the interviewer's questions. This is the time to practice all of the different responses and best ways to address the battery of questions you will face with a real employer, so that your answers become smooth and to the point, and you hone your body language and vocal characteristics while continuing to improve your "likability" factor. Go to interviews even if you think you may not get a job, and then honestly assess your performance.

More immediately, do homework on the company you are approaching. Many have brochures; many are listed in standard library references. A call to the public relations department can sometimes result in a wealth of material. Find out if the company has a Web site. Talk to people who may know the company. Ask questions at the interview about the job as well as the company's process and organization, instead of self-serving questions that indicate you are interested only in what the company can give you, such as a long vacation or high pay! Try to see how you best fit in. Know the important facts about the job, including the salary range. Prepare to bring relevant examples of your work, such as sketches, designs, or writings.

It's usually better not to ask about salary and benefits at the initial interview. It may sound as if that is your only interest in the company. Moreover, a salary discussion at the outset of the first interview or soon after the interview starts could eliminate you. If the interviewer brings up salary by asking, "What are you currently making?" try to dodge the question with comments like, "I am sure your compensation will be commensurate with the skills I bring. Would it be okay to explore the job's duties and requirements before talking about salary?" Another way to handle an interviewer stubbornly pursuing the salary issue is to deflect the question and say, "What salary range have you budgeted for this position?" Try to get the interviewer to reveal the salary range to you. If it is above what you are currently making, smile inwardly and proceed with the interview to win a second interview. If it is below what you are making, take the same tactic with the same goal. If the hiring manager really wants you, the salary and compensation issues can usually be resolved later to your satisfaction. Remember, in negotiations, the first one to throw out a number loses.

A better way is to do your homework beforehand; should salary come up in conversation you will know this information. Salary.com (**www.salary .com**) is a commercial Web site that provides salary information and ranges for jobs in major cities in each state.

In some career areas, salaries are nonnegotiable and not an issue—government, teaching, and union jobs are examples. In others, salaries are negotiable. In such cases, the interviewer may ask what salary you expect. If you have no idea of the range and were not able to find out ahead of time, ask. Unless you are a superstar, don't ask for the top of the range, but don't undervalue yourself, either. Know the minimum you'll accept—and know your worth. Place yourself somewhere in the middle and leave it open to negotiation. If you have been networking, going to business meetings, reading up-to-date material, and talking to people, you will have an idea of what a reasonable salary should be for someone in your situation. And again, don't forget to factor in other benefits such as the opportunity to own equity or stock in the company. Also, you may ask for a salary review in six months or so or make a proposal just after you have done a good job on a particular project. Ask the personnel or human resources office for brochures on company benefit plans; also check their Web site. And definitely review them before accepting an offer.

Interview Behavior

As a job seeker, you should approach each interview by being true to yourself and trusting your own judgment. You can build self-confidence by practicing ways of talking and listening effectively and by learning to answer an interviewer's questions. You also want to manage how you look and behave in those first critical few seconds when you meet the interviewer to project yourself as a positive, pleasant, capable person. The first impression the interviewer has of you sets the tone for the interview. A positive impression of you is great; a negative one puts you at a disadvantage that you must overcome quickly. Here are some key points to practice.

- *Good eye contact:* Get comfortable with and use this form of personal contact. If you like your interviewers, your eyes will communicate warmth and interest. Don't forget to smile.

- *Appropriate body language:* Be relaxed and open, interested and attentive. Become aware of ways in which your body sends messages of boredom, fear, enthusiasm, cockiness, nervousness, or confidence. Become aware of others' body language. Much of what you "say" will of course be conveyed by your manner, not your words.[9] Some experts say as much as 95 percent of our communication is nonverbal.

- *Appropriate voice:* Try to come across with vitality, enthusiasm, and confidence. Remember that low, relaxed tones convey confidence and competence; high, squeaky tones convey insecurity. Tape record your answers to expected questions so that you can hear yourself; at least practice them out loud, alone or with someone who will give you honest feedback.

- *Active listening:* Indicate that you have heard and understood what the interviewer has said. For example, if the interviewer mentions tardiness as a problem, say, "It must be difficult to have employees who are constantly late. I can assure you I'll make every effort to be on time."

- *Good choice of words:* Use language that is respectful but not overly formal. If you do your interview homework and practice, the right words should come easily.

Practice Questions

You will be asked questions about your previous work experience and education, your values, and your goals. You may be asked general questions about your family life and leisure activities, but very personal questions are not appropriate in an interview, and most interviewers today avoid specifics. Some, such as your marital status or age, are illegal.

Questions dealing with factual information should not be a problem if you have prepared well. Have on hand your own card file of all education, previous jobs, and other experience, with correct dates, place names and addresses, job titles and duties, names of supervisors, and other relevant information in case these slip your mind. Usually this information is on the application. The interview centers on clarification of points on the application and résumé.

If you have been working regularly and successfully in your field for a period of years, the interview will be mainly a chance for you to tell what you have done. If you are a recent graduate, the discussion may focus on your education and casual jobs.

If you have been in and out of the job market or have had problems in the past, the interviewer will want to explore the reasons. Be relaxed and not defensive. Look on the interview as a chance to make a fresh start. Assure the interviewer that you will not be a problem but a solution. All the questions in the interview are different ways of asking "Can you do the job?" If you keep that clearly in mind, you will be able to support your answer, "Yes, I can do the job," with all sorts of relevant data. Interviewers are looking for people who are reliable and conscientious and who can get along with others. A poor entry-level hire can cost as much as $5,000 to $7,000, according to the Department of Labor.[10]

Practice answering interview questions until you feel comfortable. Prepare concise answers so you won't ramble, keeping your answers brief and focused to avoid losing the interviewer's attention. Omit personal information and especially any negative information about your past jobs and employers. Some people get carried away and start talking about their childhood, personal problems, and all sorts of irrelevant data that wear interviewers out and hardly charm them. And of course, when talking about your present workplace, be positive about managers, coworkers, and the company in general. No one wants to hire a complainer. And you definitely do not want to divulge any company secrets to potential employers who may assume you would do the same to them. Some companies even ask employees who

ving to sign a statement that they will not do so, nor jeopardize the
y's privacy in any way.

u should be aware that interviewers, like everyone else, have personal
es for the qualities they seek in coworkers other than their employ-
ry and qualifications. Some managers prefer to hire people of a
ender, age, appearance, physical size, ethnic background, or reli-
nce, regardless of existing anti-discrimination laws. Is this fair?
appen? Yes, all of the time. Life can be unfair, and the employ-
no exception. The bottom line for you is to know your
hortcomings, be able to promote the former, and not let the
ou or the interviewer.

ne typical, commonly asked questions, along with answers

hing about yourself. This request is one of the most fre-
erviewers, so you should prepare an answer. Include rea-
background, and personal attitudes are good for the job
future with the company. You will seldom have a bet-
is to talk about yourself.

g your present job? (Or *Why did you leave your last*
s of your leaving were unpleasant or your present
, these personal problems will be the first answers
t they should be the last answers you give. Every-
n one reason, and negative reasons can be made
pressive, your coworkers were disagreeable, or
ve can provide you the opportunity for growth
lt for anyone to improve on a job when his or
ve. Here are some possible replies:

- "I   d to have reached a point where there was little potential for
  growth."

- "I have learned my job well and would like to try new dimensions in a
  growing [or larger, or innovative] company."

- "I decided to change careers, and I just got my degree."

- "I left to raise a family, and now I am ready to return to work permanently."

- "I moved [or the company reorganized or merged or cut back or slowed
  down]."

*Your application indicated that you have been in and out of the work
force quite often (or haven't worked in some years). What were you involved
with during those periods of unemployment?* Be prepared to give assurance
that your qualifications are such that you can handle the job and that you
plan to stay with the company. Knowing your abilities and what the job
demands can clarify this subject for you.

What are your weaknesses and what are your strengths? The question about weaknesses is the most dreaded one in the interview. Careful preparation will enable you to turn this question into an opportunity to show the interviewer where you shine. There are three major elements in a good response: to show the interviewer that you can (1) recognize your own deficiencies, (2) see when they affect others, and (3) take corrective action without having to be told. Here is a sample answer integrating these three elements: "I am a stickler for punctuality and get annoyed when people show up for project team meetings late. It means that I have to go over the material they missed and bore the people who were on time. Everybody gets annoyed. But, I recognize that our business is dynamic, customers call, and problems arise demanding immediate attention. So, I often meet individually with the team's members to get their input on a good time and date for our meeting. I arrange to have minutes of the meeting distributed so those late or missing can be informed. Everybody seems pleased, and we get our work accomplished." Not only is your stated weakness an asset to the company, your ability to correct yourself demonstrates valuable talents any boss will welcome.

Responding to the greatest strengths question seems easier, but it also demands preparation; make sure the stories that you prepare illustrate your important strengths, and tell them in a way easily understood by the interviewer. Using a specific example to illustrate your strengths will be a plus, especially if you can integrate your response into situations the hiring manager has already discussed with you.

Do you have any reason to feel that you cannot perform the described job duties well? In some cases, physical or mental limitations can interfere with job performance, but it is illegal for an employer to discriminate against anyone only on the basis of a disability. The Americans with Disabilities Act says it has to be clear that disabled applicants cannot do the job even if reasonable accommodations are made for them.

Made-up situations that test a person's knowledge of the job may begin with questions like "What would you do if . . . ?" The quality of your solution is not nearly as important as your attitude and your creativity under fire. A calm approach is a best bet. Cushion your statements with answers like, "One of the things I might consider would be . . ." If you commit yourself to a process of what you *would* do, and it isn't the solution the *interviewer* would like or consider, you are in an awkward position, so give your answer a cushion of several possible choices. If you have experience related to the question, then provide specifics highlighting your essential skills and talents.

Give me an example of a time when you . . . ? The question could be completed with: *successfully resolved a customer complaint, juggled several time-critical tasks simultaneously, managed a group of professionals, and so on.* These "behavioral interviewing" questions, used by savvy interviewers, are a good way for employers to assess your demonstrated skills and talents from you having handled real situations. Using a response style embodying the problem-solution-results approach described earlier for accomplishment statements is an effective way to frame your answer. Providing clear, relevant responses using specific examples from your experience assures potential employers that you could tackle such situations in the new job. For almost any question asked of you during an interview, weaving in examples where you actually used some skill or skills relevant to the job will reinforce that you are the right person to be hired.

The State University of New York College at Brockport (**www .brockport.edu/career/behave.htm**) offers some suggestions and examples for successfully handling behavioral interviewing questions.

How did you get along with . . . ? This question can be asked about supervisors, coworkers, subordinates, even teachers. Few people get along with everyone. If you generally do, say so. If you had a problem with someone, there is usually no need to tell the whole tale here. The willingness to work out problems is a plus. Be positive, not blaming or complaining.

Would you accept part-time or temporary work? Employers are more inclined to hire for full-time work from a part-time or temporary employment pool than to take a person from the outside. If you plan to stay with the company, ask if a temporary or part-time job may result in a permanent hire before you say yes. If you want a temporary job and are offered a permanent position, however, consider their cost and time of training you. It takes most employees at least several months to begin to earn their pay. "No" is a better answer if you really want temporary or part-time work when you are offered a permanent, full-time position.

Why do you want to work for our company? If someone looking for a job is more interested in getting a good job than in being particular about where they work, then this attitude can make the person appear not to care about the company. One of the most important things you should do before you go to an interview—or ask for one—is find out all you can about the company. Identify some positive aspects of policies, procedures, or products you can discuss with interest. Do your homework—so you will have work to come home from. Today, you can find out almost everything you need to know about a company prior to the interview, just by browsing their Web site.

How long do you expect to work for us? The truth is that a company will not keep employees past its ability to use their skills. And you are not going to work for a company past the time that it is good for you. The best answer may be, "As long as I can continue making significant contributions to the success of the company." Companies also do not appreciate people who do not plan to stay for a reasonable amount of time. It is very costly to recruit, enroll in benefits, and train a new employee only to have that person leave.

Do you have any questions about the company or the job? Be ready for this question by preparing some questions of your own ahead of time to show your interest. You should be asking questions throughout the interview, too, rather than just responding when asked, to determine whether the job is what you really want. You do not want to irritate the interviewer with a deluge of questions, nor do you want to interfere with the time allocated for the interview, so choose a few important questions for each interview. Just as the interviewer may want you to meet with other people in the company for their take on you, it is appropriate for you to ask to meet with a prospective coworker or another manager in the company to hear their perspective. Further, your questions are a clear and an overt demonstration of your interest in the company, something that some candidates often fail to do and that may get them eliminated from further consideration. This is an ideal time to relate your interest, enthusiasm, and commitment to the company and the job.

There are some questions you must resolve honestly ahead of time:

- Are you willing to or can you move or travel, work overtime, take a temporary or part-time job?
- Do you have plans for your next job, your next few years, starting your own business, changing fields, going back to school?

In every case, the real questions are these: *Can you do the job? Will you stay with the company?*

Sometimes you may be asked questions that startle you. If you feel unprepared, it's wise to say, "I need a few moments to think about that." Then take a few deep breaths, relax, and begin confidently. If you still draw a blank, be prepared to deal with the situation, perhaps saying, "Maybe we could come back to that later," or "I really should be prepared to answer that but I'm not." It's a learning experience and you learn that you can keep cool.

Be prepared for some difficult ("whew!") questions if you have a poor work record, have ever been fired for serious problems, or have been convicted of a crime. Take a deep breath, relax a minute, look at the interviewer, and say in your own words something like this: "Yes, I made a mistake [or have done poorly in the past], but I learned my lesson, and I'm determined that it won't happen again." Then stop. Do not keep on explaining. If you sound confident and not defensive, the interviewer will be more likely to accept your answer. Perhaps you can include some recent experience as evidence that you've made some changes in your life. Again, you need to reassure the interviewer that you are capable of doing the job.

You may be startled by inappropriate or personal questions that appear to have nothing to do with job qualifications but may indicate discrimination. Questions about age, race, religion, nationality, home ownership, credit report, physical characteristics, organizations, political views, or disabilities are improper unless the answers are job related. Also inappropriate are questions that discriminate between males and females—such as questions about family planning, child care, or pregnancy.

Decide in advance how you will answer such questions if they are asked. Sometimes you can deflect a question by thinking about why the interviewer asked it. Sometimes young women are asked, "Do you have any kids?" when the interviewer is actually interested in knowing "What would prevent you from traveling out of town on company business two weeks per month?" A good response can be, "My personal life allows me to accept a position that involves traveling." This answer may be an acceptable response, relieving the interviewer's concerns about your ability to travel and allowing the interviewer to move on to the next topic. If the questioner seems on the malicious side, then be thankful you discovered this critical information now rather than after being hired. If the issue is not really important, you may prefer to answer the question rather than risk alienating the interviewer with a refusal. You may always ask, "Can you explain how this question relates to the job?" which will help you determine what is really being asked. A good sense of humor and respect for others can be enormously helpful.

Regrettably, some questions may be outright discriminatory. Some examples and tips for handling illegal questions are presented at this site: **www.jobweb.com/Resources/Library/Interviews__Resumes/Handling_Illegal _46_01.htm.**

Nelva Shore, a California employment specialist, says, "It really doesn't matter what questions are asked as long as you can talk!" Be ready to talk positively about yourself, your goals, and your reason for applying. Practice talking. One woman who stood out in an interview later told about how she had practiced sitting down in front of a mirror; she practiced talking out loud, answering questions, making eye contact, controlling voice melody— every phase of the interview—until she felt totally at ease. Her enthusiasm came through unspoiled by anxiety. You can learn these skills, too.

Follow-Up

If the interview has gone well, you may try to get a sense of your standing by asking what the next steps are and watching to see a favorable response. Some people try something known as a "trial close" by asking, "Well, I am excited about the job. When would I start?" while watching closely for signs from the interviewer confirming the question. Tailor the trial close to suit your communication style and the situation of the interview. Any negative responses should trigger some questions from you. Maybe a question was not answered to the interviewer's satisfaction and you missed the cues when it happened. Now you have a chance to recover and regain lost ground.

Career Perfect (**www.careerperfect.com/CareerPerfect/interviewFAQs5 .htm**) is a commercial Web site offering advice on different topics and the importance of interview follow-up.

Florida State University (**www.career.fsu.edu/ccis/guides/second_inter .html**) recommends how to prepare and handle a second interview.

If you aren't told the results at the end of the interview, feel free to ask when you will hear them. In the private sector (nongovernment), it is appropriate to send a thank-you letter right after the interview that encourages a reply (see page 257), perhaps asks for more information, or accepts an offer (see page 258). Then call after a week or so if you haven't heard. It is also important to give notice promptly if you decide to decline an offer.

Sometimes there is a delay in hiring someone after an interview. Several months may go by because of changes inside the company. Tactfully keep in touch with your contact in the company or with the personnel department until you are certain there is no opening for you or you are hired. Job Shop participant Hal Thomas suggests returning after one to two weeks to learn whether the position has been filled; returning in one to two months, perhaps with work samples, to show continued interest; and then sending a letter and work samples (if applicable) in six months.

What happens if you do not get the job? Sure it is disappointing, but do not just walk away and abandon a rich opportunity for feedback and networking. Capitalize on the relationship you've built with the interviewer to find out how you could have been better or what else you could have done during the interview to be the winning candidate, If you got several steps into the interviewing process before being rejected, you could ask the hiring manager and those who interviewed you what other departments within the company could use someone with your talents and skills. If no opportunities exist within the company, leveraging your relationship with the interviewers to network could yield new contact names and companies. Sometimes the new people who are hired leave the company soon after starting for a variety of reasons. If you were the second on the final list of candidates, you might get a phone call from the hiring manager inquiring about your interest in the job.

After you are hired, you may be asked to supply such items as a birth certificate, proof of citizenship, a green card if you are an immigrant, a photograph, and proof of age. Have these items ready if you feel they may be required.

JOB OFFERS: TOO MANY OR TOO FEW?

Most people do not negotiate the parameters for their jobs very often and are usually unskilled in getting the best offer possible from the company. Students starting in their first jobs or people employed for decades have trouble at the

February 4, 2003

Dierk Van Symms
Manager of Technical Services
Effective Micro Systems, Inc.
130 Meridian Dr., Suite 411
Aurora, IL 60505

Dear Mr. Van Symms:

Thank you for the chance to discuss a work opportunity with
Effective Micro Systems, Inc. I have completed the EMS
Interview Survey, and it is attached for your review.

I am pleased about the possibility of working for EMS as a member of your team. After meeting with you and your staff, I feel that
I would fit in very well with the group and would be immediately
helpful on the retrofit project you discussed. Each of you has
confirmed what I already know—that EMS is a quality organization with dedicated and customer-focused employees.

I look forward to continuing the interviewing process at our next
meeting you have scheduled on Wednesday, February 12, 2003,
at 9:00 am. Please feel free to call me at home or work if I can
answer further questions or provide additional information.

Sincerely yours,

Joanne M. Malatia
5405 Monroe St.
Aurora, IL 60504

Enclosure: EMS Interview Survey

Figure 7-11   Thank-You Letter Following an Interview by a Systems Analyst

October 30, 2002

Ms. Jill Jones
Director of Marketing
PTT Corporation
Dogwood, AL 36309

Dear Ms. Jones:

I am very pleased to accept an internship in marketing with PTT Corporation. It will be a pleasure to associate with the people I have met at PTT. The work you outlined in your letter sounds very challenging. I appreciate the chance to further my education in this way.

I look forward to starting on February 1. Please call if you wish to discuss further any aspect of my internship.

Sincerely yours,

Chris Cross
5401 Monroe St.
Mobile, AL 36608

Figure 7-12   Acceptance Letter

negotiating table. Some people get so excited to be asked to join the company during the interview that they immediately accept the first offer presented. It pays, literally, to be a bit reserved during the negotiation process and to try to be as rational as possible when discussing the terms of your employment. The fact that you are the one who is being offered the job means that you are now in the best position to gain the most from your negotiations. To prepare yourself to make the best possible deal, take the time to list all of the items that you want from your employer beforehand. Rank order these items in terms of importance to you to negotiate knowledgeably and rationally in a give and take with your prospective boss. Sometimes the items you negotiate for in the interview with the boss may change when the official offer is presented to you. The offer may come verbally from your boss, someone from the human resources office, or in a letter. If all of the things you discuss are presented to your satisfaction, then sending a confirmation letter is all that you need to do to seal the deal. Congratulations! If, however, some things are missing from the offer or are have changed from what you had agreed to previously, then now is the time to resolve them.

The time immediately before accepting a job offer is when you have the greatest bargaining power to negotiate for your compensation package. The company has invested time and energy interviewing and investigating you to determine that you are the one best suited to fill the position. They want you to accept their offer and will be most willing at that time to sweeten the deal to get you. It is now that you exercise your negotiation strategy, having done your homework and planning in advance. Do not be afraid to ask for something that you believe to be reasonable, and be prepared with a valid rationale if asked why. If an attractive offer is made to you, even saying the simple phrase, "Oh, I thought it would have been more?" with the right combination of vocal expression and body language may net you a sweeter deal. The best technique is to be silent after asking and wait until the other person speaks, even if the delay is 10, 20, 30 seconds, or more. Once you accept the offer or start work, asking for additional compensation or perks will probably not be successful and may even antagonize your new boss.

Taking the time to adequately prepare yourself for the negotiation stage of your job search is important for you to get the most compensation from the company, which can take many forms other than salary. In fact, you are limited only by your imagination for what you can ask for during the negotiation. You must be reasonable and prudent, however, to not push your demands beyond what your new boss would consider acceptable. Those items that your boss has direct control over will most likely be granted to you, as long as you don't go overboard with your demands. If your boss has to confirm with his or her manager or go to the human resources department for possible approval, then the likelihood of you getting those requests diminishes. Having a clear idea of what you want, rank ordering those items in terms of importance, and knowing the dollar cost of those items will help you win at the negotiation table. Also, trying not to appear adversarial will be important for you to keep your boss on your side to help you get the things that you want. Being able to "read" your boss to know when you have exhausted all negotiation avenues will let you know when it is time to stop pushing on one item, time to look at another item, or time to call it quits and make up your mind.

Always ask for any verbal offers to be given to you in writing. It is also reasonable to take some time to consider an offer. If your potential boss wanted to force you to accept an offer at the end of the interview, that should send some alarm bell off to make you wonder why this is being done. Make the decision that is right for you.

You probably will not get a job offer during your first interview. But suppose you do get a job offer in this early phase of your career search. Beware quick decisions. You can easily get carried away with excitement and leap into the first job that comes along. When recruits are in short supply, companies may try to give a job seeker little time to weigh a decision. If you have researched the company and know you want to work there, your decision will be easier to make.

One suggestion that may help in your decision making is to conduct a "head and heart" analysis to select the best job. List "head" and "heart" items, rank them in order of importance, assign values and weights to them, compute the values for each, and then total the values. Examples of "head" items are salary, bonus, stock plans, benefits, commute time, etc. "Heart" items are how you feel about the job. For example, how much you like your boss or coworkers, how you feel about the company, and your office, or how much you enjoy your work and how fun your coworkers are. The job offer that receives the highest combined "head and heart" score should be accepted. If your head and heart scores are very dissimilar for a specific offer, then further evaluation and consideration are warranted.

Some jobs sound rewarding in terms of personal growth, but the salary is so low you could not live on it without making sacrifices. Another job pays very well, but the work sounds dull and disagreeable. You might even be offered a temporary job; it would fulfill your immediate needs, but you'd be back on the job market in six months or so. Should you accept one of these less desirable jobs just to get hired or to get experience? When either employer or employee is less than honest in the hiring game, they both lose.

If you aren't hired for the job you want right away, you may be only one of many well-qualified applicants. In a competitive field, you may spend months finding a job. Whether you should take a less desirable job depends on how long you can afford to wait and continue the search. If you job hunt for many months without a nibble, you may need to consider alternatives: other careers, new training, other opportunities in your present position,

"Night work! You mean when it's dark?"

© Jim Unger /distributed by United Media, 1998.

additional paid or volunteer experience that may be useful in a different kind of job.

You may have to start at the bottom and work up to the job you want. Suppose you, a business major with a fresh degree from a good university, are offered a job as a mail clerk. Or you have a master's degree in computer programming, but you are offered a job as a computer operator. You may feel such offers are beneath your dignity. But before you ride away on your high horse, consider these facts: one major oil company makes a practice of hiring as mail clerks new graduates who are candidates for all management and public relations jobs. In so doing, they have a chance to look you over before entrusting a more important job to you. And you have a chance to network inside and explore possibilities before getting too entrenched. Be wary of turning down a job that fails to meet your expectations. Ask some company employees what the offer means. Ask the interviewer what the growth potential of the job is and whether you may be given a performance review in three to six months for a possible promotion.

Job hunting requires that you keep involved in some part of the process at all times. Keep in mind a clear picture of what you want and the place you would like to work. Frustration and rejection are a normal part of the experience; both can be overcome with the passion to pursue your dreams. Although being flexible is reasonable, do not lose sight of your goals or settle for less. Focus on the changes you can make to find more satisfaction in the workplace. Be true to yourself, and be persistent.

ELECTRONIC COMMUNICATIONS, SCANNERS, AND THE INTERNET

In our electronic age, we conduct business very quickly, and job hunting is no exception. A potential hiring manager or recruiter may ask you to send your résumé right away via e-mail or fax; you may see a job ad in the newspaper that lists only a fax number and no address; or you may read about a position on a company's Web site asking for e-mail responses only. This seems wonderful; yet some caution needs to be exercised. Your résumé was designed to have its maximum positive visual impact on someone who receives your document as you printed it. Can you be assured that the résumé you carefully designed and crafted will look the same and have the same effect when sent electronically? The short answer, unfortunately, is No. The résumé that is a work of art in your hands may look common, ugly, or even illegible when received on a well-worn fax machine in need of an overhaul. The résumé you created with your word processing software and sent via e-mail can be opened by someone using a different word processor, who may see a jumble of characters and symbols rather than what you had intended. Someone may ask you to insert your résumé into the body of an e-mail rather than attach it as a separate file to avoid potential virus infection. You lose all of your formatting, your selected font, and, certainly, the dramatic impact you had hoped for. If you send your résumé directly from your computer to the recipient's fax machine, several pages of garbage characters may be printed unless you've formatted your résumé for electronic distribution.

To the dismay of the creator of the perfect résumé, many companies now use computerized scanning systems to screen applicants. The technological ease of use and affordability of these systems makes them attractive even to small companies. These systems scan a person's résumé, integrating the information into a giant database for future exploration by hiring managers. Companies have gotten sophisticated and efficient at using scanning systems to process the hundreds or thousands of résumés received to eliminate the problems of people handling and reviewing paper résumés, the time it takes, and the amount of physical space résumés occupy in storage. Managers within a company can easily access the résumé database by entering the relevant search parameters and have the résumés of matching candidates presented on monitors for further evaluation. You will probably see newspaper job ads or a company's Web site indicating résumés received will be scanned and retained by the company.

Should you compete in this electronic world given that the main thrust of everything presented in this chapter so far has been to target specific hiring managers to receive your résumé and telephone calls? Yes! You should explore all avenues when looking for a job to maximize the chances your résumé reaches a hiring manager. Just keep in mind that your résumé becoming one with thousands or tens of thousands of other résumés in a company's database does not give you the same advantage that sending your résumé directly to a hiring manager does. However, being in a company's résumé database may give you additional exposure to some hiring managers who were previously unknown to you.

There are three main considerations when preparing a résumé to be scanned. First, is your résumé in a form that can be easily scanned? Second, does your résumé contain the key words or phrases that are commonly queried for in searches? Last, is your résumé in a format that can be easily integrated—digested, if you will—by the scanning system?

Some simple rules for scannable résumés apply:

- Use white, non-shiny paper.
- Use 10- to 14-point type.
- Use standard, normal fonts, no **bolding,** *italics,* or <u>underlining.</u>
- Use white space to clearly separate text sections.
- Avoid graphics, bullets, special characters, or lines.
- Use 65 to 70 characters per line.
- Use laser printing, not dot matrix.
- Minimize or eliminate folds in résumé.

Now that your résumé is scannable, you need to ensure that the correct key words and phrases are included to generate the most "hits" when queried on a search. Résumés written to be read by people are loaded with verbs to describe action; but for your scannable résumé, stocking it with nouns and the appropriate terminology used in the industry or company is the norm. It is reasonable to have a section in your scannable résumé called "Key Words," which lists all of the relevant words you believe could be included in the search; for example, *manage, program, $100,000 budget, Microsoft WORD, Windows XT, 12 years experience, report, schedule, 15%, supervisor, B.A., M.B.A., University of Maryland, PC, college, engineer, SQL, Xerox Corporation, General Motors, automation, TQM, accountant, administrator.* A side benefit of this tactic is some résumé searching systems are programmed to look for both key search words and the number of their occurrences, with high instances of both variables required for the résumé to be sent to a hiring manger or other person for further review. When submitting your résumé to companies, it may be advantageous for you to send two versions, one to be read by a human and one to be scanned. Let the recipient know this in your cover letter. Continual innovations in scanning technology will only improve, thereby making this method more attractive for processing applicants in the future. A résumé that is suitable for scanning and has the added benefit of being formatted for successful transmission through e-mail systems and for cutting and pasting into online e-forms appears on pages 266–267.

The last thing that you must worry about is how easy it is for your résumé to be received, uploaded, and integrated into the company's computer system, whether for subsequent scanning or reception as an e-mail message. As you visit some job posting sites on the Internet and some company Web sites, you will find that they have special e-forms in which you type your résumé information directly into their system. Although tedious, this method ensures your information is integrated into a database correctly. Some of these sites let you "cut and paste" your résumé into their e-forms sections. Some sites request that you send your résumé in a special format that can be easily uploaded into their system. Now the format of your résumé becomes important, whether for uploading or transmission through e-mail systems.

Rebecca Smith's résumé site (**www.eresumes.com**) is a classic for helping people craft effective electronic résumés, providing detailed information and résumé examples.

A good source to explain the differences between scanning, e-forms, and posting sites for electronic résumés, along with reference sites to visit, is **www.computerbits.com/archive/1996/0700/resume.html.**

Beloit College in Wisconsin (**beloit.edu/~facs/onlinejobsearch/resume5 .htm**) presents tips, techniques, and link sites to writing good electronic résumés.

If at all possible, create your résumé with a standardized word processing application, such as Microsoft's WORD, which is the business standard. Two common output formats used with word processors have the highest probability of intact transmission: RTF (Rich Text Format) and ASCII (American Standard Code for Information Interchange). Outputting your résumé in RTF format, from your Microsoft WORD, PageMaker, or other word processing software, improves the chances that the formatting and overall appearance will remain unchanged when sent electronically and subsequently viewed by a hiring manager on his or her computer system using a (possibly) different word processing application. Résumés produced in ASCII format should be universally readable; but all of your formatting will be lost. If an older version of a word processing application is used to open a file created with a newer version of the same software application, or the recipient has a different computer platform, documents generated as RTF or ASCII files can save the day.

Confirm with the recipient the format and word processing application that will be used to read your résumé. You may see ads, either newspaper or Web site, specifying a format or word processing application to be used in reading received résumés. Know that what the ads ask for may or may not allow you to keep the integrity and visual impact of your résumé.

Finally, if you decide to post your résumé on a Web site in HTML format, a common language for Internet browsers like Netscape, Mosaic, or Internet Explorer, it is possible that the reader may see something different than you intended due to browser compatibility and version issues. These are good reasons why it is important to invest the extra time to ferret out the appropriate person within the company to send your résumé to directly via the mail. A personal contact can save you from getting lost in this world of virtual unreality.

It is important to know what the policy of a company is about receiving unsolicited résumés, especially résumés attached to e-mails. The use of the Internet has given rise to the spread of people sending computer viruses through e-mails and their attachments. A hiring manager he or she may be reluctant to open your unsolicited résumé attached to your e-mail, and he or she may even delete the entire message without opening it. Inserting your résumé into the body of the e-mail document via cut and paste can alleviate the concern. You may lose some of the formatting that you created for your résumé to make it appealing and compelling to read, but you will increase the chances of the hiring manager reading it. Experiment as much as possible with friends and associates to confirm that what you see on your screen and what you want a hiring manager, someone in personnel, or some other contact to see is what will actually appear on their screen.

There are job sites on the Internet that will allow you to post your résumé for potential employers to see; if an employer is interested, he or she can then contact you. Some of these sites provide a free application that lets you create a résumé online for entry into their system for subsequent display. Some sites even prompt you through the résumé writing process to make it as easy and painless as possible. Can great jobs be found this way? Of course. There is a catch, however: every potential employer who accesses that job posting Web site—and anyone else for that matter, even your current employer—can see your résumé. Plus, you are now out of the control loop on where and to whom you present your résumé. Potential recruiters may take and present it to companies unauthorized by you, which may compromise your ongoing job search efforts. This also holds true for people who post their résumés on their own Web sites as well.

Joanne M. Malatia
5405 Monroe St.
Aurora, IL 60504
jmmalatia@yahoo.com
home: (708)-555-1478
cell: (708)-555-4321

KEY WORDS

IBM3033, AS400, PCs, OS/MVS, OS/400, Windows XP, Windows 2000,
Windows NT, COBOL, BASIC, RPGII, Pascal, JCL. Assembler MS Office,
Access, Oracle SQL, SAS, SPPS, MAPPER, Systems Analyst, database,
Computer Programmer, Data Collector, raw materials, purchasing
system, Production, 37% improvement, team player, communication
skills, B.S., computer information systems.

PROFESSIONAL EXPERIENCE

Watlow Electric Manufacturing Company, Batavia, IL, 1999-Present
Systems Analyst (2001-Present)

+Develop a cross-checking system that improved on-time deliveries
for 12 major customers a minimum of 18%.

+Design and implement a computerized raw materials purchasing
system, installed ahead of schedule and under budget, that saved
$320,000 annually in excess raw materials inventory.

+Coordinate implementation of corporate-side order processing and
sales analysis system, ensuring effective transition with no
disruption to order processing or sales teams.

+Conduct semi-annual system audits (mainframe, mid-sized, and PC-
based system) to determine future needs, configure necessary
hardware and software requirements, develop system strategy, and
present findings to management, maintaining company's premier
position in the industry in all productivity per employee measures.

Computer Programmer (1999-2001)

+Defined data sets, processing problems, and objectives using MAPPER
database language to improve production run changeovers by 16%.

+Performed general maintenance on all computer hardware systems at
Batavia plant minimizing downtime and disruptions to plant
operations.

+Instructed team members and plant users (over 60 people) on a
variety of business and manufacturing computer applications.

Lovejoy Rehabilitation Center, West Chicago, IL, 1997-1999
Data Collector for Research/Education Department

+Directed a system investigation of the Materials Management
Department to determine system requirements for upgrade and
efficiency improvements. Results led to $832,000 investment in new
equipment, standardization of software applications, and
productivity improvements up to 37% in departments transitioning
from manual to computerized systems.

**Figure 7-13   Chronological Résumé of a Systems Analyst, Written to Be
Scannable and Compatible for Transmission via the Internet**

+Coordinated acquisition and installations of new system upgrades to ensure smooth transition.

+Designed and implemented software application training programs for staff to master new applications and procedures quickly.

+Conducted 130 patient telephone interviews to determine specific system needs and prepared management report with findings.

+Implemented a successful follow-up tracking system to gather patient feedback to measure service performance goals and find where new modifications could yield improved patient satisfaction.

McDonald's of Stratford, Bloomingdale, IL, 1995–1997

Administrative Assistant to General Manager

+Managed and balanced daily books and cash sheets while maintaining cash flow to ensure efficient operations.

+Scheduled and planned employee activities and supply deliveries according to management goals.

+Oriented and trained all new employees.

EDUCATION

B.S. (Computer Information Systems) DeVry Institute of Technology, Lombard, IL

COMPUTER EXPERTISE

Hardware: IBM3033, AS400, PCs
Operating Systems: OS/MVS, OS/400, Windows XP, Windows 2000,
                   Windows NT
Languages: COBOL, BASIC, RPGII, Pascal, JCL. Assembler
Applications: MS Office, Access, Oracle SQL, SAS, SPPS, MAPPER

You must be cautious about protecting your privacy from people taking the information contained in your résumé and using it for nefarious purposes. Your phone number, e-mail address, street address, and occupation are highly valuable data and should be protected. You can avoid putting detailed contact information on your posting; instead, use a special e-mail address at one of the free, Web-based sites like Yahoo or Hotmail. This protects you from a potential avalanche of unsolicited sales calls and Internet spam (unwanted e-mail messages), yet it affords an easy way for legitimate employers to contact you. Also, use only those résumé posting sites that offer privacy safeguards and protections.

Résumé posting and job listing sites are numerous and can create a false sense of security, promising that hundreds or thousands of employers will see your résumé or that you will see hundreds or thousands of jobs in your career field, quickly enabling a match to occur. You may get lucky and actually get a job this way. The data seem to indicate, however, that few job seekers and few employers find matches this way. Data from two studies summarized by Bolles[11] from the year 2000 indicated that fewer than 5 percent of online job seekers found employment via the Internet, and fewer than 10 percent of employers found new hires through this medium. As the technology capability of both job seekers and employers improves, more jobs will, no doubt, be found via the Internet, but do not rely on this method exclusively.

Monster.com (**www.monster.com**) is a huge Web site offering résumé posting, job listings, and career help. You can craft your résumé online following Monster's template.

Here is a commercial site providing résumé posting and listings for thousands of jobs: **www.employmentguide.com**.

The commercial Web site **www.nationjob.com** uses a "personal agent" (an application that automatically monitors the listings) to scan job listings continually and notify you when a job match is found, thus letting the power of the computer work 24/7 for you. This feature is common on larger sites.

USAJobs (**www.usajobs.opm.gov**) is a posting and listing service for employment in U.S. government jobs.

Another commercial Web site that uses a personal agent to inform you of a job match is **www.4work.com**.

SUMMARY

Investing the time to identify your job search objectives, develop your strategies and confirm your tactics will get you in front of the most important person in your quest, the hiring manager. You should be proactive and aggressive, going after those jobs that meet your expectations, investigating, uncovering, and creating opportunities that may not be apparent to job seekers or even potential employers. Motivation and persistence are two powerful driving forces.

Know and understand the sources from which information about jobs is obtained. About 75 percent of all jobs are found in the hidden job market, that realm of interpersonal networks leveraged by the job seeker to meet people who can help him or her meet a hiring manager. Want ads in newspapers and on Web sites and jobs gotten through recruiters and agencies account for about 10 percent each. Your goal is to use all avenues, but spend the most time in the hidden network, as the competition there can be nonexistent or minimal.

Knowing how hiring managers think is an essential competitive advantage that can help you ensure the most favorable receptivity from them. Hiring managers think when they read résumés or meet candidates, "Do I like you, and can you make me rich, make me a hero, and make my problems go away?" Your efforts to answer Yes to these questions improve your chances of gaining an audience with the manager and winning the job.

The main source for the ideal job is through the network of contacts you develop and cultivate, from close friends and acquaintances to strangers you will come to know. Job hunting is about building relationships with people who can refer and introduce you to other people and ultimately the hiring manager. You should use your own key questions when meeting new people: "Will you be my boss? Do you know my boss? Do you know where my boss may be?" to help you maximize these encounters. To make your network effective, you need to keep your contacts informed, thank them for their assistance, and do what you can to help them.

Recruiters (given the moniker "headhunters") and employment agencies are two other viable sources for jobs; but you should exercise caution when using them and know how their methods apply to you. Keep control of what you want them to do. Recruiters will not consider you if you are outside the profile of their search. Using contingency recruiters adds a fee premium to the cost for a company to hire you. Agencies can offer temporary or permanent work.

Advertised jobs in the newspaper or on Web sites are the most competitive, as everyone sees them and will respond. Avoid responding to ads that do not list the hiring company. Responses to ads are processed by human resources personnel, who are charged with the task of selecting the few best résumés from the hundreds or thousands received, or they are scanned into a résumé database for further analysis and possible selection. Either way, you face barriers to reaching the hiring manager. Do your own detective work to reach the hiring manager directly.

Your résumé is your marketing document designed to present you in the most favorable light to the hiring manager. The most important function of your résumé is to entice the hiring manager to call you. Your résumé will help you clarify your job history and serve as a source for questions during an interview. There are three basic résumé styles: chronological, which lists your employment history and accomplishments in descending order; functional, which contains groupings of your accomplishments in key skill areas; and hybrid, which combines elements of the chronological and functional résumés. Managers prefer chronological résumés, as these clearly show your work history. Having powerful quantitative and qualitative accomplishment statements indicating results of your efforts is the heart of any great résumé, is the most difficult task to do, and is what hiring managers want to see. You should design your résumé carefully, selecting paper, font, style, spacing, and content so essential information "grabs" and holds the hiring manager's attention. Writing a good cover letter will help ensure your résumé is read. Having a reference list to hand out during the interview marks you as a candidate who is prepared and shows initiative. You may be asked to complete a job application before being granted an interview, a document that may divulge much more information about you than does your résumé.

Going into a job interview having done adequate research on the job, company, and interviewer; having anticipated and prepared answers to questions; having viewed a videotape of yourself responding to tough questions in a mock interview; constantly projecting that you are a likable and capable person; and remembering to temper your answers and actions to satisfy the manager's four key questions will put you on track to advance to the next round of interviews and, ultimately, be offered the job. Using "trial closes" at the end of the interview demonstrates your interest in the job and will garner important feedback about how you did. Following up the interview with a thank-you card or handwritten note is a nice personal touch. If you do not win the job, possibly the interviewer can be a networking source for you.

It is important to know what compensation you want and the ways to negotiate for it when you receive the job offer. Having done the research up front, so that you know what the going rate is for what you want, helps you play equally in the negotiating game. Equating all elements in the offered compensation package into their dollar equivalents or going through a "head and heart" analysis of competing job offers provides a mechanism to help determine which job to accept and also how to negotiate for more.

Care must be exercised when sending résumés or other documents through faxes, e-mail, or computer networks, as what you send may not arrive intact, usually to your detriment. Scanning résumés is practiced by many companies and merges your résumé with thousands of others into a database that hiring managers mine for viable candidates based on key word searches. Using a special format, type font, and key word list will help you float in this electronic sea of data. You can output your résumé in RTF or ASCII format to be most compatible with different computer systems and word processing software packages. Putting your résumé in the body of an e-mail message avoids having the recipient delete it for fear of a potential computer virus in any attachment. Be cautious about creating and posting your résumé online, to protect your privacy and avoid unapproved use of your contact information.

SELF-ASSESSMENT EXERCISES

1. The Job Hunt Begins

a. Write your accomplishment statements. Think in terms of what problem you faced, what you did, and what the results were. Use quantitative results wherever possible.

Accomplishment 1

Problem _____

_____

Solution _____

_____

Results _____

_____

Accomplishment 2

Problem _____

_____

Solution _____

_____

Results _____

_____

b. Begin a rough draft of your résumé. Then polish and type a good copy.

Name _____

Address _____

Home phone _____   Work phone _____

Fax _____   E-mail _____

Position objective _____

Summary _____

_____

_____

Experience summary (Make chronological or if necessary hybrid or functional.)

_____

_____

_____

_____

_____

Education _____

_____

_____

Personal paragraph _____

_____

_____

_____

Special notes (honors, works published, organizations, etc.) _____

_____

_____

c. Write a cover letter to accompany your résumé.

2. Practicing an Interview

Some interviewers use a rating scale to grade your performance on various points of importance to them. Page 274 shows a scale used by recruiters who come from various workplaces to interview students on campus. Role-play an interview. Then, using the interview rating chart, rate yourself or ask someone to rate you on your interview skills. Here are some what/how/why practice questions.

Work Experience

What have you done to get to your present position?

What were your major responsibilities on your last job (or last military experience)?

What did you like most about that job?

What did you like least about that job?

What problems did you face? How did you overcome these problems?

What did you learn on your last job?

How do you feel your last job used your ability?

Why did you leave (or are you planning to leave) your last job?

What impressions do you think you left on your last job?

Why do you want to work for us?

What do you feel you can contribute?

Education

What were your favorite courses (workshops, seminars)?

Why did you choose your major?

How would you rate your instructors?

What activities and clubs were you in? How did you participate?

How did you finance your education?

What further education are you planning?

Skills and Values

How do you get along with people (supervisors, coworkers, instructors)?

What are your transferable (general) skills?

INTERVIEW RATING CHART—CONFIDENTIAL

Santa Clara University

Career Planning and Placement Office

Firm _____

Recruiter _____ Date _____

I. CHARACTERISTICS OF CANDIDATE

A = Interview preparation
B = Clarity of career objectives
C = Realistic career objectives
D = Appropriate academic preparation
E = Personal appearance
F = Communicative ability
G = Emotional maturity
H = Self-confidence
I = Motivation
J = Overall rating

II. EMPLOYER INTEREST

1 = Particularly high interest
2 = Interest with further consideration necessary
3 = Prefer not to make offer
4 = Needs placement counseling

III. ADDITIONAL COMMENTS

RATING SCALE   1) Outstanding   2) Above average   3) Average   4) Below average   5) Poor

NAME	I. CHARACTERISTICS OF CANDIDATE										II.	III. COMMENTS
	A	B	C	D	E	F	G	H	I	J		

Figure 7-14   Interview Scale

What are your work-specific skills?

What are your personality-responsibility skills?

What are your strengths?

What are your weaknesses?

How important is money to you?

How well do you work on your own?

How many days did you take off last year for sickness and personal business?

How do you feel about overtime? Flexible hours? Part-time or temporary work? Travel? Moving to a new location?

What do you do when a coworker is behind schedule?

What kind of decision maker are you?

Goals

What do you see yourself doing in five years?

How do you plan to get there?

What areas of growth and development do you plan to work on?

What salary would you like to earn?

Tell me about yourself!

3. More Interview Questions

Make up some questions you would like an interviewer to ask you.

4. The Application Form

Carefully fill out the application form on pages 276–277 and sign it for use as a future reference.

5. The Job Hunt Checklist

If you are job hunting now, establish a goal: for example, you will contact twenty-five people by information interviewing, networking, applying for jobs, writing letters, making telephone calls, and sending résumés on request. To check your progress, answer the following questions *Yes* or *No*. Use this

EMPLOYMENT APPLICATION

Personal Data

Position Applied For   Application Date   /   /

Name (last, first, middle)

Social Security Number   Driver's License Number (if required by job)

Address

City   State   Zip Code

Home phone (   )   Message Phone (   )

Date available for work ____ / ____ / ____   Have you been employed here before?   ❑ Yes   ❑ No
Are you legally eligible for employment in this country?   ❑ Yes   ❑ No
(Proof of U.S. citizenship or immigration status will be required upon employment.)
If you are under 18, can you furnish a work permit?   ❑ Yes   ❑ No
Type of employment desired: ❑ Full Time   ❑ Part Time   ❑ Temporary   ❑ Seasonal
Have you ever been convicted of a felony in the last 7 years?   ❑ Yes   ❑ No
(Such conviction may be relevant if job-related, but does not bar you from employment.) If yes, please explain.

Employment History

List your last four employers, assignments or volunteer activities, starting with most recent employer, including military experience.

From   To   Employer   Phone (   )

Job Title   Address

Immediate Supervisor & Title   Summarize the nature of work performed and job responsibilities.

Reason for leaving.   Beginning rate/salary $ per   Ending rate/salary $ per

From   To   Employer   Phone (   )

Job Title   Address

Immediate Supervisor & Title   Summarize the nature of work performed and job responsibilities.

Reason for leaving.   Beginning rate/salary $ per   Ending rate/salary $ per

From   To   Employer   Phone (   )

Job Title   Address

Immediate Supervisor & Title   Summarize the nature of work performed and job responsibilities.

Reason for leaving.   Beginning rate/salary $ per   Ending rate/salary $ per

Figure 7-15   Application Form

Courtesy of Alida Stevens, President, Smith & Vandiver, Inc., Watsonville, CA

From	To	Employer	Phone (	)

Job Title   Address

Immediate Supervisor & Title   Summarize the nature of work performed and job responsibilities.

Reason for leaving.   Beginning rate/salary $ per   Ending rate/salary $ per

Skills and Qualifications

Summarize special skills and qualifications acquired from employment or other experience that may qualify you for work with our Company.

Education Record

High school	Dates attended
Degrees or diplomas	Course of study
College/University	Dates attended
Degrees or diplomas	Course of study
Other	Dates attended
Degrees or diplomas	Course of study

References

Name	Phone number ( )	Years known
Name	Phone number ( )	Years known
Name	Phone number ( )	Years known

It is understood and agreed that any misrepresentation by me in this application will be sufficient cause for cancellation of this application and/or separation from the employer's service if I have been employed. Furthermore, I understand that just as I am free to resign at any time, the Employer reserves the right to terminate my employment at any time, with or without cause and without prior notice. I understand that no representative of the Employer has the authority to make any assurances to the contrary.

I give the Employer the right to investigate all references and to secure additional information about me, if job related. I hereby release from liability the Employer and its representatives for seeking such information and all other persons, corporations or organizations for furnishing such information.

Signature of Applicant   Date   /   /

checklist to help you set new goals for other tasks. As with any checklist, refer back to it frequently to monitor your progress, update your activities, and reward yourself for your achievements.

_____ Have you decided what you want in a job?

_____ Can you articulate these wants clearly and succinctly to others?

_____ Have you identified job titles or functions that fit your wants?

_____ Have you interviewed twenty-five people to obtain information about jobs and companies?

_____ Have you written an effective résumé for each job title or function?

_____ Have you identified and researched companies that use these job titles or functions?

_____ Have you contacted a network of at least twenty-five people who could help you?

_____ Have you identified and contacted the hiring managers in target companies for these job titles or functions?

_____ Have you gotten job interviews?

_____ Did you honestly critique yourself after each job interview?

_____ Did you write and send thank-you letters to the people who interviewed you?

_____ Did you follow up if you did not get the job to ask the hiring manager for recommendations to other managers within the company or to managers in other companies?

 ## GROUP DISCUSSION QUESTIONS

1. Who do you want to network with and why?
2. Who do you want as personal or professional references and why?
3. What concerns do you have about contacting hiring managers, and how can you resolve these concerns?
4. How will you ensure that you have a good interview?

8

Decisions, Decisions

What's Your Next Move?

 **GOALS**

- Survey the options.

- Learn a decision-making process.

- Set realistic goals.

*I*n the last half century, opportunities and choices have increased faster than at any other time in history, particularly in the affluent, technological segments of the world. Ordinary people can see other lifestyles around the globe through travel and television, talk to thousands of strangers over the Internet, become educated, control family structure, and enjoy a proliferation of consumer goods unimagined by emperors of old. These innovations create a growing array of careers. As a result, decision making is more difficult, especially when you are trying to stay true to your values in a strong popular culture.

Throughout the career search process you have been making small decisions, often without even realizing it. And because of them, you have likely zeroed in on a general career area, if not a job title, and you have focused on the background that you will need for this type of career.

Author and educator H. B. Gelatt reminds us that most people make decisions easily most of the time without thinking too much. Each personality type has its own decision-making style, ranging from the dynamic, energetic, and enterprising risk takers to conventional, slower moving, and more careful people.

Although few people can be fully defined according to personality types, one may say that, generally, the following behavior patterns commonly occur among different personality types. The social person often acts out of caring for others but is not always practical. Both the realistic and the conventional types are practical folks who tend to stay within secure societal norms. The conventional type follows the lead of others; realistic types will decide independently, often disregarding people's feelings but generally staying on the conservative side. The creative/artistic person, on the other hand, will see so many possibilities—including some that follow no known guidelines—that he or she will have difficulty making choices. And, whereas the enterprising person leaps first and gets the facts later, the investigative type keeps researching, hoping that working on a decision long enough will make the results absolutely clear and certain. What kind of decision maker are you?

> I try to take one day at a time,
> but sometimes several days
> attack me at once.
> —*Ashleigh Brilliant*[1]

Some people want things in their lives settled, so they make decisions promptly and with satisfaction. Others like to keep all their options open, so they tend to delay decisions until the last possible minute.

For anyone faced with tough decisions, for the person who tends to agonize over every decision, for those who delay decisions, organized steps can provide perspective. In this chapter we consider a *decision-making dozen:* four attitudes, four options, and a four-phase decision-making process. Its purpose is not to nail you down to a decision but to show you a structured method for reaching one.

ATTITUDES

Four attitudes can help you make a good decision: stay calm; be persistent; keep your perspective; be confident.

Stay Calm

Although a certain amount of anxiety can motivate a person to make a decision, too much can interfere with it. If you are under severe pressure, you may try to escape through fantasies: quit work or school altogether; join the Marines; end your marriage; run off with your secretary; sell everything, hitch up the wagon, and head west! The uncertainties are as numerous as the fantasies: Am I OK? Is there anything at all in life for me, or is this all there is? Will my health hold up? Will my kids ever get settled? Will I ever have kids? Will I look like a fool if I go back to school? Can I keep on succeeding? Do I even want to? Sometimes turbulent thoughts can seem like part of the decision-making process. You can practice letting them go, however, by affirming that you have made good decisions in the past and you can do so now.

Be Persistent

Take one step at a time. You rarely have to put a major life decision into action in one immediate, straight-line leap. It often takes thought and some testing to sort out all the possibilities. If a decision to get a four-year degree seems overwhelming, a small decision to look at college catalogs in the library or talk to an educational counselor or teacher may be a manageable first step. But make up your mind to keep moving toward the goal you seek.

Keep Your Perspective

Stop and occasionally review your direction. If it is helpful, use the exercises in Chapter 9 to assemble information that is relevant to a career decision. Identify your strong and weak spots as well as areas you still need to explore. Keep focusing on what you want your life to be like.

Be Confident

If you are honest, you know that you have made some good decisions in the past—from what to wear to where to work. A lack of confidence can be a giant block on the road to good decision making. As Ken Keyes, Jr., says, "Beware what you tell yourself!"[2] Compare the person who says, "I don't deserve success, I'm just not good at much of anything," with the person who may say, "Everyone—including me—deserves success." Sometimes our bad feelings can send us in search of a problem: "Don't cheer me up because it will ruin my misery program." Affirmations, those positive and negative thoughts we think over and over again, are so powerful that the authors of the children's book *Make It So!* ask children to speculate, "So—I've been wondering—could most of my problems be caused by me?"[3]

You can't know the future. Some decisions will work out; some will not. In order to improve your life, you change what can be changed, accept what can't be changed and work with it, and hope you have the wisdom to know the difference.

> When you don't know which way to turn, son,
> try something. Don't jest do nothin'!
> —*Grandpa to grandson in* Cold Sassy Tree[4]

FOUR OPTIONS

At this time you have four options. Go back to or remain in school, seek a new job or involvement, keep the same job with a new approach, or keep the status quo by deciding not to decide.

Back to School

If you are already in school, committed to staying there, and clear on your program of studies, then you have already made a decision.

More and more people are returning to school more often, staying there longer, and attending in nontraditional ways. According to researcher Arthur Levine, president of Teachers College at Columbia University, fewer than 16 percent of college students are eighteen- to twenty-two-year-olds attending full time and living on campus. Fifty-five percent work, 50 percent are over twenty-five years of age, and 42 percent attend part time. These students expect the college to serve them as adult consumers, not treat them as young-sters.[5] No one can afford to "stop learning" today. The rapid pace and complexity of change is redefining how work is done and what skills will be needed. This makes ongoing learning essential if you are to adapt to the changes taking place. The more you learn, the more you will increase your employability, your potential earning power, and your control over the kind of work that you want to do. To be truly career self-reliant in this rapidly changing world, you need to make a commitment to yourself to actively manage your work/life and learning opportunities.

> In the world of the future, the
> new illiterate will be the person
> who has not learned how to learn.
> —*Alvin Toffler*

The school you choose will likely reflect the community in which it is located and may influence your career choice. Colleges in Silicon Valley relate well to the computer industry; those in a rural, agricultural area will reflect careers that support agriculture.

Learning to learn, to be a generalist, to have a broad view of the world, to continue learning and developing abilities—these are essential skills for the future. The majority of jobs now require some postsecondary education and training; many unskilled jobs are either being automated or moving offshore. Industry is slowly realizing that trained people are more important than new hardware, but upgrading workers is more difficult than previously realized.[6]

A high school dropout is eight times more likely than a college graduate and three times more likely than a high school graduate to be unemployed.[7] Past are the days when a high school graduate could expect to get a life-lasting and decent-paying job that would support the American Dream of a family, house, car, and yearly vacation. High school dropouts are 72 percent more likely to be unemployed and earn 27 percent less than high school graduates.[8] The U.S. Bureau of Labor Statistics shows that those who learn more earn more. In 1998 the median earnings for full-time workers ages twenty-five and over showed the following:

Education Level	Median Earnings
Professional Degree	$74,560
Doctorate	$54,905
Master's Degree	$40,368
Bachelor's Degree	$32,629
Associate Degree	$24,398
High School Diploma	$18,732
No High School Diploma	$12,804

SOURCE: U.S. Census Bureau, 2000

Employment in occupations requiring at least a bachelor's degree is expected to grow 21.6 percent; jobs requiring an associate degree are projected to grow 32 percent; and jobs requiring a postsecondary vocational award will grow 24.1 percent during the 2000–2010 period. Those occupations requiring only work-related experience will increase by 12.4 percent.[9] So as you can see, postsecondary education is essential for you to achieve your goals.

And these days, with the intensity of the global economy, many people with the slightest connection to the business world seem to be thinking of going for an MBA—master's in business administration—if they haven't done so already.

On the educational scene, the picture for younger and college-educated women is improving. Though some continue to avoid pursuing degrees in the sciences, math, and engineering, even though these are pathways to lucrative professions, the numbers of women enrolled in these courses are increasing. Those who study these disciplines tend to drop out at higher rates than men because, except for those who study at women's colleges, they find the classes subtly or not so subtly male oriented. Even so, enrollment in these schools has been steadily increasing.[10]

In 2002, for adults age twenty-five and older, the high school graduation rate was slightly greater for women than men, 84.4 percent to 83.2 percent, respectively. Also, in 2002, 27 percent of adults age twenty-five and over had a bachelor's degree, a percentage point higher than in 2001. The highest percentage of college graduates in adults age twenty-five and over as of March 2002 were Asians and Pacific Islanders, followed by non-Hispanic whites (29 percent), African Americans (17 percent), and Hispanics (11 percent). Data from 2001 showed that the approximate average earnings for adults ages eighteen and older were $18,800 without a high school diploma, $26,800 with a high school diploma, $50,600 with a bachelor's degree, and $72,800 for those with an advanced degree.[11] Degrees will continue to make employment, upgrading, promotions, and raises more attainable.

And of course, there are always the notable exceptions: people with little education who make a dramatic contribution to their work. Commitment, opportunity, and sometimes hard times can spur people to achievements their circumstances would not predict. But generally, without knowledge and training, a worker's survival in the 2000s will be difficult.

If you simply cannot endure more education, face facts realistically and plan very carefully. Experience will teach you many of the skills you may need for your work. And realize that age and experience may change your motivation and ability to go back to school.

Do not let your age or your previous school record discourage you if you are older and returning to school. The average age of all adults going to school is over thirty, and there's no maximum in sight. One newspaper article described an eighty-two-year-old student who earned an associate degree in

"If I have to keep going to school, all the best jobs are gonna be snapped up."

© Jim Unger /distributed by United Media, 1998.

business sixty years after graduating from high school. She wrote and worked for the student newspaper.[12]

    People returning to school after a long time away are often fearful: "Am I too old to learn, too old to compete with younger college students?" Some people feel that they are incompetent because they had difficulties with certain subjects in their early school years. The surprise comes (and this happens with few exceptions) when reentry students report a great growth in confidence along with newfound goals, even though they may have previous school records that qualify as disasters. Because they are mature and motivated (although they don't always *feel* that way), they can reach their goals. So can you.

A Mini-orientation to College You might wonder what courses you would take if you returned to school. If your high school education was incomplete or deficient, or if you began college and picked up some poor grades, consider basic skills courses in language and math at adult education centers or community colleges. You also might find courses for personal growth and enrichment in these schools. Many are inexpensive noncredit courses that provide an easy way to start back to school. Training in communications, for example, can be a good way to gain confidence to face difficult situations both in the workplace and at home.

At the community college you can also sample various majors (areas of specialty), explore and prepare for a career, or take courses to transfer to a four-year college. Pick up a catalog at the college bookstore and look for introductory courses. The titles of these courses frequently include phrases such as "beginning," "orientation to," "introduction to," or "principles of." The catalog will tell you the required courses and general degree requirements for each major. Usually advisers or counselors are available to help you through the maze of choices. Search for someone who understands where you are now and how you feel.

If you want a four-year degree, you can do your first two years at a community college and transfer, or you can go directly to a four-year college. In either case, your course of studies will be something like this:

> *First year:* General education courses (GE), introduction to a major, and electives (free-choice courses)
>
> *Second year:* Exploration of a major, GE, and electives
>
> *Third year:* Major requirements, electives, and remaining GE
>
> *Fourth year:* Major requirements and electives

You will probably need more math if you are interested in science, health, four-year business or technical fields, architecture, or engineering. Adult education programs offer math courses at the high school level and sometimes beyond. Community colleges offer not only high school level courses but also most of the college courses at the freshman and sophomore level. Both offer remedial arithmetic. The usual sequence is this:

> *High school:* Arithmetic, introductory algebra, geometry, intermediate algebra, trigonometry, college (pre-calculus) algebra
>
> *College:* College algebra, analytic geometry, calculus (two to three semesters or five quarters), differential equations, and statistics

First, check to see how much math you need for various programs. (You may not need any at all.) Then try to start where you left off or where you feel most comfortable. Before you try to enroll in any course, however, find out whether you must complete any prerequisites first. (A *prerequisite* is a course that you need to take before enrolling in a more advanced course. Sometimes experience will take the place of a prerequisite, or a placement test may be required to determine which course you should begin with.)

Because most people will be working in the global economy or at least in areas of the United States with a diverse population, they will have contact with people of other cultures and languages. Consider enrolling in a language, history, or anthropology course as part of your general education to give you some understanding of other cultures.

Educational Possibilities   If returning to school seems impossible—because of time or distance, for example—investigate "distance learning." More and more colleges are putting classes on the Internet. No doubt, more schools will do so, though it takes a great deal of discipline for students to use these at-home methods of study. Some colleges and universities allow you to challenge a course by taking a test, which enables you to earn credit by examination. Some schools give credit for work experience. You may be required to go to the campus to take exams or to attend certain classes, but overall such programs decrease the time you need to spend on campus. Some colleges offer courses in weekend sessions that can lead to a degree.

Despite the fact that college tuition is rising rapidly, there are many ways to keep college costs within bounds without going into debt. If finances are a problem, apply for financial aid. Students of all ages can get grants and low-interest loans for education. But some graduates have found that paying back a loan is a struggle, especially if their first jobs do not pay well. Some graduates change their lifestyles; live at home; mortgage, sell, or rent their houses; sell their cars and ride their bikes; work part-time and go to school part-time. The bottom line is . . . if you want to go to school, there is a way to finance it!

> The truly educated *never* graduate.
> —*Council for Adult Experiential Learners*

Local community colleges can provide two years of your education at the lowest cost of any institution. A graduate of a four-year private college went back to a community college for courses relating to a newly found career goal. He was surprised to find excellent instructors and courses. He lamented the money his parents had spent based on mistaken stereotypes about "junior colleges," especially since his major had not resulted in satisfying employment.

Some call the two-year colleges the new graduate schools for returning students, one in four of whom has a bachelor's degree or higher.[13] Businesses in the community work closely with these institutions, advising them about the kinds of course work they would like their workers to pursue, and the colleges develop state-of-the-art programs as a result.

You may be in school wondering if you should be out. Returning is difficult once you leave, as you know already if you have ever stayed out even a short time. And if you begin working, perhaps start a family or buy a house, returning to school can become a very remote possibility very fast. On the other hand, many people have found that being out of school for a time was a good experience for them. They have worked, traveled, joined the military, and found new energy to return to school. Talk to people who have gone either way: those who have managed to survive the struggles of college learning and those who have stopped out for a time. Talk to a counselor, get some help with your studies in the meantime, and then make your decision following the steps discussed later in this chapter.

You may be working and feel that going back to school is impossible for you. But remember, further education is not. Wise people set goals to learn as much on the job as possible and learn while earning. They take on new tasks, extra tasks, find a mentor. You may even set up a development program with your manager.

You can teach yourself many things, and you can find other people who will help you learn. You can enroll in college work experience courses or seek internships where you will work at your same job and earn credit. You can join in the work of a nonprofit community organization or even get on a working board of directors and learn much about business management, marketing, fund-raising, public presentation, and other skills. A lot depends on having a goal and working toward it—and being flexible enough to see alternatives.

As you know, most jobs require only average to somewhat-above-average skills. Talking to people in the field can help you assess your motivation, especially if it looks as if your desired profession will require years of training. Remember, however, when you meet competent professionals who are all trained, experienced, and "way up there," they didn't get there in one step. The most valuable asset you can have in acquiring a high-level ability is the patience to persevere until you learn it. Hard work is fun if you are doing what you enjoy. As you go along, new horizons will open up. Before the end of your training, you may choose to stop out at a point where you feel comfortable. Instead of going straight on to become a certified public accountant, you may try working as an accounting clerk, which may lead you in a direction that you hadn't seen before. Or you may find along the way that you float sideways to a different area with similar satisfiers. The more homework you've done on your interests, the more quickly you'll be able to make such changes.

If you want to get more detailed information about your skills, your aptitudes to develop skills, or areas in which your skills need sharpening, you can contact a counselor at a local college, in your state employment office, or in private practice. They can direct you to aptitude assessments that evaluate your skills and abilities. They also can direct you to training programs that can help you develop specific skills.

VARIOUS ROUTES TO EDUCATIONAL CREDIT/TRAINING

HIGH SCHOOL CREDIT

Adults can earn high school equivalency certificates through the General Educational Development (GED) program. Contact your local school district or
GED Testing Service, American Council on Education:
http://www.acenet.edu

COLLEGE SEARCH

Commonapp distributes the common application to 230 schools and is a 501(c)3 nonprofit:
http://www.commonapp.org

Free Application for Federal Student Aid at U.S. Dept. of Education:
http://www.fafsa.ed.gov

FastWEB gives scholarship information:
http://www.fastweb.com

Hispanic Financial Aid:
http://wwwhispanicscholarships.com

Finaid.org is the most comprehensive collection of information about student financial aid and scholarships on the Web and is free to all:
http://www.finaid.org

Peterson's site for college and graduate school search, financial aid, and test preparation:
http://www.petersons.com

The Princeton Review's site for school search, financial aid, and test preparation:
www.princetonreview.com

Sallie Mae is a government-sponsored corporation that services college loans and gives basic financial aid information:
http://www.salliemae.com

Yahoo! includes a quick college search program under education:
http://dir.yahoo.com/Education

COLLEGE CREDIT: ALTERNATIVES

At various colleges, look for flexible alternatives, such as distance learning, weekend programs, credit by examination, and credit for work experience.

Credit by Examination

College Level Examination Program (CLEP) provides extensive information and resources for over 2,900 participating colleges and universities:
http://www.collegeboard.org

Credit for Noncollege Learning

The Center for Adult Learning and Educational Credentials at the American Council on Education evaluates courses given by private employers, community organizations, labor unions, government agencies, and military education programs:
http://www.acenet.edu/calec/index.cfm   *(continued)*

VARIOUS ROUTES TO EDUCATIONAL CREDIT/TRAINING *(continued)*

Credit for Experience

You can apply to institutions for college credit for your work experience.

Council for Adult and Experiential Learning (CAEL) National Headquarters:
http://www.cael.org

Intered's list of schools degree programs, and questions to ask:
http://www.intered.com

Credit for Correspondence and Independent Study

University Continuing Education Association (UCEA) sponsors a wide variety of correspondence and independent study courses that is available through its membership institutions. The association publishes *The Independent Study Catalog: The UCEA Guide to Independent Study through Correspondence Instruction:*

http://www.ucea.edu

The Distance Learning and Training Council (DETC) is a clearinghouse for distance learning information:
http://www.detc.org

The Free University Project can provide online guidance for people to receive college credit through examinations:
http://www.freeuniv.com

For additional information on accredited distance learning, contact the following organizations:

Charter Oak State College:
http://www.cosc.edu

Excelsior College: A Virtual University:
http://www.regents.edu

Thomas A. Edison College:
http://www.tesc.edu

International University Consortium distance learning sponsored by the University of Maryland University College:
http://www.umuc.edu/ide/potentialweb97/sponsors.html
http://www.umuc.edu/gen/virtuniv.html

University of Wisconsin Clearinghouse of distance-learning information:
http://www.uwex.edu/disted

Western Governors University:
http://www.wgu.edu

Specialized Programs: Degree, Nondegree, Apprenticeships

Conservation Directory (Lists college degree programs related to the environment)

National Wildlife Federation:
http://www.nwf.org/education

Institute for Social Ecology:
http://www.social-ecology.org

Back to the Job Market

For some people, seeking a job after some time out of the labor pool can seem difficult. One woman, who by choice had not worked for years, had this to say:

> Last fall, quaking and shaking, I had made up my mind I must not put off the job-hunting ordeal any longer. I told friends that I was going back to work and one responded that her husband needed an assistant. An interview was set up and I found myself two weeks later working with a fine man who has been very understanding of my initial lack of self-assurance. My 60-day performance report was a very satisfactory one (was delighted to have "initiative" get the best grading); and at six months received a 12 percent raise, but, best of all, the following remarks: "in recognition of outstanding contribution to the department." I love the work, and most of all, I love the self-assurance it's given me. Tell others as scared as I that it's not all that hard. Take that first plunge, and you've got it made. And on a second note, my family is delighted with the new and confident me!
>
> —Carol Shawhan

Same Job/New Approach

Those who are already working and have looked over the job market may find that their present job isn't so bad after all. "Then why," they wonder, "do I feel dissatisfied?" One common explanation is, "I'm not comfortable with my coworkers." Would some fine tuning in human relations/communications improve your work life?

Human relations can absorb much of your energy as you seek to accommodate the various colleagues you meet at work. Sometimes a change in yourself can make a vast difference. You can learn to communicate more effectively, assert yourself in a tactful way, grow in self-confidence, and become more considerate and understanding. Usually you will find it necessary to strike a balance: not make a federal case out of every annoyance, yet be able to make changes in a situation that clashes sharply with your sensibilities. Review your personal responsibility skills from Chapter 2.

If your job is beginning to call for new duties, such as public presentations or writing, some of your basic skills may need improving. Put energy into your job and learn as much as you can in order to grow and develop. Your self-confidence will improve along with your skills.

Some people create a job within a job by assessing the tasks they like or dislike. Sometimes it's possible to trade tasks with others, ask for a reorganization, even hire someone to work along with you if your workload warrants it. Tackling a new project, changing departments, doing the same function in a new locale—each of these can be a creative way to get a fresh start.

Amazingly, some people are so successful they are promoted beyond the level of their own self-confidence, which has to catch up with their new position. Sometimes a step down—a career direction we rarely consider—can be a welcome change. One executive, laid off and then rehired into a lower position, says, "The money doesn't add up, but for the first time in my life I don't give a damn. I haven't felt this good in years!"[14] If you are dissatisfied with yourself, consider reading about or enrolling in some personal-growth classes. If a problem is weighing on you, discuss it with a trusted friend or a counselor. Many problems have obvious solutions that we may miss when searching alone.

There may be problems in the workplace, such as discrimination, sexual harassment, and poor management, that you have not caused. You may blame yourself or believe that you can solve them alone. You may press charges where there are violations of the law, but often it's wise to get some advice first from relevant government agencies or groups, such as the National Labor Relations Board or, if you are a woman, the Commission on the Status of Women. Try to find a trusted counselor who can help you. Even if one workplace doesn't work for you, the career itself may still be a good choice. Try to separate the job from the place and people. You may simply decide to move on to a different workplace while keeping the same career.

Deciding Not to Decide

When you keep the status quo, you are deciding not to decide—which can be a good decision. You may stay in the same job, take more classes, or continue to be at home with your children. But if you feel that your life needs change, try to set a reasonable time limit for your next move. If your present situation is uncomfortable for you, take some sort of action to work toward improvement—even if it is just reading helpful books or writing out a plan.

DECISION MAKING: A FOUR-PHASE PROCESS

Those who find decision making difficult or who have not zeroed in on a career/life decision may find this four-phase process helpful: gather information, weigh and brainstorm alternatives and outcomes, check values, and design strategies.

Gather Information

Every decision calls for accurate information. In working through this book you have been gathering the information you need to make a career decision.

You have learned how to pull information from a variety of sources and resources. You have already made many decisions about who you are and what you like. This is a process of using all the small decisions you have been making throughout this book to focus on a career. You may want to stop here and review this material.

Weigh and Brainstorm Alternatives and Outcomes

Examine Possibilities There are probably more possibilities out there for you than you can imagine; that is, there are many things that you *could* do. Whichever of the alternatives you act on will have several outcomes. Before you make an important decision, try to imagine what the result will be, in both the immediate future and some years down the line. Without a crystal ball, it's hard to predict exactly how a decision is going to turn out. You make the best one you can and then see what adventures it leads to.

People are often able to picture only one type of outcome. Some, burdened by fears, see only disasters—major and minor. Other overly optimistic folks see nothing but grandiose positive effects. Most major decisions, however, produce a mixture of outcomes. You can take a job with a good salary, for example, but find that you will need training or have to work overtime. Even a dark outcome can have a light side. The extra training you get may feel like a waste of time, but later it turns out to be just the background you need for another situation. Working overtime may result in your making new friends. Hardly any decision has perfect results.

Even the most carefully reasoned, good decisions can bring disappointing results. Everyone at times makes decisions that don't bring the hoped-for outcome. In such cases, try to avoid blaming yourself; instead, give yourself credit for having taken the risk. Many alternatives seem risky only because they involve the risk of others' disapproval: What will people think? In fact, you may find yourself preserving the status quo solely out of fear of others' opinions, giving them power over your life. There is no way to change and grow without some risk. It is also important to avoid repeating the same mistakes.

Every change, however, even if it's only rearranging the garage, has an impact on others. Caring for those around you involves bringing them along with your decision making—that is, communicating your own needs honestly while listening to theirs, keeping them informed as you make changes. Hardly any change is perfect. There will be advantages and disadvantages to most moves. The idea is to *maximize the advantages.*

> It would be easier to play my part in life
> if I had a copy of the script.
> —*Ashleigh Brilliant*[15]

Brainstorm Alternatives   When you brainstorm, you write down every possibility without censoring it. Don't worry about whether an idea will work or what others will think. The important part is getting down as many alternatives as possible and then sorting them out. If you omit any, you may miss one that, on second look, may turn out to be possible and desirable for you.

You may have decided on a career for which there seem to be few opportunities. To find related alternatives, list all the functions of a person in that career. Then check the functions you think you'd enjoy most. If "history teacher" is on your list, do you like history, or appearing before an audience, or both? What can you do with history besides teach?

You could develop a unique lecture series on a topic of current interest to present to community groups. You could tutor, learn to be a docent (a person who conducts groups through such places as museums), work as a tour guide or as historian for a state park department, or get involved in history-in-the-making in politics.

If you could get along without teaching, you could develop a tour series on tape or by map; you could write news articles about historical subjects; you might work in a library, publishing company, heritage or historical center, or a bookstore where you might specialize in historical books.

Perhaps, after thinking it over again, you will decide that teaching is more important to you than history. Consider teaching other subjects (check school districts for local trends); volunteer in schools, recreation centers, and senior citizen centers; work as a teacher aide; teach small classes at home in areas such as woodworking, cooking, vegetable gardening, or auto repair; try teaching or giving lectures on these or other subjects to community groups such as the Parent–Teacher Association or Girl Scout and Boy Scout troops; or tutor or teach a class for families doing home schooling. Consider teaching recreation skills such as dancing, yoga, riding, swimming, tennis, music, bridge, exercise, skiing, golf, massage, boating. Some fitness "trainers" now visit people in their homes to show them how to use and plan a program for their exercise equipment and to monitor their progress.

With a little work, some of those activities can be parlayed into a lucrative business. A job must fulfill the needs and wants of other people to such an extent that they will part with something, usually money, in exchange for goods or services produced in that job. For people who would like to teach and earn a more secure living, an often-overlooked area is industry. Larger industries have training programs and orientations for new employees and inservice training for continuing employees. Someone must be the teacher in these industrial settings.

Working in marketing and sales, public relations, or human resources, including such areas as job development or affirmative action, can involve you in many situations similar to teaching: training, giving site tours, helping people find employment, and working with other people's problems that arise. Again, know what functions you might like to perform, and many more options may become visible.

Go back to the exercises in Chapter 2 and Chapter 3 and review the factors that are important to you. Consider related jobs again and *brainstorm* with friends, relatives, neighbors, acquaintances, strangers, or anyone who will give you five minutes of time and a dip into his or her experience pool. For just about any career you choose, there are alternative jobs that can offer you most of what you would enjoy.

If you still want more than anything to follow a career that is highly competitive, don't be afraid to face that competition. Here are some other ideas to give you a start.

- Don't overlook entry-level or support-service job skills, such as word processing and cashiering, to gain access to careers of interest to you. Often you can then work into jobs closer to your interest field, in places from art galleries to auto shops, by beginning at the bottom.

- Use your main career interest as a hobby while you work at something else to support yourself. Who knows where it will lead? Walter Chandoha pursued a business degree while maintaining his interest in photographing cats. He became a successful animal photographer and additionally wrote columns for gardening magazines. His business background may have helped his career.[16]

- Investigate training programs in various industries, government agencies, and temporary agencies like Manpower.

- Consider earning extra money, perhaps at home, in one of these areas: catering; cake decorating; woodworking; picture framing; custom design of clothing or toys; recycling or redoing clothing, furniture, or household appliances, or other tools or gadgets; auto repair; house painting; yard cleanup; pet care; growing vegetables on consignment; translating; making telephone wake-up calls or operating an answering service; providing income tax service; computer work, perhaps in a medical, technical, scientific, or legal specialty, doing bookkeeping, newsletter layout and editing, or other graphics such as designing stationery or business cards. Your telephone Yellow Pages will give you additional ideas. More people than ever are finding work at home to their liking.

- Consider direct selling for companies of good reputation, for whom you can virtually be your own boss. Ask advice from friends who have sold such items as cosmetics or cleaning products. Consider franchises. They exist in a wide variety of fields from construction to specialty foods.

- Consider temporary employment, a growing area that provides flexible time, a sense of independence, and in some cases many employee benefits.

Taking jobs through one of your local agencies can provide a way to survey businesses, make contacts, and make money on your own schedule in a wide array of jobs. Advertise your skills and classes through friends, supermarket bulletin boards, local community groups. Donate samples and do demonstrations. Be aware that finding a job in an area of your favorite hobbies may not be as satisfying as you may think. Mark Twain fulfilled his dream of becoming a full-fledged riverboat pilot, but said, "Now, the romance and the beauty were all gone out of the river. All the value any feature of it had for me now was the amount of usefulness it could furnish toward compassing the safe piloting of a steamboat." Author Lyle Crist concludes, "He [Twain] had gained the mastery . . . and lost the beauty."[17] Keep your options open. The wider your "satisfaction band," the more likely you are to achieve satisfaction. When you have done everything you can but you end up with a job you don't care for, you still have some choices.

- Volunteer experience can be extremely valuable for skill development and increased self-confidence. Some groups even pay volunteers a small stipend and provide them a place to live. Pinpoint the skills you would like to develop and ask for experience doing these things—for example, public relations, fund-raising, supervising people, organizing materials or activities. Be specific. Ask to be paired with a pro who will teach you some tricks of the trade. Be aware, however, that volunteer organizations are usually just as accountable for time and money as any business and cannot always accommodate your needs.

President George W. Bush, in his State of the Union address in 2002, called on every American to dedicate at least two years over the course of one's life to the service of others. He created the USA Freedom Corps (**www.usafreedomcorps.gov**) to support and find volunteer opportunities for every American. The Bureau of Labor Statistics indicates that 27.6 percent of Americans, or more than 59 million individuals over the age of sixteen, volunteered with a service organization between September 2001 and September 2002. Volunteering can help you acquire marketable skills while helping your country. The Corporation for National and Community Service involves Americans of all ages and backgrounds in service to help strengthen communities through opportunities like AmeriCorps and Senior Corps (**www.nationalservice.org**).

> When you help your neighbor, you help your nation.
> —*George W. Bush*

Weigh Alternatives

We will use an exercise called Decision Point (see pages 306–307) to organize and clarify the alternatives you may have brainstormed.

For example, if you were trying to decide whether to take a job in New York or one in Chicago, you would put the New York job in the balance first, and would write in such projected negative or undesirable results as longer work hours and hectic commuting conditions. On the positive side, you might list high pay, exciting work, status, closeness to family, and cultural opportunities. You would then check whether the result would be likely or unlikely to occur. You might find, for example, that high pay would not be very likely. On the other side, hectic commuting might also be unlikely if the company allowed telecommuting and flextime, or if affordable living space were reasonably close to the job site. When you indicate that a possible outcome might be unlikely, you would be wise not to let that factor influence your decision very much if at all. Going further, you might want to rank your likely positives and negatives to see which would be the most important.

Next, of course, you would weigh Chicago in the balance, for who knows what possible positives might turn up that would make the Windy City irresistible—a fabulous job and luxurious, affordable housing close to old college friends? Then you would compare the results to see which would look better to you, New York or Chicago. Overall, the positive results of one alternative might quite outweigh all the negatives. And you might choose to ignore the negatives. It's up to you! What decisions have you made in the past? How have they turned out for you? Review one of these decisions as if you were just about to make it now.

Decision-making exercises can help to organize and clarify your possibilities, but they cannot make the decision for you. They require you to use your rational, logical self. After such a process, give your intuition time to voice your sense of appropriateness and certainty about the decision. At some deeper level, you will usually know that your choice will work for you. You will feel finished and at peace after the struggle. You will be ready to let go the alternatives, perhaps with a twinge of regret, for there are good sides to everything. You will be ready to move on and take the steps you need to reach your goals.

Check Values

As you make choices, you express your value system—because values are revealed in what you do, not in what you say. Every step of this career search process has been related to your values. As a final check, consider your decision in terms of these values. If you want to live very simply, why seek a high-powered, energy-consuming job, the only reward for which is money? On the other hand, if money seems important to you, look at the bottom line. If you want both a family and a career, plan for it. You may wish to review Rating Values from Chapter 1 and any other values that may possibly be affected so that your choice reflects these priorities.

Design Strategies

This book outlines many steps you can use in making a good career decision. To carry out your next career/life decision, develop a good set of strategies—a step-by-step procedure to make it a reality. Think of each step as a goal. Your goals need to be clearly stated. It won't do to say vaguely that you will "do better in school" or "start job hunting." Rather set a **SMART** goal! One that is **S**pecific (detailed, not vague or confusing), **M**easurable (the result can be evaluated), **A**chievable (it is reachable), **R**elevant (it makes sense), and there is a **T**ime frame (appropriate target date). "I will read and outline history notes for two hours each evening and review them for half an hour every morning until the midterm," or "I will call five people tomorrow to ask for information interviews." Setting a time frame helps to discourage procrastination. When you successfully accomplish your goal, reward yourself by doing something special, and you will find that your zest for continuing will increase.

> Goals are dreams that are measurable.
> —*Anonymous*

It is important to be persistent, but it is also important to assess your strategies and to give up those that don't seem to be working for you instead of

repeating them. If time is a problem for you, learn to manage it. Some people pack their lives with so many activities that they experience failure, frustration, or frenzy instead of accomplishment. Others take on too little and end up feeling bored and uninvolved. Here are some techniques for managing time:

- List all the tasks on your agenda and rank them in order of importance.
- Keep a "very important" list, a "so-so" list, and a "nice if I can get around to it" list of tasks that need doing.
- For one week, keep track of all your activities on the weekly schedule at the end of the chapter to discover where you are spending your time.

For further help with time management, read Alan Lakein's *How to Get Control of Your Time and Your Life.*[18]

Some people want to rush ahead to that satisfying job. They may leave school without finishing a degree, leave a job too soon where they were getting valuable experience, or miss the job they really want by grabbing anything that comes along. As difficult as it seems at the time, waiting and finishing one phase of life before starting another is sometimes the best decision.

At age eighty, Giuseppe Verdi explained why he decided to write one more (and very difficult) opera. He said, "All my life as a musician I have striven for perfection. It has always eluded me. I surely had an obligation to make one more try!"[19]

JOB HUNTING . . . AGAIN? AGAIN!

Many people are rushed into a career decision these days without being the least bit prepared. The reason? They find themselves laid off. Whole towns are shocked to realize that they have depended for almost all of the employment in a community on one company that now decides to leave. Even a whole country can face hard times when it depends on one industry. The collapse of the Philippines' sugar industry due to falling prices worldwide in the 1980s put the whole country into a severe economic decline. A war, a political decision to fund or not to fund certain projects and programs, any number of happenings can lead to downsizing or restructuring as well as expansion in your workplace. Most recently, many technology workers lost jobs in the downturn of the Internet economy, and many airline employees were fired in the aftermath of the terrorist attacks of September 11, 2001.

You may have earned a degree and learned new skills in preparation for your career. You may have found that dream job that embodies your most important values and interests and in which you are encouraged to develop your skills. You may have put a great deal of energy into your job and plan to stay with it. You may have a growing family and a hefty mortgage. But even if you planned to stay at the same place in the same job for a long time, some day, burnout or boredom may prompt you to wonder, "Is this all there is?"

Even with a job that seems secure and satisfying, it is always wise to have your résumé ready and a game plan in mind in case you (or your employer) decide to call it quits. Job hunting in a tight job market with your benefits running out, the mortgage payment due, and applications that generate only rejections can undermine the strongest ego. Here is what some people do all the time: they keep up the contacts they have made by networking; they continue the self- and career-assessment process; and they keep learning new skills. Preparing for change is an important part of career development.

You may find that having a network of people in your field can prove helpful in your job. Many people call on colleagues in other companies for advice on various sorts of problems both in their careers and in their work.

It helps to be moneywise and to have a plan for lean times. Consider what you really *need* to survive and look for sources to fund your needs. Experts say people should try to have money saved that can pay their expenses for six months. They keep bills paid and pay cash instead of using credit cards. In a time of under- or unemployment, some reduce expenses, move to a less expensive location, use cheaper transportation, have a garage sale and sell off excess baggage, plant a garden of basics to save on food bills, join or start a small co-op to buy food wholesale, find people who can share resources. Your expanded activity lists from Chapters 1 and 2 may indicate what you may do to earn needed cash. Psychological as well as financial preparation will greatly enhance your confidence when the time comes for a move.

If you have been fired or laid off, evaluate the causes so that you can avoid them in the future. Despite the very real trauma involved in being jobless, you can use the experience to advantage by preparing for your next job. Ask for help with job hunting from friends, relatives, and neighbors without hiding your job loss. As everyone knows, it can happen to anyone.

If you are unemployed and haven't had a chance to prepare for it, now is the time to work out a plan of action to avoid sitting at home reading the want ads and feeling terrible. Being a couch potato will rarely bring success! First, review the data collected in this book and related resources. Second, follow good job-hunting techniques: update your résumé, renew your contacts, and collect letters of recommendation. Third, join or start a support group. Fourth, work out a daily schedule of things to do that includes not only job hunting but other important business-of-living activities like exercising, eating nutritious food, and visiting friends. In the meantime, consider temporary work, part-time work, "just any job," negotiating to share a job, or going back to school. Try to keep your life in balance on not only the physical but also the emotional, intellectual, and altruistic levels. Enjoy the "unemployment benefits" such as sleeping late some mornings, catching up on errands, or enjoying an occasional walk. The more you can relax with your new leisure, the better you'll be able to plan your next step.

Basic physical needs may seem so imperative at such times that concerns about emotional, intellectual, and altruistic needs and wants can fly out the window as you begin to believe that any job will do! But perhaps this is the time to gather some emotional support, to use every bit of your intelligence and knowledge to carve out more than a survival path. The insights you gather may be just what you need to boost your confidence and morale and open up unsuspected possibilities. Survey the skills you developed on your last job. Did that job put you in touch with new interests? What did you dislike about that job?

A layoff can be a liberating experience—if you don't get too hungry—and a good time to reevaluate a career and make changes. It is also a sobering opportunity, especially if it is your first one, to reevaluate your career and life priorities and bring them into balance. A layoff can sharpen your career savvy for your next foray into the world of work. Unemployed people have started businesses, often on a shoestring, found rewarding partnerships, and created satisfying new careers. Many people have moved from the corporate complex to small-business ownership. They have gone from designing microchips to designing sandwiches in their own delicatessens, from making hardware to making beds in their guest cottages by the sea. Numbers of individuals who were forced to make a change as a result of unemployment have been delighted with the results.

Even if a risky venture isn't for you right now, get together with others to share such resources as physical necessities, ideas, job leads, and support. Call your local school career center for help. If you are unemployed, keep busy with courage.

You will find a more balanced and satisfying life by developing your potential as far as possible in all areas. There are those who have even found that volunteering to help people more needy than themselves gave them new insights into all the resources they *do* have. A number of them have even met individuals who offered them a job.

Despite the negative press regarding enormous layoffs, the *New Yorker* says that "the job-creating capacity of the United States economy is the envy of the developed world," and that in the main, people are still finding equivalent jobs after layoffs.[20]

THE GREAT GAP

Some people complete the entire career search process without making the big decision. If you are still unable to choose a career, you may need more time to gain confidence and clarify your values. You may need to give your creativity time to work. There is a point—we could call it the Great Gap—

where you must cross over from process to action. No matter how much support you've had, how many inventories you do, and how many people you talk to, the decision is yours alone to make alone.

Perhaps you need to take a "dynamic rest" along the road to success. Read some books about the problem that's holding you back. Discuss it with a trusted friend or counselor. Paradoxically, sometimes we need to accept the status quo before we can change it.

And reassessment time will probably come around again and again because people change careers and jobs often in their lives. Some people take time each year to evaluate their situation. They review the balance in their lives among its physical, emotional, intellectual, and altruistic/spiritual components. Which of these need levels motivates *you* most? The more you grow, the more your lower needs will be fulfilled, and the more you will become a self-actualizing person who acts out of concern not only for yourself but for other people and the planet.

"In *Elegant Choices, Healing Choices,* psychologist Marsha Sinetar, Ph.D., says that elegant choices are those options in life 'tending toward truth, beauty, honor, courage.' They are choices that are life supporting, whereas choices that take one away from truth, morality, and self-respect are life-defeating."[21]

> Until one is committed, there is hesitancy, the chance to draw back, always ineffectiveness. Concerning all acts of initiative (and creation), there is one elemental truth, the ignorance of which kills countless ideas and splendid plans: that the moment one definitely commits oneself, then Providence moves too. All sorts of things occur to help one that would never otherwise have occurred. A whole stream of events issues from the decision, raising in one's favor all manner of unforeseen incidents and meetings and material assistance which no man could have dreamed would have come his way. Whatever you can do or dream you can, begin it. Boldness has genius, power, and magic in it. Begin it now.
>
> —*Goethe*[22]

CHANGE IS HERE TO STAY

H. B. Gelatt, an expert in the career management field, says,

> For those of you who are worried that I might change my mind again, let me assure you, I will. Fortunately, this is a trait whose time has come. Changing one's mind will be an essential decision-making skill in the future. Keeping the mind open will be another. Learning to be good at

being uncertain is becoming a modern-day asset in decision-making. The hard part to learn is to be positive about the uncertainty.[23]

Some people might like to avoid it, but in this age, change is inevitable. Some understanding of your past, confidence in your future, flexibility, and the willingness to accept "ambiguity, inconsistency, and uncertainty" will make the process of decision making more manageable.

Often, consciously or unconsciously, people may be searching for something new, working out the details without expressing the process to anyone. And when they reach a decision, it may seem sudden to the observer.

Sometimes people have such a powerful experience that they begin to see their lives in a totally different way. They or someone close to them may have a serious accident or become quite ill; someone they care about may die; their marriage may break apart; they may travel to and live in a very different culture. Often experiencing a war or the extreme poverty of a developing country can cause people to question their lives. A retired military man and vice-president of a bank made such a change after working in Guatemala and seeing the activities of an older couple involved in helping the rural poor in that country. He felt so alive and energized by these experiences that he went back to Yale to get a master's degree in forestry that he could use to help the environment in developing countries.

People are more than squares on a page or checks in a box. They are pain and purpose, hopes and dreams, woundedness and wholeness. They are a compendium of cultural constraints and conditioning with the ever-present possibility of breaking loose into wondrous patterns with surprises at every turn.

> I have never begun any important venture
> for which I felt adequately prepared.[24]
> —*Anonymous*

SUCCESS: NEW DIRECTIONS

We began this book by looking at success, and since then, you have been learning good things about yourself: your interests, values, and skills. You've learned how to find or make a place for yourself in the job market. You've learned to assess jobs and workplaces and how to network effectively. You've learned to change attitudes and feelings and "own" all the good things about yourself by positive affirmations. When you believe in yourself as a capable person, you are on your way to further growth, to self-actualization, to fulfillment. When you are true to yourself and all that is best in you, you will be a success.

You are unique. The person you are and could become, the success and happiness that you can achieve, can be done only when you listen to your own voice. Mythologist Joseph Campbell says, "If you follow your bliss, you put yourself on a kind of track that has been there all the while, waiting for you."[25] Some people just won't give up until they have found satisfying work and a lifestyle that is uniquely their own. Experiencing and living your dreams can be both invigorating and frightening.

"A mark of the adult is the willingness to recognize material limitations, to recognize that no single life can embrace the multitude of experiences available to humankind: climb all the mountains, chart all the seas, master all the arts," wrote Ted Berkman. "Freed from the tyranny of 'want it all,' I find that I have all I need: books and friends, the beach at sunrise, the towering silhouette of the Santa Ynez mountains. . . . There is time to savor and to serve."[26]

Success has been popularly defined as achieving your goals. But with the third millennium underway, success is much more than that, much more than media and corporate images. Success must ultimately include a balanced life in which we have taken care of ourselves and those dependent on us in the context of global concerns. Success, then, means achieving realistic goals, using effective strategies based on our interests, skills, and true values, accounting for the basic needs and the legitimate, enriching wants of ourselves and others. The most far-reaching successes are those that transform us into better people and creators of a better world. Some people create so much joy within themselves—despite facts, trends, and predictions and often against significant odds—that they are happy anywhere. Perhaps that joy, after all, is the key to success.

> The richest person in the world is not the one who has the most
> friends, nor the one who knows the most, but the one who is wise
> enough to distinguish between the essentials of life
> and the nonessentials and go forth like an adventurer,
> with the wind and the rain and the sun in his face.
> —R. L. Duffus
> The Tower of Jewels:
> Memories of San Francisco

SUMMARY

Deciding which career path to pursue can be difficult. If you have taken your time during the career search process, completed a detailed self-evaluation, researched your options and viable careers, talked to others and gathered useful information, selected specific companies and hiring managers, written a powerful résumé, and practiced interviewing techniques, then you are ready to make a good career decision, set attainable goals, and reach your objectives.

When faced with tough decisions you will want to consider the decision-making dozen. Four attitudes can help you make a good decision: stay calm; be persistent; keep your perspective; and be confident. With these four attitudes in place, you can consider your four options or a combination of options: go back to school; seek a new job or involvement; keep the same job with a new approach; or keep the status quo and decide not to decide. Now, you can work the decision-making four-phase process: gather all your information; weigh and brainstorm alternatives and outcomes; check to make sure your values align with your choices; and design a strategy to move forward.

When your decision is clear, set a SMART goal and strategies. Make sure your goal is Specific, Measurable, Achievable, Relevant, and has a realistic Time frame. After you have selected your goal and developed your strategies, make sure you reward yourself when you make significant accomplishments along the way. Periodically reevaluate your goal and modify your strategies, objectives, and timelines to keep your career on the course you want it to go.

SELF-ASSESSMENT EXERCISES

1. Decision-Making Style

How do you make decisions? Check (✓) the appropriate columns. Then mark plus (+) before items you'd like to improve.

	Usually	*Sometimes*	*Rarely*
▪ I make decisions after considering alternatives.	_____	_____	_____
▪ I make decisions easily, on time, without undue agonizing.	_____	_____	_____
▪ I base decisions on reasoned judgment of the information available.	_____	_____	_____
▪ I base my decisions on feelings and intuition.	_____	_____	_____
▪ I tend to think my decisions will turn out to be disasters.	_____	_____	_____

	Usually	Sometimes	Rarely
■ I tend to imagine my decisions will have spectacular positive results.	_____	_____	_____
■ I consult with others, but my decisions are my own.	_____	_____	_____
■ I compromise when the needs of others are involved.	_____	_____	_____
■ I make some decisions to fulfill my own desires.	_____	_____	_____
■ I "test out" major decisions ahead of time if possible.	_____	_____	_____
■ I take responsibility for the results of my decisions.	_____	_____	_____
■ If a decision doesn't work, I try another plan, without great regret.	_____	_____	_____

2. Decision Point: Selecting Alternatives

If you are on the verge of a decision but are having trouble choosing the alternative that will work best for you, list those alternatives here (for example, if you are trying to decide which geographical location will suit you, list all the possibilities; if you are deciding on a career, list those possibilities):

Alternative a. _____

Alternative b. _____

Alternative c. _____

Alternative d. _____

3. Decision Point: Weighing Alternatives

a. Write one of the alternatives you are considering: _____
b. On page 307 list as many negative and positive results as you can that might occur if you followed that alternative. Check whether they are likely or unlikely.
c. If you have many more likely negative results than positive results, you may wish to choose another alternative to pursue.
d. Rank the positive and then negative results in order of their importance to you.

NEGATIVES (Undesirable outcomes)	Likely	Unlikely	POSITIVES (Desirable outcomes)	Likely	Unlikely
_____	_____	_____	_____	_____	_____
_____	_____	_____	_____	_____	_____
_____	_____	_____	_____	_____	_____
_____	_____	_____	_____	_____	_____
_____	_____	_____	_____	_____	_____
_____	_____	_____	_____	_____	_____

e. Compare results:

■ Do the positives outweigh the negatives?   Yes _____   No _____

■ Overall, do the positives seem more likely and desirable than the negatives? Yes _____   No _____

f. Repeat this procedure for each of your alternatives. Then write a paragraph comparing your results for each alternative. Discuss how these results may affect your final decision.

g. Ten years down the path, which decision would you like to have made? What results might occur only later? Add your insights to the paragraph in f.

h. Spend time choosing your decision; spend some of it alone. Cross the Great Gap!

4. Setting SMART Goals

Write down the decision you've chosen to carry out. Make it a SMART goal. Is it specific, measurable, achievable, relevant, and does it have a time frame? After you have written your goal, state four or more steps or strategies you will take to accomplish it.

My goal is: _____

_____

I plan to achieve this goal by: _____

Is this goal realistic? _____   Does it agree with my values? _____

Steps I will take   *Date to be accomplished*

a. _____   _____

b. _____   _____

c. _____   _____

d. _____   _____

e. _____   _____

Now that you have written your goal and strategies, post copies where you can see and read them every day. Tell others about your goals. Visualize yourself completing your goal. How will your life be different? How can you reward yourself for completing a strategy that leads to your goal?

5. Back to School

If going to college is on your list of possibilities, check (✓) the answers that explain why. If college isn't for you, check any other training alternatives that appeal to you.

Why College?

_____ Not sure, but wish to explore and find out about it

_____ Personal enrichment

_____ Hope to improve basic or other specific skills

_____ Would like to obtain a high school General Equivalency Development (GED) diploma.

_____ Wish to earn a career program certificate

_____ Plan to earn a two-year degree at a community college

_____ Want to earn a BA or BS degree from a four-year college or university

_____ Want to do graduate work

_____ My mother/father/boss/spouse made me come to college.

Other Training Alternatives?

_____ Apprenticeship programs with unions in various crafts

_____ Adult education in local school district

_____ Proprietary schools (private schools that teach a special job skill)

_____ On-the-job training programs or management training programs

_____ Course work by TV, job experience, weekend college, and other options for the busy person

6. School Subjects

a. Check (✔) the columns that describe your feelings about school subjects.

	Like	Dislike	Did well	Did not do well	Avoided
Reading	____	____	____	____	____
Writing	____	____	____	____	____
Speech/Drama	____	____	____	____	____
Math	____	____	____	____	____
Science	____	____	____	____	____
Social studies	____	____	____	____	____
Arts/crafts	____	____	____	____	____
Music	____	____	____	____	____
Industrial/Technical	____	____	____	____	____
Business	____	____	____	____	____
Health	____	____	____	____	____
Agriculture	____	____	____	____	____
Physical education	____	____	____	____	____
Foreign language	____	____	____	____	____
Computers	____	____	____	____	____
_____	____	____	____	____	____

b. Circle the subjects you'd like to study further.

c. Now look at your "worst" subjects. Are there any you'd like to try again? Not try again?

Try again: _____   Not try again: _____

7. Some College Majors Arranged by Personality Type and Job Group

On the following page, check (✔) majors of interest to you.

R REALISTIC

___ Aero Maintenance/ Operations
___ Air Conditioning/ Refrigeration Technology
___ Air Traffic Control
___ Anaplastology
___ Automotive Technology
___ Biomedical Technology
___ Construction Technology
___ Electronics Technology
___ Engineering/Technology
___ Food Service Technology
___ Hazardous Materials
___ Industrial Administration
___ Laser/Microwave/Digital Technology
___ Machine/Tool Technology
___ Quality Control
___ Radiologic Technology
___ Robotics/Computer- Assisted Manufacturing (CAM)
___ Semiconductor Management
___ Solar Technology
___ Telecommunications
___ Transportation
___ Watch Repair
___ Welding Technology
___ Agriculture
___ Animal Health Technology
___ Nursery Management
___ Park Management Technology
___ Wildlife Management Technology
___ Administration of Justice/Private Security
___ Fire Science
___ Safety Engineering
___ Physical Education/ Kinesiology

I INVESTIGATIVE

___ Biological Science
___ Agriculture
___ Animal/Avian
___ Bacteriology
___ Biology
___ Botany
___ Conservation
___ Enology
___ Entomology/Pest Science

___ Environmental Science
___ Food Science
___ Forest Science
___ Genetics
___ Kinesiology
___ Marine Biology
___ Microbiology
___ Nutrition
___ Soil/Water/Wood Science
___ Toxicology
___ Zoology
___ Cybernetics
___ Engineering
___ Aeronautical/ Aerospace
___ Agricultural
___ Bioengineering
___ Civil
___ Computer Science
___ Electrical/Electronic
___ Environmental/Earth Resources
___ Material Science
___ Naval Architecture
___ Nuclear
___ Robotics
___ Science
___ Systems
___ Transportation
___ Linguistics
___ Mathematics/Statistics/ Applied
___ Medical
___ Dentistry
___ Medical Technology
___ Medicine/Surgery
___ Optometry
___ Pharmacy/Pharmacy Technology
___ Veterinary Medicine
___ Physical Sciences
___ Chemistry
___ Geology/Earth Science
___ Meteorology/ Atmosphere
___ Oceanography
___ Physics/Astronomy
___ Social Sciences
___ Anthropology
___ Consumer Economics/ Science
___ Ethnic Studies
___ Geography
___ History

___ Peace and Conflict Studies
___ Psychology
___ Sociology
___ Urban/Rural Studies
___ Women's Studies

A ARTISTIC

___ Architecture
___ Commercial Art
___ Computer-Assisted Design (CAD)
___ Fashion Design
___ Film/Photography
___ Graphics
___ Interior Design
___ Industrial Design
___ Journalism
___ Landscape Design/ Ornamental Horticulture
___ Media Specialty
___ Printing/Lithography/ Desk-Top Publishing
___ Radio/TV
___ Technical Drafting/ Modelbuilding/Illustrating
___ Technical Illustrating/ Writing
___ Art/Art History
___ Dance/Drama
___ English
___ Foreign Language
___ Humanities
___ Literature
___ Music
___ Philosophy
___ Speech

S SOCIAL

___ Community Health Worker
___ Counseling
___ Dental Assistant/Hygiene
___ Dietician
___ Health Science
___ Nursing RN, LVN, Assistant
___ Ophthalmic Dispensing
___ Pediatric Assistant
___ Physical/Occupational Therapy/Assistant
___ Primary Care Associate
___ Psychiatric Technology
___ Psychology–Clinical
___ Public Health
___ Radiology/EKG/ Phlebotomy

___ Respiratory Therapy
___ Social Service
___ Speech Pathology and Audiology
___ Cosmetology
___ Food Service
___ Gerontology
___ Leisure/Travel
___ Advertising
___ Business Administration
___ Convalescent Hospital Administration
___ Education
___ Financial Services
___ Health Care Management
___ Insurance
___ Labor Studies
___ Law
___ Library Science
___ Management/Supervision
___ Manpower Administration
___ Office Administration
___ Public Relations
___ Recreation
___ Volunteer Administration

E ENTERPRISING

___ Fashion/Retail Merchandising
___ International Trade
___ Law
___ Marketing/Sales
___ Political Science
___ Purchasing
___ Real Estate
___ Speech/Communications

C CONVENTIONAL

___ Accounting
___ Banking/Finance
___ Court Reporting
___ Data Processing
___ Insurance
___ Paralegal
___ Secretarial
___ Administrative
___ Clerical
___ Legal
___ Medical Assistant/Records
___ Unit Clerk
___ Word Processing

8. Blocks and Barriers: Finding the Keystone

To find out what is holding you back, ask yourself whether you are dealing with barriers within yourself. Place a check (✓) before any that apply:

Blocks Within You

_____ Locked into your stereotypes

_____ Too complacent to change the status quo

_____ Lacking confidence / awash in fear

_____ Weak skills

_____ Negative attitudes

_____ Caught in health or emotional problems

_____ Bogged down in transitions like divorce, death of spouse, immigration adjustment

_____ Longing for improved personal relationships

_____ Afraid to make a commitment

_____ In the habit of procrastinating

_____ Over-researching—losing yourself in the library

_____ Experiencing conflicts about values

_____ Too many "shoulds"

Barriers Outside You

_____ Poor job market / economy

_____ Societal expectations that you accept

_____ Imperative roles such as parenting

_____ Physical realities such as illness

What steps can you take to overcome these blocks and barriers?

_____

_____

_____

9. Positive Affirmations

Everyone is a mixture of faults, foibles, and failings along with skills, successes, and strengths. Check (✓) the statements that match your thought patterns. Select one *positive* statement and say it many times a day over a week's time. Know that attitudes and feelings can be changed.

Negatives	Positives
____ I don't think I'll ever figure out what I want to do.	____ I can take steps to figure out what to do.
____ I'm not interested in anything.	____ I'm interested in many things.
____ I never have much fun.	____ I enjoy many of my activities.
____ I'm dumb.	____ I can learn.
____ If my first choice doesn't work out, I'm stuck.	____ I can plan alternatives.
____ I'm tired of trying because nothing works.	____ I have the energy to make things happen.
____ I'm afraid.	____ I can be courageous.
____ No one likes me anyway.	____ I can create a good time.

____ I can make a good decision!

 ## GROUP DISCUSSION QUESTIONS

1. Describe your decision-making style. What factors might cause you to "decide not to decide"?
2. Share your educational plans. Define lifelong learning and the form it can take in your own life.
3. What new approaches can you take to improve your work/educational/life situation?
4. Illustrate how a decision you've made recently reflects your most important values. What values might take the place of work in your life?
5. How can a person prepare for unemployment?
6. Discuss with a group or write your feelings about important decisions you have made and those you would like to make.

9

Work Affects the Soul

The Final Analysis

 GOALS

- Review the career decision-making process.

- Gather personal information into one place.

- Review and update your goals.

*T*he Final Analysis is a place to summarize the information you have gathered from the self-assessment exercises in this book. It will give you an overview of the important areas of your life that are affected by work. It will help you assess your career search process and determine how effectively this process has helped you choose the career that will lead to growth and self-fulfillment on all levels. It may help you make some final decisions, and it provides a handy future reference.

To complete the Final Analysis, review the self-assessment exercises and summarize the data here. Feel free to add additional information about yourself and the career/life decisions you are considering.

CHAPTER 1
NEEDS, WANTS, AND VALUES: SPOTLIGHTING YOU

1. Review the Life Problems Checklist (p. 31) and Feelings Checkpoints (p. 32). Then list those areas you would like to develop and those you would like to change or eliminate.

I want to develop   *I want to change*

_____   _____

_____   _____

_____   _____

_____   _____

Reprinted with permission from Mal Hancock.

2. Review Needs and Wants a–c (pp. 29–30). Check the balance in your life. Do you have enough? What do you need or want on these four levels?

I have enough of   *I would like*

Physical level

_____   _____

Emotional level

_____   _____

Intellectual level

_____   _____

Altruistic level

_____   _____

Is your life in balance on these four levels?   Yes _____   No _____

If not, how can you improve the balance? _____

_____

_____

_____

3. Review Identifying Your Values (pp. 33–34). Write your top ten most important values in order of importance.

_____   _____

_____   _____

_____   _____

_____   _____

_____   _____

4. Review your autobiographical data. Summarize what you learned about yourself in exercises a–d in Drawing a Self-Portrait (p. 36).

_____

_____

_____

5. Review Candid Camera 3-D (pp. 35–36). List the four activities you enjoy most.
   a. _____   c. _____
   b. _____   d. _____

6. Describe success for yourself. _____

_____

_____

CHAPTERS 2 AND 3
PERSONALITY AND JOB SATISFIERS

1. Review the Personality Mosaic in Chapter 2. Then list your types in order from highest to lowest.

   First _____   Fourth _____

   Second _____   Fifth _____

   Third _____   Sixth _____

2. Which level of involvement with Data, People, and Things do you enjoy?

   Data   High level ____   Modest level ____   Little or none ____

   People   High level ____   Modest level ____   Little or none ____

   Things   High level ____   Modest level ____   Little or none ____

3. Write your top ten motivated skills and indicate how you want to use that skill with Data (D), People (P), and/or Things (T).

   _____   _____

   _____   _____

   _____   _____

   _____   _____

   _____   _____

   These are the skills you want to ensure are a significant part of your work life.

4. From the Personal Responsibility Skills Checklist (pp. 66–67), list your best personal skills and the ones you could improve.

   Best skills   *Could improve*

   _____   _____

   _____   _____

   _____   _____

   _____   _____

   _____   _____

5. List your work-specific skills.

_____

_____

List the work-specific skills you wish to acquire.

_____

_____

6. From the Personal Style exercise in Chapter 2, write your four-letter style.

_____   _____   _____   _____

What are three important things about your personal style, and how might they influence your career?

a. _____

b. _____

c. _____

7. List three job families and subgroups from the job charts in Chapter 3 in the order of importance to you.

Job Family	Subgroups
_____	_____
_____	_____
_____	_____

8. Tell how your top job group matches your personality, skills, interests, and work qualities. Use a separate sheet of paper if necessary.

_____

_____

_____

_____

_____

9. List the job title you would like most. _____

10. Do you want a career or "just a job"? Explain your answer.

_____

_____

11. How does your career choice match your values?

_____

_____

_____

CHAPTER 4
WORK: CHALLENGES, OPTIONS, AND OPPORTUNITIES

1. Tell which one of the major challenges listed on page 133 is most important to you and why.

_____

_____

2. List three careers you would like to be involved with to meet your most important challenge and tell what you would like to do.

_____

_____

_____

3. Does your career choice enable you to be involved with any of these options? How?

_____

_____

_____

4. What does the *Occupational Outlook Handbook* (or similar references) say about the employment outlook for the career of your choice?

_____

_____

_____

5. What is the salary range for the career of your choice? _____

Would this career support your lifestyle?   Yes _____   No _____

6. List three alternate careers you would consider. List one positive and one negative feature of each.

Career	Positive feature	Negative feature
a. _____	_____	_____
b. _____	_____	_____
c. _____	_____	_____

7. Do you have beliefs about the future that could hinder you from achieving your career goals? If so, what are they? What can you do about them?

_____

_____

_____

CHAPTERS 5 AND 6
WORKPLACES/WORKSTYLES/TIMESTYLES

1. Use findings from your research to describe the ideal workplace. Consider size and complexity, type of environment, emotional rewards, and work routine you would like.

_____

_____

_____

_____

_____

_____

2. Review the Career Ladder (p. 143). How far up the ladder do you want to go? Explain your answer.

_____

_____

_____

3. Review Researching Workplaces (pp. 200–201) and Workplace Checklist (pp. 203–206). Then list the four corporate values that are most important to you (see Workplace Values, pp. 150–152).

a. _____

b. _____

c. _____

d. _____

4. Review the roles you'll play as you enter the diverse workplace of the future.

Circle those major role components of your life that are most important: career, family, marriage, children, ethnicity, religion, leisure, education, friends, (other) _____

List three of the roles that are most important to you and tell how they will be affected as you move forward.

a. _____

b. _____

c. _____

How do you want to improve one of those roles?

_____

5. Describe your ideal job.

_____

_____

_____

_____

6. Describe your ideal boss.

_____

_____

_____

7. Describe your ideal work day.

   _____

   _____

   _____

8. Describe your ideal balance of work and leisure.

   _____

   _____

   _____

9. If you were to decide to open your own business, what steps would you take first?

   a. _____

   b. _____

   c. _____

10. Workplace first choice:

    a. Where would you like to work?

    _____

    b. How does this workplace present challenges of interest to you?

    _____

    _____

    c. What positive options does it have that fit your values?

    _____

    _____

11. What does work mean to you? Describe your personal work ethic.

    _____

    _____

    _____

    _____

CHAPTER 7
THE JOB HUNT: TOOLS FOR BREAKING AND ENTERING

To prepare for the job hunt:

1. Name the title of a job you might apply for. _____

2. List five of your characteristics that relate to that job and tell how.

    _____

    _____

    _____

    _____

    _____

3. Write your "30-second" introduction of who you are, what you have to offer, and what you want. Be clear and concise, but make sure you include enough information so that others will understand your strengths.

    _____

    _____

    _____

    _____

    _____

4. Write your three most powerful accomplishment statements. Remember to include the problem you tackled or solved, the solution you used, and most important, your quantifiable results.

    a. _____

        _____

    b. _____

        _____

    c. _____

        _____

5. Think of the three most difficult questions you could be asked during an interview and write your response to each. Remember the problem-solution-result approach.

a. _____

_____

b. _____

_____

c. _____

_____

CHAPTER 8
DECISIONS, DECISIONS: WHAT'S YOUR NEXT MOVE?

1. Write your SMART career decision goal.

_____

_____

_____

What steps have you taken so far to reach your goal?

_____

_____

_____

Are there any barriers that might stand in the way of achieving your goal? If so, what and how might you overcome the barrier?

_____

_____

_____

What is your next step toward your goal?

_____

_____

_____

2. Educational planning sheet

    a. Do you now have the skills and training you need to obtain a job in the field of your choice?   Yes _____   No _____

    If you need more preparation, which of the following do you need?

    _____ College   _____ Workshops or seminars   _____ Apprenticeships

    _____ On-the-job training   _____ Other _____

    b. If you need more education, which of these alternatives are you considering?

    _____ A few courses   _____ A BA or BS degree

    _____ A certificate   _____ Graduate school

    _____ An AA or AS degree   _____ Other _____

    c. List an appropriate major (or majors) for your career choice (see pp. 309–310).

    _____   _____

3. I plan to complete my degree (or training) by (date): _____

    I plan to be employed in the job of my choice by (date): _____

4. Review the inventories and your autobiography. Check each item in the Final Analysis. Does it all hang together?   Yes _____   No _____

5. Are you on the road to a successful future?   Yes _____   No _____

> Wherever the future may lead,
> May you always have the
> wisdom and strength to
> follow your dreams,
> The courage and ambition
> to meet new challenges,
> And may you always know the
> happiness and pride that
> comes with success!
> —*Anonymous*

Notes

CHAPTER 1
Needs, Wants, and Values:
Spotlighting YOU

1. Page Smith, *Redeeming the Time: A People's History of the 1920s and the New Deal*, Vol. 8 (New York: McGraw-Hill, 1986), p. 953.
2. Denise Veneble, "The Wage Gap Myth," *National Center for Policy Analysis*, Brief Analysis: No. 392, April 12, 2002.
3. "Potpourri," Financial Resource Center, Santa Cruz, California, May 1992.
4. Jim Frederick, "The End of Eureka!" *Working Woman*, February 1997, p. 40.
5. *INC*, February 1995, p. 6.
6. Bill Cane, *Through Crisis to Freedom* (Chicago: Acta Books, 1980), p. 21.
7. Victor Frankl, *Man's Search for Meaning* (New York: Washington Square Press, 1963).
8. Eileen R. Growald and Allan Luks, "A Reason to Be Nice: It's Healthy," *American Health Magazine*, reprinted in the *San Francisco Chronicle*, March 4, 1988, p. B-4.
9. "For a Better World," *World Monitor*, January 1989, p. 95.
10. World Bank, June 1996, in *Ministry of Money*, August 1996, p. 2.
11. *Ministry of Money*, August 1996, p. 6.
12. David Shi, "Thoreau Rides with Today's Commuters," *Christian Science Monitor*, December 13, 1996, p. 19.
13. See Gary Carnum, "Everybody Talks about Values," *Learning*, December 1972; S. B. Simon, S. W. Howe, and H. Kirschenbaum, *Values Clarification* (New York: Hart, 1972), pp. 30, 113–115.
14. Edward Goss, "Patterns of Organizational and Occupational Socialization," *Vocational Guidance Quarterly*, December 1975, p. 140.
15. Ken Keyes, Jr., *Handbook to Higher Consciousness* (Saint Mary, KY: Cornucopia Institute, 1975), p. 52.
16. Adapted from Abraham Maslow, *Motivation and Personality* (New York: Harper & Row, 1954), p. 91; see also Marilyn M. Bates and Clarence Johnson, *A Manual for Group Leaders* (Denver: Love Publishing, 1972), and Keyes, *Handbook to Higher Consciousness*.
17. Carter Henderson, "The Frugality Phenomenon," in John G. Burke and Marshall C. Eakin, eds., *Technology and Change* (San Francisco: Boyd & Fraser, 1979), p. 233.
18. *Sojourners*, February 1987, p. 13.
19. Pat Mathes Cane, "The Call to Be Brothers and Sisters," *Integrities*, Spring 1989, p. 8.
20. Michelle Locke, "Labor Secretary Speaks at Berkeley," *Register-Pajaronian*, May 10, 1995, p. 7.
21. Rebecca Smith, "The Power of Persuasion," *San Jose Mercury News*, February 27, 1995, p. D-1.
22. David Suzuki, "Towards a New Ecological Future, the Importance of Grass Roots," *Talking Leaves*, Winter 1992, p. 3.
23. *Catalyst*, Summer 1991, p. 16.
24. U.S. Department of Health, Education, and Welfare, *Work in America* (Cambridge, MA: MIT Press, 1973), pp. 186–187.
25. Lance Morrow, *Time*, May 11, 1981, p. 94.
26. S. Norman Feingold, "Career Education: A Philosophy," B'Nai B'rith Career and Counseling Service, 1640 Rhode Island Ave., N.W., Washington, DC, September 1973, p. 11.
27. Virginia Y. Trotter, "Women in Leadership and Decision Making: A Shift in Balance," *Vital Speeches*, April 1, 1975, pp. 373–375.
28. Fernando Bartolomé and Paul A. Lee Evans, "Must Success Cost So Much?" *Harvard Business Review*, March/April 1980, p. 142.

CHAPTER 2
Personality and Performance:
Pieces of the Puzzle

1. John Holland, *Making Vocational Choices: A Theory of Careers* (Englewood Cliffs, NJ: Prentice-Hall, 1973). Six-personality typology adapted with special permission of John Holland and Prentice-Hall.
2. Rose Marie Dunphy, "Why I Sew," *Christian Science Monitor*, May 20, 1985, p. 34.
3. Wynne Busby, "Chips Off the Old Block," *Creation Spirituality*, Winter 1994, p. 47.

4. *This Time,* from H.O.M.E., Fall 1988, p. 7.
5. *Regeneration,* September/October 1989, p. 10.
6. Jean Houston, "The Church in Future Society," taped address to the Lutheran Brotherhood Colloquium, University of Texas, Austin, January 1979.
7. See Sydney A. Fine, "Counseling Skills: Target for Tomorrow," *Vocational Guidance Quarterly,* June 1974, and "Nature of Skills: Implications for Education and Training," *Proceedings,* 75th Annual Convention of the American Personnel Association, 1967.
8. Nancy Gibbs, "The EQ Factor," *Time,* October 2, 1995, p. 60.
9. Daniel Goleman, *Emotional Intelligence* (New York: Bantam Books, 1995).
10. David Keirsey, *Please Understand Me II: Temperament, Character, Intelligence* (Del Mar, CA: Prometheus Nemesis Book Company, 1998).
11. Paul D. Tieger and Barbara Barron-Tieger, *Do What You Are: Discover the Perfect Career for You Through the Secrets of Personality Type,* 3rd ed. (Boston, MA: Little, Brown & Company, 2001).
12. Donna Dunning, *What's Your Type of Career? Unlock the Secrets of Your Personality to Find Your Perfect Career Path* (Palo Alto, CA: Davies-Black Publishing, 2001).

CHAPTER 3
The Career Connection:
Finding Your Job Satisfiers

1. Bureau of Labor Statistics, U.S. Department of Labor, *Occupational Outlook Handbook, 2002–03 Edition.*
2. U.S. Department of Labor, Employment and Training Administration, *Occupational Network O*NET OnLine,* http://online.onetcenter.org.
3. U.S. Department of Labor, *Dictionary of Occupational Titles,* 1978.
4. J. M. Farr, L. Ludden, and L. Shatkin, *Guide for Occupational Exploration,* 3rd ed. (Indianapolis, IN: JIST Works, 2001).

CHAPTER 4
Work: Challenges, Options,
and Opportunities

1. John Peers lecture at Mission College, November 11, 1982.
2. Thomas Merton, *Raids on the Unspeakable* (New York: New Directions, 1996), p. 70.
3. Jeremy Rifkin, "The Clocks That Make Us Run," *East West Journal,* September 1987, p. 44.
4. "The Invisible Farmer," *Christian Science Monitor,* October 20, 1993, p. 18.
5. "The Invisible Farmer," *Christian Science Monitor,* October 20, 1993, p. 18.
6. James Burke, *Connections,* a PBS Series.
7. Jonathan Rowe, "Just Words, but They Linger," *Christian Science Monitor,* May 17, 1989, p. 12.
8. Stephen J. Kline, "What Is Technology?" *Reporter,* January 1986, p. 1.
9. Priscilla Enriquez, "An Un-American Tragedy," *Food First Action Alert,* Summer 1992, p. 4.
10. Thomas J. Peters, "Competition and Change," *Santa Clara Magazine,* Summer 1989, p. 10.
11. Sarah van Gelder, "A New Civilization," *In Context,* Winter 1995–96, p. 6.
12. George Gendron, "Small Is Beautiful," *INC Special Report 1995,* p. 39.
13. Lester R. Brown, Christopher Flavin, and Sandra Postel, "A Planet in Jeopardy," *Futurist,* May/June 1992, p. 10.
14. Letter, Acción International, Fall 1998.
15. Michael Renner, "Chiapas: An Uprising Born of Despair," *World Watch,* January/February 1997, p. 12.
16. Don Monkereed, "Nix the Tax Cut: Close the Rising Gap Between Rich and Poor," *Register-Pajaronian,* January 18, 2003, p 5.
17. Sharron Cordaro, "Readers' Forum," *In Context,* Winter 1995–96, p. 5.
18. David C. Korten, *When Corporations Rule the World* (West Hartford, CT: Kumarian Press, 1995), p. 221.
19. "So Many Lists, So Little Time," *USA Weekend,* March 15–17, 1996, p. 4.
20. "The Page That Counts," *YES! A Journal of Positive Futures,* Spring 1997, p. 11.
21. "The Page That Counts," *YES! A Journal of Positive Futures,* Winter 1997/1998, p. 11.
22. Lance Morrow, "The Weakness That Starts at Home," *Time,* June 4, 1979, p. 81.
23. Korten, *When Corporations Rule the World.*
24. Helena Norberg-Hodge, Director, International Society for Ecology and Culture, "Lessons from Traditional Cultures," *Futurist,* May/June 1992, p. 60.

25. Laura Van Tuyl, "Her Design Is to Save the Earth," *Christian Science Monitor,* January 28, 1991, p. 14.

26. *Comic News,* Resource Center for Nonviolence, January 1994, p. 8.

27. Marshall Ingwerson, "Tales of Golf-Ball Gulping 'Gator and Reptile's Return to Florida," *Christian Science Monitor,* July 2, 1986, p. 3; Rushworth M. Kidder, "Agenda for the 21st Century," *Christian Science Monitor,* September 23, 1986, p. 1; see also p. 37.

28. Brad Knickerbocker, "Conversations with Outstanding Americans," *Christian Science Monitor,* August 15, 1997, p. 11.

29. Source unknown.

30. Robert Gilman, "Ecological Limit," *In Context,* Fall 1993, p. 12; Molly O'Meara, "The Risks of Disrupting Climate," *World Watch,* November/December 1997, p. 10.

31. Thomas Gartside, "Planting 1,000 Trees," *Christian Science Monitor,* March 6, 1990, p. 18.

32. Peer Weber, "Neighbors under the Gun," *World Watch,* July/August 1991, p. 35.

33. Christopher Flavin, "Climate Change and Storm Damage, the Insurance Costs Keep Rising," *World Watch,* January/February 1997, p. 10.

34. "One-fifth of Americans Said to Be Drinking Dangerous, Dirty Tap Water," *Register-Pajaronian,* June 1, 1995, p. 2.

35. Sandra Postel, Last Oasis, *Facing Water Scarcity* (New York: W.W. Norton, 1997); www.worldwatch.org.

36. David Clark Scott, "Retailers Move Early to Foil Yule Grinch," *Christian Science Monitor,* November 18, 1985, p. 31.

37. Curtis Runyan, "Ecological Footprint: Taming the Consumer Culture," *World Watch,* July/August 1997, p. 35.

38. Gilman, "Ecological Limit," p. 12.

39. Runyan, "Ecological Footprint," p. 35.

40. Gilman, "Ecological Limit," p. 12.

41. "Matters of Scale," *World Watch,* January/February, 1994, p. 39.

42. "Matters of Scale," *World Watch,* January/February, 1994, p. 39.

43. Colin Woodard, "Troubles Bubble under the Sea," *Christian Science Monitor,* September 10, 1997, p. 1.

44. "Vital Signs," *World Watch,* May/June 1990, p. 6.

45. Arthur Getz, "Community Supported Agriculture," *Earth Save,* Spring/Summer 1992, p. 8.

46. "Spotlight, the Loaves and the Fishes: 1980s Style," *Regeneration,* March/April 1989, p. 5.

47. Alan B. Durning, "Trends: U.S. Poultry Consumption Overtakes Beef," *World Watch,* January/February 1988, p. 11.

48. Karen Free, "Poverty Housing Sets Families Adrift," *Habitat World,* February/March 1998, p. 2; www. fedstats.gov/ index20.html.

49. "Quinientos millones de personas viven sin hogar en las ciudades que no paran de crecer," *Perspectiva,* January 1996, p. 8.

50. Lester R. Brown, "Facing Food Scarcity," *World Watch,* November/December 1995, p. 10.

51. Barbara Marx Hubbard, "Critical Path to an All-Win World," *Futurist,* June 1981, p. 31.

52. Francois Dusquesne, "The Making of a Sacred Planet," *One Earth,* 2, p. 6.

53. Sandra Postel, *Last Oasis* (New York: W.W. Norton, 1992), p. 23.

54. Sharron Cordaro, "Readers' Forum," *In Context,* Winter 1995–96, p. 5.

55. "Almanac," *Organic Gardening,* April 1985, p. 126.

56. Howard Youth, "Iguana Farms, Antelope Ranches," *World Watch,* January/February, 1991, p. 36.

57. Jo Roberts, "Rubber Tapper Chico Mendes Murdered," *Catholic Worker,* March/April 1989, p. 1.

58. "New Ground," *Organic Gardening,* July/August 1989, p. 12.

59. Alan Weisman, "¡Gaviotas! Oasis of the Imagination," *YES! A Journal of Positive Futures,* Summer 1998, p. 11.

60. Kathryn True, "Healing Technologies," *In Context,* Fall 1995, p. 24; The Green Center, 237 Hatchville Rd., Falmouth, MA 02536.

61. Thomas Gartside, "Planting 1,000 Trees," *Christian Science Monitor,* March 6, 1990, p. 18.

62. "'Global Releaf' Project," *Greenhouse Gazette,* Spring 1989, p. 11.

63. Brad Knickerbocker, "Draft Horses Pull Their Weight for Endangered Fish," *Christian Science Monitor,* September 9, 1997, p. 13.

64. Alexandra Marks, "Seal of Approval," *Christian Science Monitor,* June 24, 1997, p. 10.

65. Eliot Coleman, "Living Soil," *Organic Gardening,* October 1989, p. 67.

66. "Who Gardens? Most Are Women," *Register-Pajaronian*, March 29, 1996, p. 25.

67. Cathryn J. Prince, "All Built Up, Places to Grow," *Christian Science Monitor*, September 17, 1997, p. 1.

68. Christina Waters, "Natural Phenomenon," *Metro Santa Cruz*, April 4–10, 1996, p. 11.

69. Christina Waters, "Seeding the Future," *Metro Santa Cruz*, September 5–11, 1996, p. 5.

70. Lester R. Brown, "Facing Food Scarcity," *World Watch*, November/December 1995, p. 10.

71. "Americans Spending Billions on Offbeat Medical Treatments," *Register-Pajaronian*, June 27, 1993, p. 1.

72. "Almanac," *Organic Gardening*, April 1985, p. 126.

73. Christopher Flavin and Molly O'Meara, "Solar Power Markets Boom," *World Watch*, September/October 1998, p. 23.

74. Craig Savoye, "An All-Solar Home in the North Country? It Can Be Done," *Christian Science Monitor*, April 14, 1983, p. 14; "Superinsulation Means Super Savings in Canada's Cold," *Christian Science Monitor*, July 14, 1983, p. 14.

75. Terri Franklin, "Building Houses Made of Straw," *Habitat World*, June 1995, p. 12.

76. Peter Tonge, "Fuel-Stingy Z Stove: Could It Be the Answer for Fuel-Poor Third World?" *Christian Science Monitor*, January 6, 1984, p. 25.

77. Christopher Flavin, "Power Shock: The Next Energy Revolution," *World Watch*, January/February 1996, p. 10.

78. Darren Waggoner, "Wind Energy Picks Up Speed in the Midwest," *Doing Democracy*, Spring, 1997, p. 9.

79. Seth Dunn, "The Electric Car Arrives—Again," *World Watch*, March/April 1997, p. 19.

80. Rhea Wessel, "Is There No Time to Slow Down?," *Christian Science Monitor*, January 9, 2003, p. 13.

81. Marcia D. Lowe, "Bicycle Production Rises Again," *World Watch*, September/October 1994, p. 38.

82. Christopher Flavin, "Conquering U.S. Oil Dependence," *World Watch*, January/February 1991, p. 28.

83. Christopher Flavin and Seth Dunn, "Kyoto: The Days of Reckoning," *World Watch*, November/December 1997, p. 21.

84. "Eco-Actions," *CO-OP America Quarterly*, Winter 1992, p. 8.

85. James R. Woosley, Amory B. Lovins, and L. Hunter Lovins, "Energy Security: It Takes More Than Drilling," *Christian Science Monitor*, March 29, 2002, p. 11.

86. Amory B. and L. Hunter Lovins, "Carbon Reductions Can Make You Money," *Christian Science Monitor*, December 22, 1997, p. 16; Bill Cane, "Study Guide for Group Leaders," *Circles of Hope* (New York: Orbis Books, 1992), p. 6, Rocky Mountain Institute, 1739 Snowmass Creek Rd., Snowmass, CO 81654.

87. Robert Gilman, interview with Bob Berkebile, "Restorative Design," *In Context*, 35, 1993, p. 9.

88. David W. Orr, "Breaking Ground," *YES! A Journal of Positive Futures*, Winter 1998/1999.

89. Michael N. Corbett, *A Better Place to Live, New Designs for Tomorrow's Communities* (Emmaus, PA: Rodale Press, 1981).

90. Sarah van Gelder, "Cities of Exuberance," *In Context*, 35, 1993, p. 46.

91. Robert Rodale, *Regeneration of Health and the Human Spirit* (Emmaus, PA: Rodale Press, 1986).

92. Stuart Cowan, "A Design Revolution," *Yes! A Journal of Positive Futures*, Summer 1998, p. 27.

93. Cowan, "A Design Revolution," p. 27.

94. Howell Hurst, "Focus," *INC*, February 1991, p. 15.

95. Frank Swoboda, "Labor Secretary Challenges National 'Competitiveness' Issue," *Register-Pajaronian*, September 24, 1994, p. 22.

96. Cindy Mitlo, "A Matter of Principles," *CO-OP American Quarterly*, Spring 1996, p. 18.

97. *National Green Pages 1998*, CO-OP America, 1612 K St. N.W., #600, Washington, DC 20006.

98. Muhammad Yunus, "A Lesson in the Price of Bamboo," *World Ark*, Summer 1997, p. 28.

99. "Green Business," *CO-OP America Quarterly*, Winter 1994, p. 25.

100. Trickle Up Program, 54 Riverside Dr. PHE, New York, NY 10024-6509.

101. Greg Ramm, "Community Investment Is Coming of Age," *Building Economic Alternatives*, Spring 1987, p. 9; *Custody & Finance World*, May 1997.

102. Jeremy Rifkin, *The End of Work* (New York: G. P. Putnam's Sons, 1995), p. 241.

103. Hazel Henderson, "Will the Real Economy Please Stand Up," *Building Economic Alternatives,* Summer 1986, p. 3.

104. "New Loans," *ICE Update,* April 1998, p. 3.

105. *Adobe Magazine,* Autumn 1998, Cover.

106. Beth Burrows, "Ethics and Other Irrational Considerations," *Boycott Quarterly,* Spring 1994, p. 20.

107. Quotes from Christopher Cerf and Victor Navask, *The Experts Speak* (New York: Pantheon Books, 1984).

108. TRW advertisement, 1985.

109. *Catholic Women's NETWORK,* March/April 1998, p. 13.

110. "Responsible Investing," *CO-OP American Quarterly,* Spring 1998, p. 13.

111. May 1998 phone bill.

112. Oscar Arias, "Global Demilitarization," *Christian Science Monitor,* November 3, 1997, p. 15.

113. Kirsten A. Conover, "Public Groundswell Sways Organic Guidelines," *Christian Science Monitor,* May 14, 1998, p. 14.

114. "World's 'Vital Signs' Getting Better," *Register-Pajaronian,* October 19, 1992, p. 1.

115. Responsible Wealth, c/o United for a Fair Economy, 37 Temple Pl., Fifth Fl., Boston, MA 02111, *Update,* February 1998.

116. Ann Japenga, "Why Med Schools Teach Meditation," *USA Weekend,* February 21–23, 1997, p. 8.

117. "Odds and Ends," *Ecology Action Newsletter,* October 1992, p. 4.

118. "Odds and Ends," p. 4.

119. "Odds and Ends," p. 4.

120. "Odds and Ends," p. 4.

121. John Young, "The New Materialism," *World Watch,* September/October 1994, p. 37.

122. Michael Renner, "Monitoring Arms Trade," *World Watch,* May/June 1994, p. 21.

123. Campaign against Arms Trade, 5 Caledonian Rd., London NI 9DX.

124. Flavin and Dunn, "Kyoto: The Days of Reckoning," p. 21.

125. "Indicators," *YES! A Journal of Positive Futures,* Winter 1997, p. 7.

126. Paul H. Ray, "The New Political Companies," *Yes! A Journal of Positive Futures,* Summer 2002, p. 47.

127. David R. Francis, "Sizing Up the Yuppies and the Dinks Gives Population Insights," *Christian Science Monitor,* April 11, 1988, p. 14.

128. Hunter Lovins and Michael Kinsley, "Ingredients for Success," *Idea Bulletin,* Summer 1987, p. 3.

129. John O'Donohue, *Anam Cara* (New York: HarperCollins, 1997), p. 148.

130. Virginia Y. Trotter, "Women in Leadership and Decision Making: A Shift in Balance," *Vital Speeches,* April 1, 1975, pp. 373–375.

131. Adapted from Leonard Steinberg, Long Beach State University, Long Beach, CA.

CHAPTER 5
Workplaces/Workstyles:
Companies That Work

1. Adele Scheele, "Moving Over Instead of Up," *Working Woman,* November 1993, p. 75.

2. Statistics of U.S. Business: 1999: All Industries United States, www.census.gov/epcd/susb/1999/us/US-.HTM.

3. Erving Goffman, *Asylums* (New York: Doubleday, 1961).

4. Barbara Garson, "Women's Work," *Working Papers,* Fall 1973, p. 5.

5. *Nations' Restaurant News,* December 1984.

6. "MIT's Engineering Students Seek Better Ways to Coat M&Ms," *Register-Pajaronian,* January 2, 1991, p. 20.

7. Robert Levering and Milton Moskowitz, "The Workplace 100," *USA Weekend,* January 22–24, 1993, p. 4.

8. Christy Heady, "Time Is Now for Women to Take Control and Start Investing," *Christian Science Monitor,* June 16, 1997, p. 8.

9. Cecil Johnson, "Southwest Airlines Is a Model of Management Success," *San Jose Mercury News,* February 2, 2003, p. D-4.

10. James Kouzes and Barry Posner, "Credibility Makes a Difference," *Santa Clara Magazine,* Fall 1994, p. 12.

11. www.newbusinesscentre.com/statistics.html.

12. James C. Collins, "Building Companies to Last," *INC Special Issue: The State of Small Business,* 1995, p. 83.

13. Dale Kurschner, "The 100 Best Corporate Citizens," *Business Ethics,* May/June 1996, p. 24.

14. U.S. Trust gets such information from a variety of sources—companies' annual reports, Securities and Exchange Commission reports,

findings of the Investor Responsibility Research Center, the National Labor Relations Board, the Council on Economic Priorities, and the Interfaith Center on Corporate Responsibility.

15. Dawn-Marie Driscoll and W. Michael Hoffman, "It May Be Legal, But Is It Ethical?" *Christian Science Monitor,* December 8, 1997, p. 15.

16. Ron Scherer, "Eye on Firms That Use 'Cheap Labor' Abroad," *Christian Science Monitor,* November 14, 1997, p. 3.

17. Jeffrey W. Helms, "Green Investing," *Gardenia,* Winter 1994, p. 6; Anne Zorc, "Checking Up on Corporate Claims," *CO-OP America Quarterly,* Fall 1991, p. 16.

18. Jill Andresky Fraser, "Changing of the Card," *INC 500 97,* p. 84.

19. Loretta Graziano, "I'm Optimal, You're Optimal—an Economist's Way of Knowledge," *Propaganda Review,* Winter 1988, p. 36.

20. "Eco-Actions," *CO-OP America Quarterly,* Summer 1997, p. 7. Graduation Pledge Alliance, MC Box 152, Manchester College, North Manchester, IN 46962 or NJWollman @Manchester.edu for online brochure or questions.

21. "Worth Repeating," *Money Matters from Working Assets,* Fall 1994, p. 4.

22. Robert Levering and Milton Moskowitz, "The Workplace 100," *USA Weekend,* January 22–24, 1993, p. 4.

23. Kouzes and Posner, "Credibility Makes a Difference," p. 12.

24. William Bridges, "A Nation of Owners," *INC Special Report: The State of Small Business,* 1995, p. 89.

25. "Doubting Sweden's Way," *Time,* March 10, 1975, p. 42.

26. Sabrina Brown, "The Diversity Advantage," *Santa Clara Magazine,* Spring 1994, p. 22.

27. Elie Wiesel, "The Foreigner in Each of Us," *Christian Science Monitor,* August 7, 1991, p. 23.

28. "Bar Association Honors Lawyers Who Fought for Women's Equality," *Register-Pajaronian,* August 7, 1995, p. 8.

29. Denise Venable, "The Wage Gap Myth," *Brief Analysis No. 392,* National Center for Policy Analysis, April 12, 2002.

30. "Statistically Speaking: Issues Women Face," *Habitat World,* April/May 1998, p. 14.

31. "Facts Out of Context," from the United Nations Development Report, *In Context,* Winter 1995–96, p. 13; Toni Nelson, "Women's Work Undervalued by $11 Trillion," *World Watch,* November/December 1995, p. 7.

32. "Facts Out of Context," p. 13; Nelson, "Women's Work Undervalued by $11 Trillion," p. 7.

33. "Facts Out of Context," p. 13; Nelson, "Women's Work Undervalued by $11 Trillion," p. 7.

34. "Statistically Speaking: Issues Women Face," p. 14.

35. "Statistically Speaking: Issues Women Face," p. 14.

36. "Statistically Speaking: Issues Women Face," p. 14.

37. Cassandra Burrell, "Census: Half of U.S. Poor Are Children," *Register-Pajaronian,* August 19, 1996, p. 1.

38. "Women and Work Factsheet," *Women at Work* (Washington, DC: Wider Opportunities for Women, 1997).

39. Shelley Donald Coolidge, "At Home: Career Change for the 90s," *Christian Science Monitor,* December 8, 1997, p. B-1.

40. Household Data Annual Averages, 2002, U.S. Census Bureau, ftp://ftp.bls.gov/pub/special .requests.lf.aat37.txt.

41. Nelson, "Women's Work Undervalued by $11 Trillion," p. 7.

42. Peggy McIntosh, "Unpacking the Invisible Knapsack," *Creation Spirituality,* January/February 1992, p. 33.

43. Lisa Genasci, "Women's Work, More Take on Non-traditional Jobs," *Register-Pajaronian,* March 11, 1995, p. 11.

44. *Women and Nontraditional Work,* National Commission on Working Women of Wider Opportunities for Women (1325 G St. N.W., Lower Level, Washington, DC 20005), November 1989, p. 1.

45. Shelley Donald Coolidge, "Climbing Career Ladder Tips Balance at Home," *Christian Science Monitor,* July 15, 1997, p. 1.

46. Mark Lloyd, "Affirmative Action: Solution or Problem?" *Christian Science Monitor,* January 18, 1991, p. 19; "Final Hearings Held on the Glass Ceiling," *Register-Pajaronian,* September 27, 1994, p. 14.

47. Mitch Finley, "My Three Sons," *Santa Clara Magazine,* Fall 1990, p. 47.

48. James A. Levine and Todd L. Pittinsky, "Working Fathers," *INC,* July 1997, p. 83.

49. "Millions of Youngsters Live in 'Blended' Families, Census Bureau Analysis Shows," *Register-Pajaronian,* August 30, 1994, p. 15.

50. Shira J. Boss, "Let's Honor Fathers—Single Fathers, Too," *Christian Science Monitor,* June 13, 1997, p. 19.

51. "Fewer Households Are Made Up of Married Couples," *Christian Science Monitor,* July 2, 1997, p. 2.

52. "Obstacles Remain for Women and Working Mothers, U.N. Says," *Register-Pajaronian,* February 16, 1998, p. 9.

53. Anne-Marie Foisy-Grusonik, "The Superwoman Fallacy," *Santa Clara Magazine,* Winter 1992, p. 44; cf. Pamela Kruger, "All Twentysomething Women Want Is to Change the Way America Works," *Working Woman,* May 1994, p. 61.

54. Nancy K. Austin, "What Balance," *INC,* April 1997, p. 37.

55. "Family-Leave Law Goes into Effect," *Register-Pajaronian,* August 3, 1993, p. 3.

56. Scott Baldauf, "More Stay-at-Home Dads Drop Baby Bottles for Briefcases," *Christian Science Monitor,* March 26, 1997, p. 1.

57. Randolph E. Schmid, "Minding the Kids," *Register-Pajaronian,* October 8, 1997, p. 9.

58. Lillian Hellman, *An Unfinished Woman: A Memoir* (Boston: Atlantic Monthly Press, 1969).

59. Zalman Schachter-Shalomi and Ronald S. Miller, *From Age-ing to Sage-ing* (New York: Warner Books, 1995).

60. Ann Crittenden, "Temporary Solutions," *Working Woman,* February 1994, p. 35.

61. Political letter, 1988.

62. "Snapshot of America: Older, More Interracial," *Christian Science Monitor,* March 27, 1997, p. 14.

63. William H. Carlile, "All Anglo No More, a Latin Phoenix Rises," *Christian Science Monitor,* August 6, 1997, p. 1.

64. Lucia Mouat, "Despite Minority Gains, Gap between Races Still Looms Large," *Christian Science Monitor,* November 21, 1990, p. 8.

65. Gregory Rodriguez, "Multiracial Americans Deserve Better Than 'Other,'" *Christian Science Monitor,* October 14, 1997, p. 19.

66. "Reaching New Heights," *Vista,* September 1996, p. 23.

67. *1997 Economic Census Surveys of Minority- and Women-Owned Business Enterprises,* www.census gov/csd/mwb.

68. *1997 Economic Census Surveys.*

69. The Wage Gap by Education, Race, and Gender, Data Source: U.S. Census Bureau, Current Population Survey, March 2001, www.imdiversity.com/villages/woman/Article_Detail.asp?Article_ID=3990.

70. Terence Wright, "Liberation, My Nation, Migration," *Diaspora,* Fall 1980, p. 1.

71. Adair Lara, "If You're So Smart, Why Are You So Stupid?" *San Francisco Chronicle,* August 4, 1994, p. E-10.

72. Susanna Heckman, "ADA Burden Not All on Business," *Register-Pajaronian,* March 14, 1992, p. 11.

73. Shelley Donald Coolidge, "Finding Love, 1990s Style: Cupid Strikes at the Office," *Christian Science Monitor,* February 13, 1997, p. 1.

74. Hans Selye, 1936, 1950, cited in David Barlow and Mark Durand, *Abnormal Psychology* (Pacific Grove, CA: Brooks/Cole, 1995), p. 335.

75. "Pieces," *Good Money,* November/December 1984, p. 7.

76. Shelley Donald Coolidge, "Vacations Feel the Pinch, as Workers Feel Pressure of Changing Workplace," *Christian Science Monitor,* June 3, 1997, p. 1.

77. David Holmstrom, "Leisure Time in the '90s: TV Soaks Up the Hours," *Christian Science Monitor,* June 3, 1997, p. 13.

78. "Fit Employees Keep Health Costs Down on the Job," *Register-Pajaronian,* September 20, 1995, p. 19.

79. John Kenneth Galbraith, "The Economics of an American Housewife," *Atlantic Monthly,* August 1973, pp. 78–83.

80. Marilyn Gardner, "Striking for Home Time, Not Dollars," *Christian Science Monitor,* February 4, 1998, p. 1.

81. Bernard Lefkowitz, *BREAKTIME: Living without Work in a Nine to Five World* (New York: Hawthorn, 1979).

CHAPTER 6
Timestyles/Workstyles: Alternatives That Work

1. Elyse M. Friedman, ed., "Almanac, a Statistical and Informational Snapshot of the Business World Today," *INC Special Issue,* May 20, 1997, p. 120.

2. Marilyn Gardner, "Wanted: Employees to Work 30-Hour Weeks," *Christian Science Monitor,* March 30, 1997, p. 10.
3. Charlotte-Anne Lucas, "Bechtel Employees Like Short Week," *Register-Pajaronian,* January 3, 1991, p. 16.
4. Gardner, "Wanted: Employees to Work 30-Hour Weeks," p. 10.
5. Employed and unemployed full- and part-time workers by age, sex, and race, U.S. Department of Labor Bureau of Labor Statistics, 2001, ftp://ftp.bls.gov/pub/special.requests/lf/aat8.txt.
6. Paula Ancona, "Temporary Workers in Demand," *Register-Pajaronian,* October 8, 1994, p. 24.
7. Manpower Inc. Fact Sheet, March 1998.
8. Stephen Barr, "Government Issues Rules on Temporary Employees," *Register-Pajaronian,* September 21, 1994, p. 14.
9. Krishna Kundu, "Telecommuting: Work Is Virtually Something You Do, Not Somewhere You Go," *Future Trends: Contemporary Issues in Employment and Workplace Policy,* November 23, 1999, www.epf.org/etrend/tr991123.htm.
10. *Women and Office Automation: Issues for the Decade Ahead* (Washington, DC: U.S. Department of Labor, Women's Bureau, 1985), p. 24.
11. *Futurist,* February 1984, p. 82.
12. Franchise Fact Sheet, International Franchise Association, 1350 New York Ave., N.W., #900, Washington, DC 20005 (202) 628-8000, Spring 1994; Echo Montgomery Garrett, "The 21st-Century Franchise," *INC,* January 1995, p. 79; Echo Montgomery Garrett, "Looking for a Unique Work Environment?" *INC,* April 1997, ad pages.
13. Ylonda Gault, "Rising-Star Franchises," *Working Woman,* November 1993, p. 85.
14. Vivian Hutchinson, *Good Work, an Introduction to New Zealand's Worker Co-operatives,* Taranaki CELT, P.O. Box 4101, New Plymouth East, New Zealand.
15. "Global Cooperation," *CO-OP American Quarterly,* Summer 1994, p. 22.
16. Associated Press, "UAL Workers Sport 'Owner' Buttons," *Register-Pajaronian,* July 13, 1994, p. 16.
17. Tom Richman, "The Hottest Entrepreneur in America," *INC,* February 1987, p. 50.
18. Editor's Notebook, "The State of Small Business 1997," *INC Special Issue,* May 20, 1997, p. 11. See also Chapter 5, this volume.
19. "Women and Work Factsheet," *Women at Work* (Washington, DC: Wider Opportunities for Women, 1997).
20. Jerry Useem, "Start-up Chasers Track New-Bis Story," *INC,* April 1997, p. 22.
21. "Small Businesses Cast a Big Shadow at White House Conference," *Small Business Success,* April 1996, p. 2.
22. Michele Wucker, "Keep On Trekking," *Working Woman,* December/January 1998, p. 32.
23. Jim Frederick, "The End of Eureka!" *Working Woman,* February 1997, p. 38.
24. Tom Ehrenfeld, "The Demise of Mom and Pop?" *INC,* January 1995, p. 46.
25. Luke Elliott, "$1,500 and a Kitchen Table," *Back Home,* Winter 1990–91, p. 20.
26. Jeremy Joan Hewes, *Worksteads* (Garden City, NY: Doubleday, 1981), pp. 5, 7; see also Bernard Lefkowitz, *BREAKTIME: Living without Work in a Nine to Five World* (New York: Hawthorn, 1979).
27. "CEO's Notebook," *INC,* July 1997, p. 105.
28. Brochure, The Drucker Foundation, 666 Fifth Ave., 10th Fl., New York, NY 10103.
29. Author visit and tour, September 30, 1994.
30. Heather MacLeod, "Crossover," *INC Special Issue,* May 20, 1997, p. 100.
31. Elyse M. Friedman, ed.,"Almanac, a Statistical and Informational Snapshot of the Business World Today," *INC Special Issue,* May 20, 1997, pp. 108, 117.
32. John Case, "The Wonderland Economy," *INC Special Issue 1995: The State of Small Business,* p. 14.
33. "Hotline Plugs Honest Mechanics," *Register-Pajaronian,* April 28, 1993, p. 5.
34. "Ethnic Marketing, Turning Obstacles into Opportunities," *Small Business,* Spring 1995, p. 42.
35. Marilyn Ferguson, *Aquarian Conspiracy: Personal and Social Transformation in the 1980s* (Los Angeles: J. P. Tarcher, 1982).
36. Richard Pitcairn and Susan Hubble Pitcairn, *Dr. Pitcairn's Complete Guide to Natural Health for Dogs and Cats* (Emmaus, PA: Rodale Press, 1995).
37. Bill Cane, *Through Crisis to Freedom* (Chicago: Acta Books, 1980), p. 8.
38. Tom Shanks and Peter Facione, "The Case of the Cyber City Network," *Santa Clara Magazine,* Winter 1996, p. 25.
39. David Brewster, "Civil Society, Democracy and the Yearning for Community," *YES! A Journal of Positive Futures,* Fall 1996, p. 17.

40. Suzanne Morse, "Reweaving the Fabric of Democracy," *YES! A Journal of Positive Futures,* Fall 1996, p. 33; Arlene Hesthering-ton and Lou Piotrowski, "Democracy in the Woods," *YES! A Journal of Positive Futures,* Fall 1996, p. 41.

41. Robert Marquand, "Wendell Berry, Plowman-poet," *Christian Science Monitor,* October 10, 1986, p. 1.

42. *Occupational Outlook Quarterly,* Spring 1983, p. 11.

43. Shelley Donald Coolidge, "Mentors Give a Tug along Career Path," *Christian Science Monitor,* July 22, 1997, p. 8.

CHAPTER 7
The Job Hunt:
Tools for Breaking and Entering

1. Mark Granovetter, *Getting a Job: A Study of Contacts and Careers,* 2nd ed. (Chicago: University of Chicago Press, 1995).

2. U.S. Department of Labor, Bureau of Labor Statistics, *Jobseeking Methods Used by American Workers, Bulletin 1886* (Washington, DC: Government Printing Office, 1975).

3. John Molloy, *New Dress for Success* (New York: Warner Books, 1988).

4. Martin Stoodley, "Choosing the Right Tool," *National Business Employment Weekly,* January 14, 1990, p. 9.

5. John Lucht, *Rites of Passage at $100,000+* (New York: Viceroy Press, 1998).

6. James L. Tyson, "As Lawsuits Rise, Companies Use Detectives to Cull Job Applicants," *Christian Science Monitor,* February 12, 1997, p. 1.

7. "Franchise Inc.," *INC,* June 1997, ad pages.

8. *Personnel Administrator,* May 1981, pp. 71–78.

9. Toni St. James, interview workshop, California Employment Development Department, 1977.

10. Lorie Parch, "Testing . . . 1, 2, 3," *Working Woman,* October 1997, p. 74.

11. Richard Boles, *What Color Is Your Parachute?* (Berkeley, CA: Ten Speed Press, 2003).

CHAPTER 8
Decisions, Decisions:
What's Your Next Move?

1. Ashleigh Brilliant, *I Have Abandoned My Search for Truth, and Am Now Looking for a Good Fantasy* (Santa Barbara, CA: Woodbridge Press, 1985), p. 128.

2. Key Keyes, Jr., "Oneness Space," Living Love Recording (St. Mary's, KY: Cornucopia Center; Ken Keyes College, The Vision Foundation, 790 Commercial Ave., Coos Bay, OR 97420).

3. Betts Richter and Alice Jacobsen, *Make It So!* (Sonoma, CA: Be All Books, 1979).

4. Olive Ann Burns, *Cold Sassy Tree* (New York: Dell, 1984), p. 379.

5. Bill Schackner, "College Students' Attitude: Give Us Latitude," *Register-Pajaronian,* August 21, 1997, p. 8.

6. "Worker Training: Competing in the New International Economy," OTA *(Office of Technology Assessment) Report Brief,* September 1990.

7. Editorial, "Candidates Avoid the Hard Choices," *Register-Pajaronian,* September 8, 1994, p. 24.

8. U.S. Department of Labor, "So You Are Thinking About Dropping Out of School . . . ," www.dol.gov/asp/fibre/dropout.htm.

9. Bureau of Labor Statistics, U.S. Department of Labor, *Occupational Outlook Handbook, 2002–2003 Edition.*

10. Jonathan P. Decker, "Howard University Becomes 'Hot Pick,'" *Christian Science Monitor,* June 2, 1997, p. 12.

11. "Graduation Rate Rises for Blacks," *Register-Pajaronian,* September 5, 1996, p. 7.

12. Chris Eftychiou, "At 82, She's a Student, Reporter, Senior Citizen," *Register-Pajaronian,* April 30, 1997, p. 11.

13. Suzi Parker, "In Ever-Changing Workplace, Two-Year Colleges Fill Niche," *Christian Science Monitor,* October 27, 1998, p. 3.

14. Susan Ager, "After Exiting the Executive Suite," *San Jose Mercury News,* October 25, 1981, p. 6-E.

15. Brilliant, *I Have Abandoned My Search for Truth,* p. 118.

16. Walter Chandoha, *Book of Kittens and Cats* (New York: Bramhall House, 1973), p. 8.

17. Lyle Crist, "Twain's River Holds Depths for Exploring," *Christian Science Monitor,* May 16, 1989, p. 17.

18. Alan Lakein, *How to Get Control of Your Time and Your Life* (New York: N.A.L. Dutton, 1989).

19. Peter F. Drucker, "My Life As a Knowledge Worker," *INC,* February 1997, p. 76.

20. John Cassidy, "All Worked Up," *New Yorker,* April 22, 1996, p. 51.
21. Feature, *Catholic Women's Network,* September/October 1994, p. 10.
22. *Lotus,* Fall 1991, back cover.
23. H. B. Gelatt, *Creative Decision Making* (Los Altos, CA: Crisp Publications, 1991), p. 11.
24. Robert Klose, "A Son Begins to Widen His Orbit," *Christian Science Monitor,* October 10, 1997, p. 16.
25. Joseph Campbell, *The Power of Myth* (New York: Doubleday, 1988), p. 91.
26. Ted Berkman, "Wanting It All," *Christian Science Monitor,* January 27, 1983, p. 21.

Index

Kathy Stewart:
678-908-7000
Africa Missions Trip